*Teaching and Learning
Primary Science*

Wynne Harlen began her professional life as a teacher and college lecturer, after graduating in physics at Oxford University. She has been engaged in research, curriculum development and evaluation in the context of primary science since 1965. She gained a PhD whilst working at Bristol University through research into evaluation procedures and her first book, *Science 5/13: A Formative Evaluation*, was published in 1975. Since then she has published, either as author or co-author, 18 books, including the first edition of *Teaching and Learning Primary Science* in 1985, and contributed to 25 other books. After four years as researcher at Reading University, she moved to London University, where she was deputy director of the APU science project at the then Centre for Science and Mathematics Education, from 1977 to 1985. She left London to become Professor of Science Education at the University of Liverpool. In 1990 she moved to Edinburgh on being appointed director of the Scottish Council for Research in Education. She was awarded the OBE for service to education in 1991.

She has worked for regular short periods abroad, particularly in developing countries, producing for Unesco the first volume of *New Trends in Primary Science Education*, 1983, *The Training of Primary Science Teacher Educators*, 1985, *Source Book of Activities for Primary Science Teacher Education* (1992) and various workshop materials and reports. Her particular concern in work both at home and abroad is to encourage children's learning with understanding, through the use of process skills, and the development of attitudes which promote curiosity about and respect for the environment.

Teaching and Learning Primary Science

2nd Edition

Wynne Harlen

P·C·P
Paul Chapman
Publishing Ltd

Paul Chapman Publishing Ltd
144 Liverpool Road
London
N1 1LA

British Library Cataloguing-in-Publication Data.

Harlen, Wynne
  Teaching and Learning Primary Science. -
  2Rev.ed
  I. Title
  372.35044

  ISBN 1–85396–185–X

Typeset by Inforum, Rowlands Castle, Hants
Printed and bound by
Athenæum Press, Gateshead, Tyne & Wear.

F G H   9 8

Contents

Acknowledgements

I wish to thank the many friends, colleagues, students and members of my family who have, consciously or unconsciously, contributed to the ideas in this book. It is a theme of the book that the ideas one understands and feels to own evolve by being tested against new experience and compared with alternative ways of looking at things. Inevitably, therefore, others' ideas have influenced mine and I have endeavoured to acknowledge this where I am aware of it. But the process is often unconscious and I apologise for any failure to give due acknowledgement.

I am grateful to the following publishers for permission to quote copyright material: Hodder and Stoughton Ltd., David Fulton Publishers, Cassell plc., Transworld Publishers Ltd (Bantam Press), The Open University, Simon and Schuster, Harper and Row Inc. and Collins Educational.

Wynne Harlen
Edinburgh, 1993

Introduction

In the eight years since the first edition of this book, the teaching of science in primary schools has been the area of the curriculum experiencing more profound change than any other, except perhaps technology. As a consequence some parts of the first edition of *Teaching and Learning Primary Science* were in need of revision and some new material was required. The main purpose of the book, however, remains as before, to provide a theory-based view of school and classroom practice in science. It continues to be founded in the view that decisions about the curriculum and everything relating to teaching should be based on a clear view of the kind of learning that is intended. The notion of 'kind of learning' embraces both the way children learn and what they learn, both of which are dependent on the role of the teacher and the organization of the school.

The most obvious change in these last few years is that science has become established as a central part of the primary curriculum and that in many countries national curricula, some underpinned by law, have been introduced to ensure that all pupils have opportunities for learning science. However, other changes, though less prominent and public, have been no less significant. The greater amount of attention to research in primary science has extended understanding of how children develop ideas about the scientific aspects of the world around and has drawn attention to the implications of this for the sorts of activities that promote learning. Research has also helped to underline the close interaction between skills and concepts. The arguments about the relative importance of content and process are largely a thing of the past. Learning with understanding demands a close interaction of the two; ideas which are understood are those which the learners have worked out for themselves by using their own ideas, or ideas suggested to them, and by trying them out against experience. As a result the initial ideas may be modified, rejected or strengthened in the light of evidence. Which of these happens depends on *the way* the ideas are related to evidence as well as on what the evidence is, so the development of skills of selecting, applying and testing ideas is fundamental to the development of those ideas. These skills are described here as process skills, comprising observing, hypothesizing, predicting, investigating, drawing conclusions and communicating.

There is always the danger of the pendulum swinging too far, in this case, of the recognition of the importance of conceptual understanding being interpreted as a case for focusing on learning *about* content rather than learning basic ideas *through* content. National curricula generally try to avoid this by expressing what is to be learned in terms of general ideas and skills. However, when their meanings are exemplified in terms of specific content, the examples may be taken as too strong a guide to what is to be taught. A further danger in the swing towards content and towards defining measurable outcomes of learning is that the development of attitudes is left out. Indeed one of the unfavourable changes in the last few years has been the neglect of attitudes in official documents. This is quite evident in the National Curriculum for Science for England and Wales (DES, 1991a) where attitudes are conspicuous by their absence, although they have been retained in the Scottish Curriculum Guidelines for Environmental Studies (SOED, 1991).

These arguments have resulted in the retention in this edition of the rationale for the importance of process skills and attitudes (Chapter 2). The particular list of process skills has been slightly modified to bring it into line with current views, but the extended discussion of what the skills and attitudes mean in practice (Chapter 4) and how teachers can help children to develop them (Chapter 7) have been retained.

A significant area of change surrounds the matter of assessment and record-keeping. While this has affected all areas of the curriculum its effect has been particularly radical in science, where there was hardly any assessment and records in the early 1980s (Clift, Weiner and Wilson, 1981). The role of assessment in helping teaching has been advocated for many years (Match and Mismatch, 1977) but only now widely accepted. Implementation, however, requires practical problems to be solved at school and class level. In view of these developments two new chapters have been created to discuss the theoretical (Chapter 8) and the practical (Chapter 9) aspects of assessment.

At the same time as assessment has been gaining a greater acceptance as a process to keep learning under review, so has school self-evaluation, as a process to keep teaching under review. School-based evaluation, within the context of school development planning, is seen as a positive process that helps schools review their progress in relation to agreed indicators and performance criteria. Discussion of these matters in relation to science now forms the final chapter of the book, although this does not imply in any way that it follows after other considerations.

Enduring themes, such as the importance of language and the recognition of the value of discussion, receive updated attention. The case of the greater appreciation of whole class and small group discussion is another example where it is important to maintain a balance and not to interpret this as licence for talking about science rather than experiencing it. Leading discussion at appropriate points, particularly to help pupils articulate their ideas and later to interpret their findings and to rethink their initial ideas, is a crucial part of the teacher's role, as is handling children's questions, also discussed in Chapter 5.

A final point to note is perhaps that in Chapter 3 there is an attempt to address what I perceive as an inconsistency between the constructivist view of learning, which permeates thinking about education not only in this book but more widely, and the objectives-based, step-wise structure of the National Curriculum. Rather than to prescribe steps in learning, some of which do not articulate well into an overall progression, it seems more useful to try to identify the main ideas and skills that all pupils should be helped to develop to some degree through their activities; to say what progresses without claiming to dictate the progression. The ideas and skills take on a more sophisticated meaning for older and more experienced pupils but for all they indicate the important ideas to which they are moving through testing and modifying their own ideas. Since the route taken in developing these ideas must allow for individual variations, if pupils are to retain ownership of the ideas, then it is not appropriate to predetermine too closely the steps in development. It helps teachers to have some guidance about the ideas pupils may be expected to have reached at certain points, but it may be sufficient to do this at the end of the infant and junior stages of education, as suggested in Chapter 8.

The provision of opportunities for all children to learn science throughout their schooling takes us into a future which will be as different again from the present as the practice of the 1980s was from the practice of the early 1990s. We do not know how children's capacity for learning will develop when they have been building up experience and ideas progressively throughout the primary years, under the guidance of teachers with increasing confidence and competence in science and with the help of computer technology to extend the range of information and evidence available to them. We may well need to revise our views about what can be achieved by children and how we should be supporting their learning. It seems, therefore, thoroughly appropriate that we should view our present knowledge of teaching and learning as tentative. It is in this spirit that the ideas in this book are offered, knowing that they are bound to be overtaken if we approach our teaching of science in a scientific way.

1

Science and Children's Education

Changes in the curriculum since 1987 have turned attention in the UK and elsewhere from the arguments about *whether* science ought to be taught at the primary level to *how* it should be taught. The questions which are of immediate concern now seem to be those about the advantages and disadvantages of topic work as a context for teaching science, the role of specialist teachers, the timetabling and organization of science activities, the assessment of pupils and the keeping of records, to mention just a few. The major battle for science in the primary curriculum has been won but there remain many areas of combat yet to be decided.

These important questions concerning practice are addressed in later chapters. There are, of course, no single or easy answers, since they depend so much upon the particular circumstances of a school; for example, on the training and confidence of the teachers, on the resources available, on the way in which the rest of the curriculum is organized. But before engaging with these practicalities it is essential to be clear about what we are trying to achieve. Practicalities should not dictate values; even if they prevent us achieving our 'ideal', as they usually do, we should be able to keep in mind a vision of what we want to work towards. This gives a direction to long-term planning, a purpose for decision-making and a basis for evaluating progress.

Thus, even though the aims and objectives of the curriculum may have been specified, this is no reason for ceasing to be concerned with why we teach science and what kind of science we want to teach. It is important to have a clear idea of why science is important in young children's education so that, in the *way* we implement it, these purposes are actively furthered. It is always possible to teach to the 'letter of the law' without regard for the spirit of the subject. It takes some effort to teach science in a way which engages children's ideas, imagination and activity and this effort will only be made if a teacher is convinced of the value of teaching this way. There must also be a vision of the nature of learning in science to inform the moment-to-moment decisions which can never be dictated by any curriculum document.

This initial chapter is therefore concerned to offer a restatement of reasons for the importance of primary science and some ideas about the nature of scientific activity within and outwith the school.

The values of teaching science at the primary level

If education is 'to fit children for the society into which they will grow up' (CACE, 1967), then a prime reason for giving science a place in the curriculum from the start is the increasingly central part that it plays in society. Developing countries, for whom the scientific and technological changes have been more rapid, acted on this and made science a part of primary education before more developed countries (Morris, 1990). Being 'at ease' with key scientific ideas is as necessary to functioning in society today as is being 'at ease' with numbers, with percentages, with rates of change, or with the various forms (genres) of language.

The analogy with the basic understanding of language has helped to coin the phrases 'scientific literacy', 'technological literacy', 'numeracy', and so on. These phrases sum up what is involved in being at ease with some overall, general ideas and methods relating to the understanding of particular aspects of living in society today, but without necessarily having a detailed grasp of every principle or a comprehensive knowledge of facts. The extent of agreement on whether scientific literacy is a realistic aim is limited (e.g. Shamos, 1988) and this is not the moment to be diverted into a discussion of how feasible it is to have a population able to follow or take part in the discussion of major science-based issues. The point to be made is that the only chance we have of developing understanding of general principles in anyone, and especially in school pupils, is to begin with the objects and events familiar to them. As we shall discuss further in Chapter 3, understanding of a particular event or system can be linked up with ideas from related but different examples to give ideas with greater power (because they help to explain more events) which themselves are linked in broad theories or principles. The process cannot proceed in the opposite direction, since the broad theories are necessarily highly abstract and indeed meaningless if they do not evoke the many real situations which they link together. Thus, for example, if children develop, through investigation and observation, an understanding that there is interdependence among plants and animals in their own environment – their back garden, the park, the stream or the hedgerow – they may eventually understand the reasons for protecting the rain forests. But if the big issues relating to this conservation are the starting point, they may be understood at no greater depth than slogans and the relationships never more than superficially grasped.

These arguments still leave open the question 'why start in the primary school?' Why is it not sufficient, as has effectively been the case into the 1980s in many western countries, to start at the secondary level?

There are two kinds of answers to these questions. The first come from experience, backed by research, about what happens when we do delay the start of science until the secondary school. These concern *children's own ideas* and *fostering positive attitudes*. The second kind arise from the recognition of *the interaction of processes and concepts*, relating to the nature of scientific activity, whether of children or of scientists, considered in a later section of this chapter.

Children's own ideas

There is ample research, some to be reviewed in Chapter 3, to show that children's ideas of the world around them are being built up during the primary years, whether or not they are taught science. But without intervention to introduce a scientific approach in their exploration of the world, the ideas the children develop may be non-scientific and may obstruct learning at the secondary level. Research by groups in the USA, Canada, UK, France, Australia and New Zealand, working mainly in the 1980s with secondary pupils, reached remarkably similar conclusions about the ideas the pupils bring with them to their secondary science education.

At first these ideas were called 'misconceptions' (e.g. Johnstone, Mac-Donald and Webb, 1977) but soon it was more appropriate and acceptable to call them 'alternative frameworks' (Driver, 1985) or 'children's ideas' (Osborne and Freyberg, 1985) as studies revealed that they were the result of thinking and reasoning by the pupils and indeed made sense to them. Because of this they were difficult to change and certainly were not to be overturned by teaching the 'right' ideas. Of course, science teachers did not need years of research to tell them how difficult it is to bring many children to an understanding of scientific principles but what this research did was to help them recognize why this was the case and to suggest some ways of addressing the problem. The findings of the groups working in New Zealand exemplify what has been uncovered by interviewing pupils and observing them in science lessons (Osborne and Freyberg, 1982). Their three main findings can be summarized as follows:

- Children approach the topics in their science lessons with quite firmly held ideas of their own, not with empty minds ready to fill with new ideas from their teacher.
- The children's ideas are often different from the scientific ideas used by their teachers and might well make better sense and seem more useful to children (for example, the scientific principle that moving objects continue in motion unless there is a force acting to stop them seems a less useful way of explaining daily observations than the idea that moving objects stop unless there is a force to keep them going).
- Formal science lessons at the secondary school often leave children's own ideas untouched and therefore much of what is presented to them makes little sense.

We shall come back later (Chapter 2) to the question of how children's own ideas are formed and how, once formed, they may be changed, but the immediate point is that there is a role for primary science in reducing this gap between the ideas children have and the ones that would enable them to benefit more from their later science education.

Fostering positive attitudes to science

Ormerod and Duckworth (1975) indicated that children's interest in science is established at an early age. Already in 1959 research into the factors affecting secondary school pupils to choose science at the age of 13 years found that 'the scientists had long-standing stable attitudes favourable to science which were formed more than two years earlier, whilst non-scientists did not make up their mind until nearer the time of choice' (Kelly, 1959). Duckworth (1972), confirming this, found in addition that the attributes which favour the selection of science in the secondary school are evident in girls even earlier than in boys.

Although selection of science at the secondary level, usually meaning 'opting out', is now officially not a problem, where science in some form has to be part of the curriculum throughout the compulsory years of education, this will not have eliminated lack of interest or 'mentally opting-out.' If children's first encounter with the subject called 'science' is one in which ideas are presented which are different from their own and do not seem to make sense in terms of everyday experience it is not surprising that a negative attitude is established fairly generally. Clearly, one step towards preventing this is to ensure that children's first encounter with science activities is not of this kind (which has implications for both secondary and primary science), but another is to make sure that science has some real first-hand meaning for them from an early age as something that can be enjoyable and useful.

It is perhaps worth emphasizing that the concern here is not for the minority who go on to study science, but for the education of the majority. The level of general skills of analytical and critical thinking, to which science makes an important but not unique contribution, required of everyone in the era of information technology is much higher than in the past. Further, there is a danger of a gulf opening up between those who understand and operate complex scientific technology and those whose lives are governed by it, unless there is a higher degree of scientific understanding throughout society. In preventing this damaging rift science education has a unique part to play. Thus there are important societal needs which have to be met by ensuring that both the general process skills and the specifically scientific ones are developed by everyone. This cannot be done if science education begins only at the secondary level.

The interaction of processes and concepts

Since the early developments in primary science in the 1960s there has been much study of both a theoretical and a practical nature of the processes of and influences on children's learning. As a result, statements then made about the relative importance of learning the processes of science and learning the content are now seen to be naïve and untenable. For example, the Nuffield Junior Science Project (1967) made the assumption that it did not matter what children investigated, what was important was how. The reason for this can be readily understood. The primary science curriculum projects of the 1960s were anxious to make a clean break from the type of science typified by the 'object lesson' in which children were merely told about things and not given opportunity to gather and use evidence and to think things out for themselves. The Nuffield Project made the distinction very clear: 'At this level we are concerned more with the development of an enquiring mind than with the learning of facts.' This was echoed by Science 5/13 (1972–1975) in defining the main aim as 'development of an enquiring mind and a scientific approach to problems.' It was recognized that in achieving this children would be 'developing basic concepts and logical thinking' and 'acquiring knowledge and learning skills' as well as skills and attitudes. However, the knowledge and concepts were treated as if they were a by-product of the process and not as an integral part of the process.

What is now realized is that process skills cannot be used and developed independently of concepts and knowledge and, conversely, that concepts and knowledge cannot be learned with understanding without the use of process skills. The two-way interdependence can be readily exemplified, so readily, in fact, that it seems obvious. But then it is often the case that effective ideas have a quality of obviousness about them that makes them almost familiar and thereafter quite ordinary (Bruner, 1964a).

Take the first part, the dependence of the use of process skills on existing knowledge. In making an observation, planning an investigation, giving an account, or contributing to a group discussion, there has to be some content and what the content is, and particularly what is already known about it, makes a considerable difference. It is not neutral. A nice example is given by Finlay (1983), describing a geologist looking at a thin section of rock under a microscope, seeing details which are significant as indicators of sedimentary particles beginning to undergo metamorphism. Someone without the knowledge of the geologist would see only a variety of shapes and colours and would probably not even observe the same details quite apart from making similar interpretations of what they see. Similarly, children observe what previous understanding suggests to them is significant to observe:

> Take the example of the teacher who was hoping to show a group of children that a candle under a jar would burn for longer the larger the jar. He had three jars of different size and explained to the boys how to put

them over three burning candles all at the same time. It worked well. So when the teacher asked them what differences they saw between the jars he was disappointed in their reply. 'Nothing. It was the same for all of them. All the candles went out.' None of the boys had observed what the teacher hoped they would notice – the difference in time of burning in each jar, a difference quite large enough to be noticed by someone looking for it. The teacher might easily have assumed that because the difference was observable it therefore had been observed.

(Harlen and Symington, 1985)

It is not just observation which is conceptually driven. An investigation planned about something with which we are familiar, where we know what variables are likely to affect the result, is more likely to be adequately controlled than one about something of which we know nothing. The point becomes obvious if we think of a nine-year-old successfully investigating the relationship between how a ball bounces and the surface it bounces on, but being unable to tackle the investigation of the relationship between the concentration of a solution and its osmotic pressure. The fact that a skill can be performed in a particular way in one situation does not mean that it will be deployable in another.

The other side of the two-way relationship between processes and ideas follows with particular force from the view of learning which is now widely supported and is presented in the next chapter. To anticipate, this view acknowledges the ideas that learners bring to a new situation and it regards learning as change in these ideas. The change may involve modification or rejection of initial ideas or the adoption of alternative ones which make more sense of the evidence then available. Whatever the change is, however, if it is carried out on the basis of the learner's own reasoning then the new idea becomes 'owned' by the learner and is learning which is understood.

In this process it is evident that what emerges as the initial ideas are changed, and whether what emerges really are the ideas which best fit the evidence, depends crucially on the collection and use of evidence and on the reasoning processes. Two things follow. In the first place, if concept development depends on process skills, as suggested, then it is important to give attention to process skills at the same time as concepts. Secondly, if children base their ideas on existing knowledge and ways of dealing with it (both necessarily limited by experience), then their ideas will often be different from those of adults and from accepted scientific views. This should not be a matter for concern as long as current concepts are seen in a developmental context. At any time children's ideas should be consistent with their experience and their ways of dealing with that experience. As either or both of these change, so will their ideas and indeed it is the function of school science to make sure that existing ideas are developed and gradually changed into more powerful and widely useful ones.

The realization that the ways in which children use and develop process skills in their current investigations depend on their existing ideas challenges the assumption that the subject matter of activities is unimportant. This is not to suggest that children cannot think and enquire scientifically in a social project or in a topic about local history, but that their scientific thinking will not develop if these are the only kinds of topics they encounter. As well as the more general skills, such as observation and interpretation of data, there are more specifically scientific skills to be developed and these require more specifically scientific activities. To some limited extent the scientific approach can be engendered in the methods used across the curriculum but the skills of enquiry cannot be fully developed unless children's activities include investigation of their physical and natural surroundings from an early age.

The main values of primary science

These various points about the role of primary science in children's education can be drawn together under four main headings. There is a need for science in primary education because it can:

1. Make a contribution to children's understanding of the world around them; understanding is seen as a developing mental structure which changes in response to children's broadening experience.
2. Develop ways of finding things out, checking ideas and using evidence; it is the way in which children interact with the things around them which will assist their learning not only in science but in other subjects also.
3. Build up ideas that will help rather than hinder later learning in science; this does not mean beginning to learn secondary science concepts in the primary school, but exploring and investigating in such a manner that children's own ideas can be put to the test.
4. Engender more positive and thoughtful attitudes towards science as a human activity; instead of unthinking reaction to the popular image of science, children need to experience science activity for themselves at a time when attitudes towards it are being formed which may have an influence for the rest of their lives.

The nature of scientific activity

A clear notion of the nature of the subject being taught, whatever it may be, is essential for the teacher. It may not be, and perhaps will not be in the case of science at the primary level, that the subject is taught separately from other subjects, but its distinctive qualities ought to be identified in the mind and the features which separate it from other subjects clearly recognized. Indeed it might be said that only when the identity of the subject, in this case science, is clearly recognized is it possible to teach it effectively within a topic or as part of an activity where it is integrated with other subjects. Otherwise, there may be very little of the activity that is truly scientific. The issues surrounding topic work are ones we shall take up later (pp. 134–6). Here the message is that we must know what science is and what makes it different, say, from technology, from mathematics, from history, from geography, all of which, at some point and in some degree, share the same methods and processes.

The characteristics of science which, in combination, define it can be expressed as follows:

- The physical world around is the *ultimate authority* by which the validity of scientific theories and principles is to be judged. Whatever the logic there seems to be in hypothetical explanations or relationships, they are only useful in so far as they agree with reality.
- Science is about *understanding*, that is, arriving at relationships between observed facts which enable predictions to be made.
- The understanding, the theories, at any particular time are subject to change in the light of new evidence and so must be regarded as *tentative* at all times.
- Science is a *human endeavour*, depending on creativity and imagination, and has changed in the past and will change in the future as human experience and understanding change.

In the following discussion of each of these points there is the opportunity to distinguish science from its closest neighbours – mathematics and technology. First, however, there should be some consistency brought to the use of words such as theory, principle, idea, concept and fact, which may seem otherwise to be used arbitrarily.

A *theory*, according to Stephen Hawking,

is a good theory if it satisfies two requirements: It must accurately describe a large class of observations on the basis of a model that contains only a few arbitrary elements, and it must make definite predictions about the results of future observations.

(Hawking, 1988, p. 9)

A *principle* is not much different from a theory, except that it is often less all embracing and relates to a more restricted group of events. *Concepts* are generalizations which describe rather than explain the features of related phenomena. They are the result of abstracting features which object or events have in common and of ignoring others. They depend upon the perception of the common and varying features but are much more than simple descriptions of these perceptions. Judgement and reasoning are involved in selecting the aspects which form the basis of concepts. *Ideas* are the building blocks of either concepts or theories and, like them, enable us to understand *facts* which arise from observations.

Reality as the ultimate test of scientific theories

It may seem obvious that, if science is about understanding the world around, then its theories must be judged by how well it does this. In practice, however, testing how well a theory fits is not always easy. Evidence may not be available, or may be contested or may depend on such complicated mathematics that few people understand it.

In the history of science there are many examples of factors other than the fit with evidence being used to assess a scientific theory. It took a hundred years for the ideas of Copernicus, that the earth and planets moved round the sun, to be accepted even though this model fitted the observations far better than Ptolemy's model of the universe, mainly because the latter's earth-centred model had been adopted by the Christian Church. There are contemporary examples of theories based on cultural mores which are preferred to scientific theories in certain societies. The extent to which science is culturally neutral is the subject of current, and complex, debate.

So the statement that reality is the ultimate test of a scientific theory is not as uncontentious as it may at first seem. It raises the question of 'whose reality' for one thing. But, while not assuming a single view of science, the statement does help to distinguish the broad area of science from other disciplines. For example, in mathematics the ultimate test is the internal logic of numbers and relationships. There is no need for the predictions from mathematical theories to relate to reality (non-rational numbers are an example), in sharp distinction to the theories of science.

Science as understanding

In both learning science and doing science the aim is to understand, meaning to have an *explanation* for what is known from which predictions are made fitting the available evidence.

In arriving at an explanation – a theory – a scientist uses existing ideas, makes predictions based on them and then makes observations to see whether the predictions fit the facts. If they do not fit, the theory has to be changed, assuming that the 'facts' are not disputed. Reference has already been made to Copernicus' model (theory) of the universe, which put the sun at the centre of planets moving in circular orbits. Although this was a great improvement on the Ptolemaic model, the predictions made about the movement of the planets did not coincide with how the planets were observed to move. Johannes Kepler then modified the theory, proposing that the planets' orbits were elliptical, not circular. Newton elaborated the model, providing an explanation for the elliptical orbits in terms of the 'law of gravitation', which gave predictions fitting the observations well – that is, until the technology existed for previously undetected phenomena to be observed. Then it was Einstein's theory which fitted the events better.

These changes exemplify the gradual development of understanding, where each step is taken from the position reached by a previous one. A scientist does not come to a new phenomenon, or revisit a familiar one, without ideas derived from what is already known. In the same way, a pupil learning science has ideas derived from previous experience which are brought to bear in making his or her personal understanding of events and phenomena. These ideas are tested out against the evidence and modified so that they become ones which fit better what has been observed.

While there are, of course, many differences between the ways of working of the scientist and of the child learning science – to be explored in Chapter 2 – they are both aiming for understanding and there are broad similarities in the way that understanding is developed. These similarities are certainly enough to support the claim that learning science and doing science are basically the same activities. Enough also to justify the claim that science education is about learning (doing) science and not learning *about* science.

The concern with understanding, which is characteristic of science, enables it to be clearly distinguished from technology. Technological activity is closely connected in practice with scientific activity. Both are relevant in the education of young children but one should not be mistaken for the other. Technology is about solving problems by designing and making some artefact, whereas science is about understanding. They are, however, more closely related than this simple statement seems to suggest. In the pursuit of scientific activity, problems are often encountered which require technology, as for example in devising ways of observing (a microscope results from the application of technology to such a problem) or in handling data (a computer). At the same time the solution of problems by technology involves the application of concepts arrived at through science (the understanding of reflection and refraction of light in the case of the microscope, for instance). Technology is also involved in the solving of problems in other areas of the curriculum outside science.

While closely related, even at the primary level, science and technology are quite distinct. There is more to science than solving practical problems and more to technology than applying science concepts.

It is not only the aim of the activities which differ, but the nature of the knowledge which is applied. Layton (1990) argues cogently that scientific knowledge has to be 'reworked' before the technologist can use it. Scientific knowledge is expressed in terms of theories which are general and widely applicable, while technology requires knowledge that is particular, specific and tailored to the particular situation.

> It is structured by the tension between the demands of functional design, on the one hand (that is, it must enable the achievement of some design purpose), and the specific constraints of the ambience, on the other (that is, the contextual constraints such as cost-limits, deadlines, ergonomics and durability requirements, individual and societal preferences).
>
> (Layton, 1990, p. 13)

The introduction of technology into the curriculum has brought about a need for greater appreciation of the meaning of technological activity, while at the same time sharpening understanding of the differences between science and technology.

The tentative nature of scientific theories

Reference above to the successive models of the solar system and theories of the universe provide an example of how certain ideas have changed. We can confidently add 'and will change', for there is no reason to suppose that this process will not continue. Einstein would have been the last to claim that he had arrived at some kind of final word on the subject. Many many examples of changes in ideas in other branches of science could be cited. Without labouring the point, what these changes mean is that, at any particular time in the past – or indeed in the present – the only certainty is that the current theories, although believed to be the most perfect insights, are only passing stages in human understanding. The consequence of recognizing this is that any theory must be regarded as subject to change and therefore as only tentative knowledge.

For a theory to be worthy of the name, as Hawking points out in the words quoted on p. 8, it must be capable of yielding predictions which can be tested against evidence. Thus there is always the possibility of evidence which disagrees with it. Even though a theory may provide predictions which accord with all existing evidence for centuries (as Newton's did) there is always the possibility of further observations which do not fit (as indeed eventually happened in Newton's case). Hawking expresses this with clarity and authority:

> Any physical theory is always provisional, in the sense that it is only a hypothesis: you can never prove it. No matter how many times the results of experiments agree with some theory, you can never be sure that the next time the result will not contradict the theory. On the other hand, you can disprove a theory by finding even a single observation that disagrees with the predictions of the theory . . . . Each time new experiments are observed to agree with the prediction the theory survives, and our confidence in it is increased; but if ever a new observation is found to disagree, we have to abandon or modify the theory. At least that is supposed to happen, but you can always question the competence of the person who carried out the observation.
>
> (Hawking, 1988, p. 10)

If this applies to the theories of scientists, how much more seriously must it be taken in relation to the individual theories of learners? At any particular time learners' ideas are those which best fit the evidence available, but soon there are likely to have to be changes in the light of further information or observations. However, if we see for ourselves the evidence which brings the need to change there will be no confusion, but greater clarity. If children are taught science in a way which reflects the tentative nature of all theories it will seem natural for them to adapt their own ideas as new evidence is presented. It is only when others tell them to adopt different ideas for which they as yet see no reason, that confusion is likely.

Science as a human endeavour

Much of what has been said about the other characteristics of science is relevant to this point, underlining the origin of ideas in the way human beings make sense of their experience. So it is perhaps surprising that science is so often depicted as being some kind of objective picture of the world 'as it is', as if facts and theories exist *in* the objects or phenomena themselves to be teased out by those clever enough to do so. An unfortunate consequence of the term 'discovery learning' is that it gives this impression. We can agree that the answers to how things work *do* reside within them in that they are to be found by investigation and experimentation, but there is an important difference between regarding the process as 'finding *the* explanation of what is happening' and 'finding the best way for me to explain what is happening'. The difference is not trivial for the latter formulation admits that there may be other ways of explaining things.

This brings us to a point which has been skated over in the story of the changing theories of the universe. How did major changes in ideas come about? How did Kepler come to hit upon elliptical orbits as providing a better model than circular ones? How did Newton arrive at the universal theory of gravitation? In Newton's case we have the apocryphal story of the falling apple, but it still leaves a big question as to how any thinking about an apple was connected up with the solar system. There are always many gaps between the realization that an existing idea is failing and the idea which replaces it. Biographies sometimes help to provide an explanation of an event, but inevitably they present it with hindsight, from the position of knowing that the new idea was in fact a useful one. From this perspective the new idea always appears so obvious that it seems surprising that it was not thought of before. At the time, however, it probably emerged from creative reflection, even day-dreaming, rather than rational thinking. Creativity and imagination have played a part in the successive changes which have led to our current state of understanding. The ideas, which appear sometimes to 'come out of the blue', have been seized upon and selected from others by a mechanism which Einstein described as 'the way of intuition, which is helped by a feeling for the order lying behind the appearance' (Einstein, 1933).

Science includes much more than controlled experiment, objective measurement and the careful checking of predictions. It depends on these but just as much on creative thinking and imagination; a truly human endeavour. Learning science through experiencing it this way is more likely to appeal to, and excite, pupils (and future citizens) than learning it as a set of mechanical procedures and 'right answers'. In particular it is more likely to appeal to the female half of the population who currently feel excluded from science because of its masculine image (see Chapter 6).

Clearly it is important for teachers to understand science as it is described by the four characteristics discussed if they are to provide opportunities for pupils to learn science in this way. Science education should enable them to become at ease with it as an important part of human experience, past, present and future, as well as a means to improving the quality of life.

2

Children's Learning

In the last chapter a parallel was proposed between the successive changes in scientific ideas and the change in children's ideas. Now we look more closely at how children's ideas change, what fosters change towards more scientific ideas and what inhibits it. A model of the learning process is presented which is intended to have, as all good theories should have (see p. 8), a predictive function. What it predicts are the effects on learning of different kinds of experience, with consequent implications for the classroom.

We begin, however, not with the theory, but with the classroom experiences. An extended account of children's interactions with objects and with each other provides an anchor in reality against which subsequent theory must be constantly tested.

Children and science in action: an example

The following are transcripts of the conversations of several of the groups within one class of 11-year-olds all working on the same problem. Each group was given four blocks of varnished wood of similar size and shape but different density and labelled A, B, C and D, a bowl of water, spring balance, ruler and an activity sheet as shown on p. 15.

The first group of five will be called group 1. They are all girls and have begun to digest the task.

Jenny	Yes, one person to write down . . .
Anya	I know why – it's the varnish
Cheryl	Just a minute! How do you know it's the varnish when we haven't even looked at it?
Anya	Yes, but look, they . . .
Felicia	That one
	(putting block A into the water) Does it float?
	(all bend down to have a good look at the floating blocks)

Manjinder	Yes, half and half
Others	Half and half
Jenny	(Beginning to write this down) Right!
	(Felicia, Manjinder and Anya each pick up one of the remaining blocks)
Felicia	Shall I put B in?
Manjinder	I'll put C in
Anya	I'll put D in
Cheryl	Leave this A in there
Jenny	Now put B in there

1. Float your blocks on the water Look carefully at the way they are floating What do you notice that is *the same* about the way all the blocks float? What do you notice that is *different* between one block and another about the way they float? Get one person to write down what you notice, or make a drawing to show how the blocks are floating Check that you all agree that the record shows what you see Put the blocks in order from best floater to worst floater 2. What other things are the same about the blocks? What other things are different? Think about their size, their mass, colour and anything else Weigh and measure them Make sure you keep a record of what you find	3. Now discuss all the things that are the same about the blocks Get one person to put down a list of things that are the same Now discuss all the things that are different and make a list of them For each thing that is *different* about the blocks you should put down what you found about each block Discuss with your group the best way to do this 4. Now look at your results of things that are different Do you see any patterns in the differences? Write down any pattern you find

Meanwhile a second group of four boys (Ahmed, Richard, Pete and Femi) and one girl (Rachel) have started in a similar way, putting one block in at a time and so far A, B and C are floating on the water. Five heads are crowded round the bowl and before D is put in one of the boys says:

Ahmed	C's nearly all gone, so D must sink
Richard	D must sink
	(block D is then put in and floats very high in the water)

Pete	Ah, D's floating on the top
Femi	D's the best floater
Pete	Now why is D the best floater?
Ahmed	Got more air in it
Richard	Got more air
Femi	. . . air bubbles
	(Ahmed takes block D out of the water to look more closely at it)
Ahmed	It's lighter
Richard	It's the lightest
Rachel	It's balsa wood
Pete	(taking the block from Ahmed) Yes, that *is* balsa wood
Rachel	Balsa (taking block and putting it back in the water)
	(meanwhile Ahmed picks up the spring balance as if to suggest weighing but puts it down again as the attention of the group turns again to the other blocks in the water)
Pete	Now which is floating the worst?
Richard	This one – C
	(he picks C out of the water and hands it to Femi)
	Now feel that one
Femi	That's
Richard	That's terribly heavy
Pete	That's why it's still floating – all wood floats – but, if – the heavier it is the lower it floats
Femi	Yes
Richard	Yes, but it still floats
Femi	(taking B out of the water)
	B's pretty heavy
Pete	(picking up pencil to begin making a record) So A . . .
Rachel	– A is sort of –
Femi	A is half-way down, and B's . . .
Richard	B sort of flops. It's half way –
Rachel	– down at one side
Pete	(concerned to have an agreed record) So how shall we describe the way A floats?
Rachel	A equals about half
Ahmed	A sinks half way and floats half way
Femi	I think . . .
Pete	(writing) A is medium weight. Block A
Rachel	No, A block –
Ahmed	(to Pete) Yes, block A
Pete	(speaking as he writes) Block A . . .
	Ahmed turns to Richard while Pete writes and points to blocks B and C)
Ahmed	(to Richard) They're both the same
Richard	(to Ahmed) They're not, that one's lopsided

Pete	(speaking as he writes) . . . is medium . . .
Femi	(joining in with Richard and Ahmed) It's probably because of the varnish it's got on it
Rachel	(also joining in) Right
Pete	(summarizing what he has written) So, block A is medium weight and so . . .
Femi	B
Richard	B's lopsided
Pete	(still writing) . . . and so it . . .
Femi	Yes, B's the worst one
Richard	No, C's the worst one
Pete	(reading what he has written and regaining the attention of the others) . . . so it floats with half the wood under the water
Femi	Yes – about that (there is a pause, they all look again, putting their heads as low as possible to place their eye level near the water level)
Femi	Use a ruler – are you sure? (he goes to fetch a ruler)
Femi	Here's a ruler

Before going any further there is enough here in these children's activity to illustrate several points about the children's own ideas, mental skills and attitudes as they explore the material given to them. Right at the start Anya throws in what appears to be a wild hypothesis: 'It's the varnish'. There is no evidence for this, as Cheryl immediately points out to her, but it does show a desire to explain. In this case the 'explanation' is a low-level one, stated in terms of an observed feature (the varnish) without any attempt to propose a link between the supposed cause and its effect, although this may have been tacitly assumed. Cheryl's intervention indicates an attitude of willingness to use evidence. They then proceed to gather that evidence by putting the blocks in the water systematically. Their first 'result' is a rough one, 'half and half', but it is recorded at the time.

The second group is also making statements ahead of observation at the start of the quoted extract. They have already put three blocks in the water and noticed a pattern (quite accidental) that each one floated lower in the water than the last. Block C has been observed to be 'nearly all gone' and they predict 'so D must sink'. They accept the evidence when they see it, however, and find that D floats higher than any other block. So they are quite willing to change their ideas in the light of evidence. Immediately there is some further hypothesizing as to why block D floats best. The initial hypothesis, about air inside it, is overtaken by one taken up by the group, that D is lighter. (Perhaps to the children these are not alternative hypotheses but different ways of saying the same thing: things with more air in them are lighter than things with less air.) They also use their previous knowledge to identify block D as balsa wood.

At the point where the floating of block D seems to have been explained by its being 'the lightest' there is in fact no evidence of this at all. The children have not even 'weighed' the blocks in their hands in any way which would have allowed comparisons to be made. The process of interpreting observations is clearly way ahead of actually making the observations in this case. But a realization of the lack of evidence for their statement may be what makes Ahmed pick up the spring balance. He does not persist at this point, sensing that the group interest has passed on to other things, but much later (in the continuation, to come) he is the one who does introduce the balance and initiates the weighing of the blocks.

The hypothesis about the weight of the blocks of wood being related to the way they float seems to direct the next section of their work. Notice how Richard, when he identifies block C as the worst floater, hands it to Femi and says 'Now feel that one'. He is referring to 'feeling' the weight and the observations he is making about the wood are clearly focused and narrowed down by the idea he has in mind. Pete puts the suggested relation clearly, 'the heavier it is the lower it floats', after reminding himself, from previous knowledge, that 'all wood floats'. Pete then directs his attention to writing down what they have found (he is the recorder). But is it what they have found? What he writes is 'Block A is medium weight and so it floats with half the wood under the water.' Their observation was about the floating not about the weight; in fact they have no evidence about how the weight of A compares with that of other blocks. The statement recorded seems to have given an assumption the status of an observation and made their observation (of the floating) into an explanation for it. The ideas they have, based apparently on no more than jumping to conclusions, have influenced the process of gathering information. But they are still exploring the blocks, the water and the equipment and as long as the real things are in front of them there is the opportunity for them to reconsider and test out their ideas.

While Femi was explaining to Rachel why a ruler was needed, Richard was looking closely at block B floating in the water.

Richard   I can't understand why this is lopsided
Rachel   Well, look, see, it goes down that side
Richard   Yes, that's what I mean, I can't understand it
Pete   (who has not noticed this lopsided debate, having been busy writing the record, finishes writing about A) Now how is B?
Richard   Lopsided
Ahmed   Lopsided
Pete   (taking B out of the water) Now B is . . .
Rachel   Hang on a minute
           (she takes block B from Pete)
Pete   Now is B heavier than A, or lighter?
Rachel   Let's see if it's . . .
           (she uses the ruler to measure the thickness of the block at all four corners; all the others close round to see what she is doing)

Richard	(answering Pete's earlier question) Sort of lopsided, Pete
Femi	Lopsided
Rachel	(after finishing the measuring of B) Yes, it's the same length all the way down, but it's lopsided
Pete	(picks up blocks A and B, weighing them in his hands) Now which one is heavier, do you reckon?
Ahmed	(reaches for the spring balance again) Try this
Pete	(picks up the pan to use with the spring balance) If we try this, we can use this – who knows how to set up something like this?
Femi	Well, you put it on the hook . . . (he hooks the pan onto the spring balance) . . . now you can weigh something on it
Richard	(who has put blocks A and B back in the water and is looking at block B) Lopsided, in'it?
Pete	(picking block A out of the water) Now shake all the water off. Try A first (Rachel holds the spring balance while Pete puts block A on the pan)
Rachel	Just put it on
Pete	Now what's it come up to? (he ducks under Rachel's arm so that he can put his eye right in front of the scale)
Femi	(also closing one eye and peering at the scale) . . . about sixty
Richard	(also trying to look) . . . about sixty-three
Pete	Is there something we can hang it on, 'cos if you hang it on your hand you're likely to bounce it about

They then seek and find a way of steadying the spring balance. In the course of this they notice the zero adjustment, take the block off and use the zero adjustment and then discuss the reading of the divisions of the scale. From this point their investigation takes on a much more business-like air. They are not content with the rough 'feel' of the weight nor with describing the floating as 'half way' for they begin to measure the parts of the block below the water. Pete finds a neat way of recording this by drawing the blocks upside down like this:

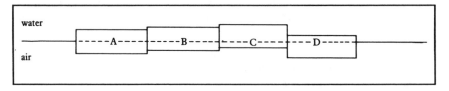

so that it is easy to see the direct relation between the length of the submerged part and the weight of the block.

The group showed what appeared to be a considerable progression in the way they approached the task. Starting from rather gross qualitative observations, of both the weight and the floating, they proceeded to use measurement to refine their observations. It appeared that this early period of rough observation was one of working out for themselves what the problem was. Once they defined it in their own minds they tackled it in a more systematic and precise manner. This may have taken some time (about 30 minutes) in this particular case because the task had been presented to them on a sheet; it was not of their finding. But evidently they did become interested in it and made it 'their own'. When children work on problems they have found for themselves there is no need for this period of 'coming to terms' with it. When they take on problems given to them, and they are generally very willing to do this, time may be needed for rough exploration before they begin to apply mental skills and ideas at the more advanced level of their capabilities. This is not unlike the scientist who takes rough measurements to 'get a feel' for the problem before setting up conditions for more precise measurement.

The observations, and later measurements, of this group were very strongly focused by their idea that the floating was related to the weight of the blocks. This idea was introduced early on, it was not something they 'discovered' by induction from their observations. It was, in fact, stated before enough evidence had been collected to support it and became the framework for the observations and measurements they made later. It seemed that there was an immediate attempt to find a relation that might explain initial observations and that later observations were focused by the desire to test this relation. In the process another relation might be suggested which was then tested. Thus all the observations were made for a purpose and not just to gather any information which later would be put together to find patterns and relations. It is entirely reasonable that this should be so, for without a purpose it would not be possible to decide what information to gather. The idea was in the children's minds and their investigation was carried out to test it.

To see if this applies to others than just this one group, here is another group working on the blocks activity and apparently making much more open-ended observations. There are five girls, Kay, Lisa, Mena, Nicola and Ann (who is the recorder).

We join them after about 20 minutes of exploratory activity with the blocks, when Ann has just summarized what they have so far done and is rereading the activity sheet to make sure nothing has been omitted.

Ann   (reading) What do you notice about the way they float?
             (answering herself) Well, we've found out that they all . . .
Nicola   . . . don't sink
             (brief laughter at this jokey statement of the obvious)
Mena   I know what it is, none of them float lopsided

Nicola	(who has taken two blocks out of the water and is holding them touching each other) They're magnetic!
Kay and	
Mena	(repeating what N has done) Yes, they're magnetic
Mena	And if you put them in like that, they go flat, look (she puts the blocks in with the largest face vertical and they settle with this face horizontal)
Kay	And D goes flat
Mena	Test with D and B
Lisa	They're getting water-logged now, aren't they?
Mena	This one goes flat last I think
Nicola	Hang on, let's put them all in and see which goes flat last (they do this)
Mena	C
Lisa	C
Kay	No, it may have been B
Mena	I think it shouldn't be that, it should be D
Lisa	That one's the heaviest, so it should go over first because it's heaviest (four pairs of hands go into the bowl, placing the blocks in vertically)
Mena	I think B should go over first and D should go over last
Nicola	Why?
Lisa	(to Ann) And they're magnetic
Mena	Yes, they're magnetic when they're wet (to Ann, who has been writing all this down) Write that down. They're really magnetic
Lisa	(reading from the worksheet) What other things are different?
Mena	Yes, look, the colour. The lightest in colour is the lightest in weight (Mena and Nicola take up the blocks and 'weigh' them in their hands)
Nicola	. . . and the darkest in colour is the heaviest in weight
Kay	Yes, the darkest in colour is the heaviest
Nicola	Yes, you know it's like white is very cool and dark is very hot . . .
Mena	Yes, you see this is the lightest and it floats the best and this is the darkest so it doesn't float so well
Nicola	The lightest is . . .
Ann	(leaving the report writing) Let's put it against the side (she picks up the two blocks in question, the heaviest and the lightest and directly compares their dimensions) You see, they're all the same size
Lisa	(pointing to the heavier one) It hasn't got so much light in it
Nicola	They're magnetic as well
Mena	That's probably only chance

Lisa	If you get them really wet and then put the sides together
Mena	(puts two blocks side by side)
	No, hang on – no, they are – even though they're shorter, this one's wider
Nicola	They're all the same size, then
Ann	The darkest is the heaviest and the lightest is the lightest
Lisa	Look, get them all wet . . .
	(dips two blocks in the water and holds them with the largest surfaces together)
Nicola	(does the same as Lisa, holding up one block with another clinging beneath it) Yes, they do, look. They're definitely magnetic
Mena	You've got to get them really wet
Kay	Try C and D
Nicola	Try the heaviest and the lightest
	(they try various combinations and find that the heavier block falls off when hanging beneath a lighter one)
Mena	The heaviest ones don't work very well
Kay	A heavy and a light work, but not two heavies

(A moment or two later they start weighing and measuring each block; Kay holds the spring balance)

Nicola	Put D on first
Ann	We can see that they're the same length
Nicola	Put D on, then we'll measure them all with the ruler
	(Kay puts D on the pan)
Nicola	That is . . .
Lisa	(interrupting) But we should dry them all off first because the water may affect them
Mena	But they're water-logged already . . .
Kay	Here you are, here's some dry towels
Lisa	The water may affect them. The water will affect to – er – thing
Kay	(pointing to the wet balance pan) This is wet – better dry that
Lisa	But that's going to be the same in all of them – so it won't matter
Ann	(still measuring with the ruler) They're about 12cm

(Some time is spent taking measurements of the blocks. They decide to find the average dimensions, for some reason, and Lisa sits aside from the rest of the group doing this. The others are stood round the bowl apparently doing nothing in particular, but they are in fact watching the movement of blocks 'stuck' to the side of the bowl. The movement is very slow . . .)

Mena	They'll never come off

Kay	I know, I'll give it a little jog and see which comes down first (both bang the sides of the bowl) They're not going to come down
Ann	This one should come down first
Kay	Yes, that one came down when I pushed (on the sides) but that one was harder to push down
Ann	So D came down, then A (Goes to record this. Nicola takes her place and continues to experiment in the same way, with Kay)
Nicola	We got to find patterns, what patterns have we got?
Kay	Well, we've got 2 dark ones and 2 light ones
Nicola	That's not a pattern
Kay	I know but . . .
Mena	We've got to find out what sort of pattern the weight goes in – there may be a pattern in the weight
Nicola	Start with D, then A, then C, then B (weight order)
Ann	Press them all down to the bottom and see which comes up to the surface . . . I should say D should come up first
Ann	One, two, three, let go!
Nicola	D, A, C, B, so that went in the heaviest order, because we found that B was the heaviest and D is the lightest
Kay	. . . and D came up first
Ann	. . . so it came out right, so we know our facts are right

There are more widely ranging observations made by this group than the earlier one and some attempt to explain each observation. Not all the ideas are tested, sometimes because other observations divert their attention, and the validity of many of the tests could be questioned. At the start of the extract the girls are following up their observation that if the blocks are placed in the water with the largest face vertical they do not float that way but turn over and 'go flat'. They have noticed a difference in the time taken for the blocks to 'go flat' and, at least in Mena's view, this is connected with the weight of the blocks. They decide to test all the blocks together rather than in pairs. The result does not satisfy Mena who says 'I think B should go over first and D should go over last', even though she saw that C was last. Nicola begins to question the assumption Mena is making and this might have led Mena to reconsider it, either by the force of argument or evidence or both.

They are interrupted, however, by the excitement over the discovery of the 'magnetism' of the blocks. It is interesting that none of the group members questions the use of the term 'magnetic' in relation to the blocks. They may indeed consider the effect to be exactly the same as found with a magnet or they may be using the word metaphorically. In either case the influence of previous knowledge in this interpretation of their observations is clear. The magnetic power of the blocks is tested by seeing if one block will support another hanging beneath it. They find the blocks differ in their ability to do this. Neither the test nor the conclusion from it is very soundly based but there is no challenge, from the teacher or the group, to make them reconsider it. Thus the idea that the blocks were 'magnetic' remained with them and was later reported as a finding from their group work.

The magnetism sequence is briefly interrupted when Lisa reminds the others that they are to look for other things that were different about the blocks. The colour of the wood is an obvious difference and Mena leaps immediately from the observation of difference to a relation which is more of an inspired guess than a pattern based on evidence ('the lightest in colour is the lightest in weight'). Indeed it is *after* this statement that the weights of the blocks are estimated by 'feel'. Nicola goes a stage further to try to explain the relation, 'you know it's like white is very cool and dark is very hot', again using previous knowledge, in this case of differences relating to colour.

In the final part of the extract the group of girls repeat in a more systematic way something that they had already done earlier (not covered by the transcript). They had held the blocks at the bottom of the bowl and noticed a difference in the rate at which they came up when released. These earlier qualitative observations were then being replaced by quantitative ones when they looked, not just for differences, but for whether these differences fitted their prediction. The pattern based on their ideas was indeed confirmed.

The only special thing about the discussions and activities of these children was that they were recorded. Such exchanges go on among children whenever they are truly co-operating and collaborating on a shared problem. Daily events in any classroom where opportunities exist for genuine group interaction and investigation would provide similar examples.

In such examples, the following points are the recurring themes:

1. The constant importation by the children of knowledge from previous experience, some relevant and some not.
2. The explanations, so readily offered, which seem like guesses preceding the evidence of whether or not they fit the observations.
3. The initial period of activity in which many predictions and explanations are aired during what seems superficial and non-quantitative exploration, followed by more focused, quantitative investigation.
4. The display of ability to use many of the process skills (observation, prediction, measurement), but carried out erratically, rather than combined in a systematic approach.
5. The challenging of each others' ideas by the children which provokes them to look for evidence to support their ideas, but still leaves many ideas untouched even though they are not supported by the evidence.
6. The neglect of attention to interpretation, to drawing observations together and reflecting on their meaning.

7. The opportunities, many of which are missed in practice, for timely intervention by the teacher which would help the children to develop their ideas and skills.

A model of children's developing ideas

A model of change in ideas has to represent reality as far as possible and to be able to account for failure to learn in certain circumstances as well as for the incidences of learning. It must also do this in as simple a way as possible if it is to serve as a mental framework for action. But any model of how children learn is no more than a hypothesis. There is no certain knowledge of how children's ideas are formed or how change in them can be brought about. All that anyone can do is to study the evidence in children's behaviour, put forward possible explanations for it and then see which of these hypotheses seems to be contradicted the least. This is what Piaget (1929) and Bruner, Goodnow and Austin (1966) and their associates have done; they looked in detail at children sorting pebbles, swinging pendulums, solving problems involving physical principles, and so on, and hypothesized about what might be going on in children's minds to explain the outward behaviour they observed. Evidence of this kind is always open to various interpretations and sometimes the evidence itself is disputed. What a child does with some pebbles or a pendulum depends on so many other things than the concepts and skills (s)/he has; it depends on whether (s)/he has seen the same or similar things before, on how interested (s)/he is in them or in other things instead, on how they are presented to him/her and by whom, on whether (s)/he is in company or alone, on what (s)/he did immediately before, how tired or alert (s)/he feels. Any generalization about children's learning must be interpreted as being an account of what is likely to be happening but not one which necessarily will hold in all incidents of learning and for all children.

The starting point for the model is the evidence that ideas from previous experience are called upon in trying to make sense of a new experience. There are probably several ideas which could be used in a particular situation and these are represented by circles in Figure 1.

Which of these existing ideas is 'activated' by being linked to the new experience will depend on the observation of similar features or properties (the ability of one block to hold another without apparent connection calling up the ideas of magnetism, for example). It may also depend on words, which can readily form links (though not always helpful when a metaphorical use of words is taken literally). The linking constitutes a hypothesis – that what worked or explained the previous situation must be working in the new one. In other words an existing idea is used to explain the new experience. This is represented in Figure 1 by the arrow. In practice more than one idea may be linked apparently at the same time, as when the boys proposed (p. 16) that it was air and then weight which accounted for the behaviour of the wooden blocks. However, for

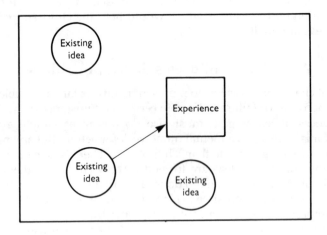

Figure 1

simplicity we show only one idea linked.

Whether the idea is useful in explaining the new experience is then tested. First the reasoning that 'if it is this . . ., then it follows that . . .' results in a prediction. Then available evidence is used, or more is sought, to see if the prediction fits and the explanation can be said to work. Figure 2 represents the linked idea being tested out to see if it fits observations from the new experience.

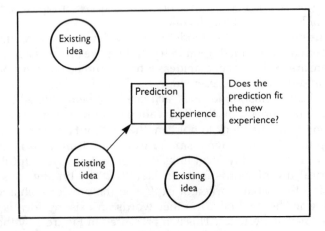

Figure 2

The possible outcomes of the testing are that (a) the linked idea is found to 'work' and emerges unchanged, but strengthened by the extension of its range; (b) the idea does not work but can be made to by some modification and so emerges as a modified idea; (c) it does not and cannot be made to work, in which case, the only way to try to make sense of the new experience is to start again and link another existing idea to it.

In all three cases (and in the range of possible variations on these three), learning occurs. In (a) and (b) existing ideas are strengthened or modified and thereby become more widely applicable. In (c) the idea that fails to explain the current experience is not dismissed as useless for explaining other experiences but its applicability is limited and it may gain a more specific definition.

Before taking the model further let us see how it accounts for the events in some examples. There were several occasions in the group discussion on pp. 14 to 23 when children made predictions about what might or might not happen. After the girls tested to see which block 'went flat' last, Mena said, 'I think it shouldn't be that, it should be D'. Mena made a prediction tested it and found it did not fit. Later, they pressed the wet blocks against the side of the bowl, above the water level and waited to see which would slip down first. Ann said, 'This one should come down first' based on some idea she had that the force holding them varied among the blocks. There was also the prediction by Richard's group of the connection between the weight of the blocks and the level at which they floated. This was eventually tested by predicting the relative weights from the way the blocks floated and then weighing them to see if the order was the same. Quite separately, Mena's group, having put the blocks in order of weight, predicted the order in which they would rise to the surface if all the blocks were held down at the bottom and released together. They predicted correctly and concluded 'so it came out right, we know our facts are right.'

The hypothesis that the blocks which stuck together were magnetic was not used to make a prediction and was not tested. It remained an untested assumption, along with several others, for example, about the colour of the blocks being significant. To suggest why this might be we return to the model and this time focus not on the change in ideas but the linking and testing processes which connect ideas to the experience.

The role of process skills in developing ideas

The model in Figures 1 and 2 suggests how ideas are changed by new experiences. When this process results in ideas which do indeed fit the experience, this is the path of learning. But the process does not automatically lead to the acceptance or development of ideas which really do fit the evidence. It is necessary to look at how the ideas are brought to bear on the experience to suggest why learning, in the sense just described, may not occur.

There are three parts of the process to consider:

- linking (involving observing, hypothesizing, predicting)
- testing (planning and carrying out a fair test, involving observing, measuring, recording)
- interpreting (recognizing patterns, drawing conclusions, reflecting)

What emerges from the attempt to understand the experience in terms of ideas depends on all of these. An idea which is linked may not be used predictively and so not tested; the test may not be a controlled and fair one, so that an idea which ought to have been rejected is accepted, or vice versa; the result may not be interpreted in terms of the initial idea, so that the latter may remain unchanged even though it ought to have been modified. In other words, *the way* in which the processes are carried out crucially influences the ideas which emerge. This is the basis of the claim made in Chapter 1 that the development of ideas depends on the use and development of the process skills.

It is important to note that when appropriate ideas do not emerge it may appear on the surface that similar things are happening – there are observations, predictions may be made, investigations may be carried out. But these may not be carried out in a way which we would call scientific. Observations may be narrowly focused on the evidence which confirms initial ideas, ignoring contrary evidence; the supposed prediction may involve a circular argument, not going beyond what is already known; the investigation may leave significant variables uncontrolled. The process skills have to be used rigorously if useful ideas are to emerge. Hence the importance of attention to developing these as scientific skills in children.

So we see that whether or not the children's ideas change as a result of seeing if what they predicted does or does not happen depends on more than just what happens; it depends, too, on the way they reason about it, on the nature of their own idea and their readiness to change their idea for a better one. This is a crucial matter for teaching. It is not enough to show children something that is in conflict with their ideas and expect this to bring about change. The children not only have to see for themselves that there is a conflict but to develop, again for themselves, an alternative explanation that is more effective in that it leads to a prediction that does fit the evidence.

What happens if an idea is not supported by the evidence but there is no alternative available? This may well happen with young children whose range of prior experience and ideas is more limited than for those who are older. However, it will be a possibility at any time depending on the novelty of the experience encountered. Rather than leave a vacuum and tolerate the discomfort of not being able to explain something, there is a tendency to hold onto existing ideas despite contrary evidence, or to 'bend' the idea to fit. We might interpret the girls' conclusion that the wooden blocks were only 'magnetic when they're wet' in this way.

Another example illustrates how different existing ideas and experience determine the outcome of children's attempts to understand phenomena. A group of children of a wide age range were discussing the common experience that expanded polystyrene feels warm to the touch. They had a big block of the plastic which was going to form part of the props for a school play. There was general agreement at first that 'there is something hot inside'. The younger children apparently found this quite a reasonable explanation. Their experience, after all, of large warm objects such as hot-water bottles and radiators, was that there was something inside that was hot and stayed hot for a considerable time. So their prediction was that the polystyrene block would stay warm, and it did.

The older children, however, brought to this problem the more complex idea that hot things generally cooled down if there was nothing to keep them hot. They knew that there was nothing but polystyrene right through the block and so predicted that if it was warm at one time then it should get cooler as time went on, and it didn't. They even tried to make a piece cool down by putting it in a fridge and it obstinately refused to feel cold. It was quite a puzzle to them and they had to think of some altogether other way of explaining the warmth they felt. In the event they came to it through playing with some other pieces of polystyrene in the form of very small pellets. They ran their hands through the pellets and one said 'It's like putting on warm gloves'. 'But gloves aren't warm, they just keep you warm' said another. 'That's what's happening with the blocks, it just keeps your hand warm, it isn't warm itself.' Here was a possible explanation (though expressed with a great deal of certainty, it was still a hypothesis) and an associated prediction. If the idea was right then the block would not be any warmer than anything else around. This could be checked with a thermometer, and it was.

Note that the 'new' idea was not new in the sense of being discovered from the observations, it was only new in that it had not been brought to bear on the problem before. In itself it was well known to the children that gloves and clothes keep them warm without having any heat source to do this. What they had to do to use this existing idea was, first, to recognize the possible connection, secondly, create a possible explanation (hypothesis) based on it, thirdly, to use it in making a prediction and, fourthly, to test the prediction.

In reality the thinking often happens in a flash and it is in no way being suggested that children consciously think through from one step to another. After all, we have seen that it is not possible to account in a rational way for how scientists arrive at new ideas. The steps are a convenient way of looking at what happens. In the polystyrene example the same processes led to different emerging ideas for the younger and older children: the younger finding their ideas confirmed and therefore not needing to change them and the older finding a conflict because their existing ideas were different and did not fit the evidence.

Similar developments take place in other ideas and the influence of the mental processes of applying, hypothesizing, predicting and checking predictions can be traced. Take ideas about dissolving, for instance. Younger children accept that sugar stirred into water 'disappears' in the sense that it is no longer there. The ideas they bring do not conflict with the observation for they do not include the concept that matter such as sugar does not just disappear in this sense. The experience of older children will probably have led to the idea that matter usually turns up again when you think it might have disappeared and it makes more sense to them to consider the disappearance as only apparent. They may find a way of checking this hypothesis readily: for example, if the sugar is still there you should be able to taste it. If it works, then the idea might be accepted or confirmed that substances like sugar are able to change in some way so that they cannot be seen in water but are still there. This is an advance on the earlier 'disappearance' idea but may itself not last for long. Other problems may require a more sophisticated idea, one which suggests an explanation of what happens to the sugar when it becomes invisible in the water. Generally, children will have wider experience and will probably have reached the secondary school, when the need for a more advanced explanation occurs and they can then call on a greater range of ideas that can be tried in searching for the explanation.

The origin of ideas: old wives' tales or products of thinking?

So far the discussion of the model has not touched upon the origin of 'existing ideas'. Some of these will be the product of changes in earlier ideas, for clearly there is a continuous cycle of using developed ideas as experience expands and developing them further. The changing ideas about dissolving exemplify this process. This raises the intriguing question: where do they start? Are children born with 'existing ideas'? At the same time, not all ideas evolve through thinking and reasoning. We are all bombarded every day with ideas from the media, casual conversation and direct instruction – ideas which are not the product of our thinking. A second question, then, concerns the status of these imported ideas. We will look at these two questions separately.

Where does it all start?

The clearest guide seems to come from the work of Piaget, who did more than anyone else to show that children have their own ideas which make sense to them in terms of their own logic. Piaget also studied the behaviour of very young children. His ideas suggest that for young children (in what he called the sensorimotor period) actions take the place of thought. Children at this stage appear to 'know' the world through patterns of their own action. Gradually, these patterns of action are internalized and the child's world is no longer essentially centred on himself.

These internalized actions later become the thoughts and thought processes. External experience can then be considered separately from internal ideas but before this they are as one.

It seems likely then that the answer to whether it is ideas or experience which comes first is that it is neither. The young child's actions are all that exist and these gradually separate into what later are described as 'ideas' and 'experience'. Once distinguishable the interaction of these may, according to the suggested model, bring about the development of ideas in the course of which they pass through a range of stages such as Piaget's work described.

The question we now turn to is whether all ideas are formed by the processing of experience and existing ideas or whether ideas can be received or generated in other ways. It is sometimes hard to believe that some of the more strange ideas of children (and of adults) come about through experience. An adult interpretation of experience often suggests something totally different from what children appear to believe. If, as suggested, though, children's ideas are a product of the way they process the experience as well as their existing ideas, then it is easy to see that these may not always lead to what an adult would view as a logical outcome. Either the existing ideas or the way of thinking about them, or both, may differ considerably from their counterparts in adult thought.

The notion of ideas being formed from experience is not therefore contradicted by the fact that children's ideas seem very strange and illogical to adults. Piaget's later work provides an example of apparently strange ideas having a basis in children's earlier experience. Joan Bliss, who worked with Piaget at that time, tells of how children were shown a smooth board across which balls could be 'fired' by a spring-loaded device. They were asked to predict the direction in which the ball should be fired to bounce off the edge at a given angle. Their drawings of the expected paths of the balls across the board were not straight. When asked about this they explained it in terms of how they knew balls to behave. In their experience, of rolling balls across bumpy paths or grass, it was quite natural for balls to move erratically. Their ideas were not fanciful but based on experience. This point is underlined by the examples in Chapter 3.

Response to 'ready-made' ideas

A different problem is posed by the ideas current in everyday life, some amounting to 'old wives' tales' and some forced on us by advertisements or political activists. 'Nothing tastes better than butter' is not usually an idea developed from experience. So does it have the same status in making sense of experience as an idea which has been developed, as it were, from within? There are plenty of ideas around that would have a confusing influence on children's scientific understanding if they were taken seriously. For example, my mother 'taught' me that if the sun shone through the window onto the fire it would put the fire out, that maggots were made of cheese and developed spontaneously from it, that placing a loose-fitting lid on a pan of boiling water made it boil at a low temperature, that electricity travelled more easily if the wires are straightened out. In my science education I found that these ideas did not stand up to the test of experience (but my mother still believes them). Many similar examples can be found every day, where people (and some of them science teachers!) are explaining things in terms of ideas which can very easily be shown not to fit experience.

These everyday examples are only some of the 'ready-made' ideas to which children are exposed. The expression 'ready-made' is used to denote generalizations or facts which have been created by someone else and not generated through the processes of applying, testing out and modifying existing ideas. Many more and more potentially useful ideas are deliberately presented to children in lessons at school. These presented ideas are not necessarily inferior to children's own ideas (indeed they are intended to be better in explaining scientific events) but they will not be immediately available for use in understanding events in the same way as the 'owned' ideas which are already part of the children's way of thinking. In order for the presented ideas to become part of the web of existing ideas, they have to be tried out as alternatives to existing ideas and judged in terms of their value in making sense of experience. Unless, or until, this happens the presented ideas will not be used; the children will stick to the ones which arise from previous experience. There are implications here for the way in which new ideas are presented to children; they should come as additional ones to try out against their own and to be tested in the same way as their own. Any implication that they are necessarily correct and not subject to any testing will leave them outside the set of ideas which are understood as if they were the children's own.

It must be remembered, however, that the result of testing an idea depends on the way the testing is done as well as on the idea. This may well explain why so many 'old wives' tales' stay alive and believed. Does the idea lead to a prediction which fits the evidence? The answer is likely to depend on how the 'prediction' is made and tested. Consider, for example, the 'old wives' tale' that the sun shining on the fire will put it out. Here is how it might be incorporated into a person's own ideas:

Ready-made idea   The sun puts the fire out
Prediction   If this is true, when the sun shines on the fire it will
                    burn less brightly
Test of prediction When the sun shines on the fire the flames cannot be
                    seen and it glows less brightly
Result   The evidence is consistent with the idea; it works

Here is another way in which this idea might be tested:

Ready-made idea   The sun puts the fire out

Prediction	If this is true, a fire on which the sun has shone will go out more quickly than one on which no sun has shone
Test of prediction	The sun makes no difference to how quickly the fire goes out
Result	The evidence is not consistent with the idea; it doesn't work

Probably the same observation which led to the rejection of the idea created a link with another idea that was the basis of an alternative hypothesis; perhaps the sunshine only appears to make the fire die down:

Prediction	If the effect is only apparent, then the fire will not be permanently affected by the sunlight on it
Test of prediction	Shade a fire that seems to have been 'put out' by the sun and see if it remains less bright (or apply a more elaborate test, depending on equipment available)
Result	The evidence is consistent with there being no detectable effect; the new idea has not been rejected

The difference between the prediction and the test in the case where the 'everyday' idea, or old wives' tale, is accepted and in the case where it is rejected is central to the distinction between a scientific and an 'everyday' approach. A scientific approach involves a prediction which is a logical result of applying the idea and the test of it involves doing something to obtain relevant evidence, in this case perhaps timing how long a fire burns with and without the sun shining on it. The 'everyday' approach does not extend the prediction beyond what is already known; a circular argument replaces a logical prediction. The test is therefore bound to be confirmatory, for no new evidence is sought. The process of relating the idea to experience is once again shown to be as important as the nature of the idea. 'Everyday' ideas can be accepted because whether or not they 'work' is judged in an 'everyday' way.

These arguments can account for the acceptance by my mother and others of her generation that cheese maggots are spontaneously created from cheese, whereas I and others of my generation regard such an idea as strange and would not accept it as our own. My mother, having had no science education, would seek and notice only confirmatory evidence. I and my generation would not only find this evidence unconvincing but would also have alternative ideas which are more convincing (that is, give predictions which fit the evidence better).

Before going further I must apologise to my mother if I overstate the position to make a point. She is not, of course, the only one to have strange ideas. Thurber's mother apparently thought herself surrounded by devices which had to be treated in particular and peculiar ways to prevent all kinds of disaster:

The telephone she was comparatively at ease with, except, of course, during storms, when for some reason or other she always took the receiver off the hook and let it hang. She came naturally by her confused and groundless fears, for her own mother lived the latter years of her life in the horrible suspicion that the electricity was dripping invisibly all over the house. It leaked, she contended, out of empty sockets if the wall switch had been left on. She would go around screwing in bulbs, and if they lighted up she would hastily and fearfully turn off the wall switch and go back to her *Pearson's* or *Everybody's*, happy in the satisfaction that she had stopped not only a costly but dangerous leakage. Nothing could ever clear this up for her.

(Copyright © 1933, 1961 James Thurber. From *My Life and Hard Times*, published by Harper & Row)

In more serious vein the chance of acceptance of ready-made ideas handed to children at school must now be considered. There is no doubt that some scientific ideas seem as strange to pupils as 'old wives' tales' seem to teachers. 'What we're taught in science is often difficult to believe' is a remark from a thoughtful 12-year-old, really trying to make sense of some ready-made ideas handed out by her teacher. She found the teacher's ideas difficult to believe because she tested them out in an 'everyday' way, not in a scientific way, and they did not fit experience as well as 'everyday' ideas. Take the idea that air has water vapour in it. This was used by the teacher to 'explain' the formation of dew on the grass. But the girl already had an explanation for this in her own idea that the coldness of the grass created the water. Her own idea also fitted other experience: the coldness of a fridge created water drops on bottles and cans taken out of it. What she was unable to do was to test either her own or the ready-made idea in an adequate way. Although the teacher's idea did not make sense to her, she was not free to reject it; it remained as an idea which she knew about, and could recall if asked, but it was not her own idea.

Children are exposed all the time to ideas of others (their teachers, other children, parents) and those which come through the media. There is no way in which children can be cut off from these other ideas and be allowed to form their own, nor would this be desirable. They must have access to a range of ideas which may be different from their own and challenge their existing ideas. If they are to consider these alternatives rationally, and not simply recite the ones which are forced hardest on them, they must have the mental and other skills needed to test them adequately against experience.

Some implications for changing children's ideas

In trying to draw together the threads of the argument in this chapter it seems best to proceed from the more general to the more particular points. If children are to achieve the aims of science education of developing understanding of the world around them, then we must cater for change in both their ideas and their process skills. If process skills are not gradually made more scientific and logical then 'everyday' ideas will not be challenged and potentially more useful ideas will be rejected. If initial 'everyday' ideas are not gradually transformed into more useful ones then process skills will be limited in their effect and so in their contribution to understanding.

From this it follows that the aims of science teaching must include the following:

• to help children become aware of their own ideas and to have access to those of others (peers, teacher and other sources) to set against them.
• to help children apply ideas (their own and others) to a problem or situation, and to test the usefulness of the ideas in particular cases.
• to help children reflect critically on how ideas have been used and tested and to find more effective ways of doing these things.

In working towards these aims experience shows that it is worthwhile avoiding certain situations and trying to supply others. Some of the ones for teaching to avoid include:

• ignoring children's own ideas or assuming that children do not have ideas about an experience or problem which is new
• introducing ready-made ideas without opportunities for children to try them out and compare them with their own ideas
• expecting children to accept the wider usefulness of ideas introduced to explain a contrived classroom experience which has little obvious parallel in their experience of everyday life
• accepting from children judgements about whether or not ideas work without asking them to explain their reasoning and show how evidence has been used
• confining children to tasks so circumscribed that they are not free to discuss and share thinking with others.

Some of the more positive things that are suggested about teaching are that it should provide the following:

• opportunities for children to investigate problems and events from which useful ideas can be developed
• opportunities for children to think of alternative explanations or solutions and test them fairly
• the introduction of ready-made ideas in such a manner that they are regarded as alternatives worth considering, not as right answers
• opportunities for children to share in groups a task or problem where they are responsible for the ideas and ways of testing them
• invitations for children to explain the thinking which led to a solution or idea being put forward in terms of how the idea came to their mind, how it led them to make a prediction and how the prediction was tested
• acceptance of the ideas and explanations of children which are consistent with their limited experience and ways of processing evidence even though these may require refinement later in the light of wider experience and knowledge.

3

Children's Ideas

The model presented in the last chapter described the process of developing ideas through using process skills. These ideas gradually become closer to the accepted scientific view of things as children's experience expands and as their process skills and ways of reasoning become more controlled and rigorous. The focus in this chapter is the developing ideas, the form they take *en route* to the more widely applicable scientific view. We shall look at what research has revealed about the ideas children have at different points and ask the questions: what are the general characteristics of these ideas? what are the implications for teaching? In the next chapter similar questions will be considered in relation to children's developing skills and attitudes related to learning in science.

In order to tackle these questions it is necessary to identify and define the ideas we are aiming for children to develop. This identification could be avoided by simply adopting the 'knowledge and understanding' targets of the National Curriculum. However, it has to be remembered that this is only one curriculum, whose definitions and structure have been moulded by a particular framework – one of behavioural statements at various levels. Even within the UK there are two other versions of a common curriculum for science, and elsewhere there are many more different approaches.

We propose here to use a list which is readily related to all of these various curriculum formulations; it originates, as most such statements do, in the view that science education should help children to understand the world around them and relate to their experience of it. This helps to identify some broad areas of understanding in relation to which the development of children's ideas will be discussed.

Areas of understanding and main ideas relating to them

The following six broad areas of understanding have been chosen as the framework for the subsequent discussion of children's ideas:

- The variety and characteristics of living things
- The processes of life
- Materials, their properties, uses and interactions
- Energy sources, transmission and transfer
- Forces and movement
- The Earth and its place in the Universe

There is little point in trying to explain this list; it has much in common with other similar lists and represents equally arbitrary divisions within the full set of scientific ideas. In the process of breaking down the whole into parts to be examined separately it is important to keep in mind a view of the gradual but uneven development of this whole. Figure 3 attempts to represent this. There is a time axis from left to right and the lines represent strands of developing ideas: sometimes merging, as broader concepts are formed from the recognition of overarching similarities between phenomena previously seen as distinct; sometimes diverging, as ideas are elaborated.

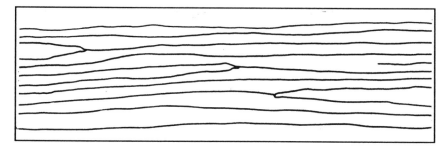

Figure 3

Each of the six areas of understanding is itself a set of developing strands, as suggested in Figure 4, which could be defined at a range of levels of detail.

In working towards an identification of the strands it is helpful to identify criteria to be used in defining appropriate statements of intended knowledge and understanding. One criterion, already used in identifying the six areas, is that they concern children's immediate everyday experience. This criterion is regarded as a central one for two related reasons. The first is that it means that children are developing concepts about the things around them; the growth of understanding of these things is a large part of the reason for learning science. The second is that it is to these ideas that children can most readily relate their own experience and first-hand knowledge. It is through being applied and used that ideas develop and become part of children's own ways of understanding. Ideas that do not link in with experience are unlikely to remain long in children's minds, however simple they may be.

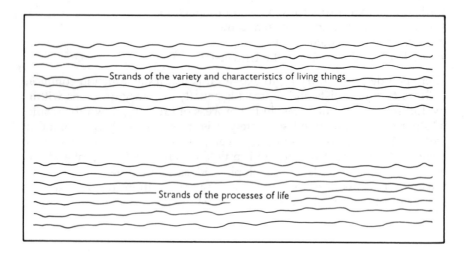

Figure 4

A second criterion indicative of the level of ideas that children can be expected to develop relates to their ways of thinking. There is no doubt that these are limited for primary children and whether the reason for this is argued in terms of their experience or mental maturity is to some extent irrelevant. The point is that experience indicates that the understanding of many of the abstract concepts of science is reached later in the secondary school and then only by some pupils. It can be argued, as it is here, that such understanding is helped by earlier exposure to concrete examples of the phenomena to which the abstract concepts will later be related. It is likely, too, that with this experience many more children than at present would achieve a better scientific understanding. But this is not an argument for introducing abstract ideas and generalizations at the primary level. Rather the reverse, for a sound foundation of ideas tested and tried in a variety of practical contexts is far more useful to later learning than a superficial knowledge of theoretical ideas.

A closely related criterion, but one that is distinct because it acknowledges that the concepts being identified are scientific ones, concerns their accessibility to children through the use of process skills. Children should be able to collect evidence and see that it is consistent with the ideas being generated; they should be able to use the ideas to make predictions which can be put to the test; they should be able to see for themselves whether or not the ideas 'work' in a range of cases. This does *not* mean that the ideas are only taken from among those which are the children's existing ideas, as was noted in Chapter 2 (p. 32). It is the usefulness of an idea that gives it meaning for children, not the source. Useful ideas can and do come from other pupils, from teachers, books, television and radio. Nor does the condition that children should be able to 'make the idea their own' by the use of process skills mean that we are only concerned with ideas about things children can physically touch and manipulate. Many of them will be, and should be, of this kind but it is important not to exclude ideas about events in children's experience which cannot be manipulated, such as ideas about the sun, moon and stars and about the weather. Children can develop these ideas by the use of process skills. Careful observation and recording reveal patterns and give rise to hypotheses and predictions which can be checked by further observation.

A fourth criterion concerns continuity in science education. Ideas developed in the primary years should link with those developed at the secondary and further levels of education.

In summary, then, ideas relating to the six areas of understanding should be selected according to these four criteria:

• They should help children's understanding of everyday events and the world around them and be applicable to their experience
• They should be within the grasp of primary-school children, taking into account their limited experience and mental maturity
• They should be accessible and testable through the use by children of science process skills
• They should provide a sound basis for further science education.

When these criteria are applied, the main ideas arrived at are those set out for each area of understanding in Figure 5. The main idea of each strand is a developing one, meaning different things at different points in development. Some of these ideas are illustrated later in this chapter. However, the individual variation in children's ideas is such that it is not possible to identify a sequence of development in close detail. It is only appropriate to do this at well separated points in time and to describe the nature of changes which indicate development as is necessary to guide the assessment of pupils' achievements. The end of the primary and secondary phases of education seem useful points for this and suggestions are made for this in the context of assessment in Chapter 8 (p. 145).

At this point the concern is to describe the curriculum in a way that provides access for all children whatever their age, experience or ability. So, for example, all pupils will be able to develop ideas about 'the relationship between the properties of materials and their uses'. For the younger and less experienced this will mean exploring materials to see how they differ and what can be done with them; for older and more experienced pupils it will involve investigating how the materials can be combined and structured to achieve required properties. Some will achieve aspects of the understanding suggested for pupils aged 7/8 (p. 145):

that materials vary in properties; that they are used for different purposes because of their properties.

The characteristics and variety of living things

The variety of living things called animals
The variety of living things called plants
Adaptation of living things to their habitats
Competition among a community of plants and animals
The effect of pollution and other human activities on living things

Processes of life

The conditions needed by plants and animals for life and growth
How plants and animals pass through life-cycles
The different functions relating to life processes of different parts of the human body
Dependence of animals and plants on each other to sustain life

Materials, their properties, uses and interactions

The wide variety of natural and processed materials with different properties (solubility, hardness, transparency, etc.)
The relationship between properties of materials and their uses
Changes in materials that are reversible but other that are not
Combustion as a reaction of a fuel with oxygen which releases energy
The composition of materials as pure substances, mixtures or compounds

Energy sources, transmission and transfer

Sounds originating from vibrating objects
Sound travelling through different materials but not space
Light passing through space but stopped by some materials forming shadows
White light splitting into colours when passing into water or glass
Reflection of light and sound at surfaces
Flow of an electric current in a simple circuit of conducting material
Control of the flow of electricity by devices such as switches and relays

Forces and movement

The effect of forces in changing the motion and/or shape of things
Changing forces by using simple machines
Describing movement of objects in terms of their speed and acceleration
Gravity as a downward force on all objects on the Earth

The Earth and its place in the Universe

The daily variations and seasonal patterns in the elements that make up the weather
The apparent movement of the Sun, Moon and stars relative to the Earth
How the Earth's movement relative to the Sun gives rise to day and night and seasonal differences
The Earth as a source of materials which need to be conserved
Function of the soil in providing for plants to grow

Figure 5   Main ideas within the areas of understanding

While others will achieve the more developed ideas appropriate to pupils aged 11/12 (p. 145):

> that the properties of materials (including solid, liquid and gas) can be explained by their composition and structure; that manufactured materials can be designed to have required properties.

But for all, the strand identifies one of the main ideas to which children's activities with materials should contribute. Others are given in Figure 5.

This way of describing the curriculum is an attempt to provide enough structure to act as a guide for planning teaching and learning but to leave freedom for teachers to pursue the development of ideas by following the route of children's understanding. It avoids the rigid framework of 'targets' at 'levels' which can dictate the steps in learning too closely for consistency with the sort of learning described in the last chapter.

The form in which these ideas are expressed needs some explanation. They might be regarded as statements of fact, for example, 'How plants and animals pass through life-cycles' but such a fact, if rote-learned, would be meaningless. It has meaning only if it arises from observing the life-cycles of a range of plants and animals, involving, for example, germinating seeds, tending seedlings, looking after the developed plants through flowering and setting seeds again. It will also involve observing the life-cycles of a variety of animals, from stick insects to hamsters and finding out about others through pictures, films or reference books. So these apparently simple statements imply the acquisition of a great deal of knowledge gained through investigation, first-hand observation and from secondary sources.

Children's developing ideas

The course that a particular child's understanding takes along the strands of the main ideas in Figure 5 is individual, since it depends upon the sense that (s)he is making of experiences within and outwith school at various times. However, there are obvious similarities in children's experiences and these are reflected in commonalities in their developing ideas. Research has confirmed this and indeed it is striking how similar the ideas of children in different parts of the world have been found to be.

The following examples of children's ideas are offered in illustration of the course of development of some of the main ideas and to provide evidence for some general characteristics which have implications for teaching. The examples can only sample the strands and for a more comprehensive account the research references and particularly the SPACE research reports can be consulted.

Variety of life

The idea that there is a group of living things called 'plants' and another called 'animals', basic to biology, is not a simple matter of definition. Some research by Bell (1981) in New Zealand established that:

children often have a much more restricted meaning for the word plant. In a sample of 29 children, she found 10-year-olds, 13-year-olds and 15-year-olds who considered a tree was not a plant.

'No, it was a plant when it was little, but when it grows up it wasn't, when it became a tree it wasn't.' (10-year-old)

Other children suggested that a plant was something which was cultivated, hence grass and dandelions were considered weeds and not plants by some 13- and 15-year-olds. Further, almost half the pupils interviewed considered that a carrot and a cabbage were not plants; they were vegetables. Over half those interviewed did not consider a seed to be plant material. Despite considerable exposure to science teaching many of the 15-year-olds held similarly restricted ideas to the 10-year-olds.

(Osborne and Freyberg, 1985, p. 7)

Following the individual interviews, Bell and colleagues carried out a survey of much larger samples of pupils. Some of their findings are given in Figure 6, which shows the percentages of pupils at various ages who considered a tree, a carrot, a seed and grass to be plants.

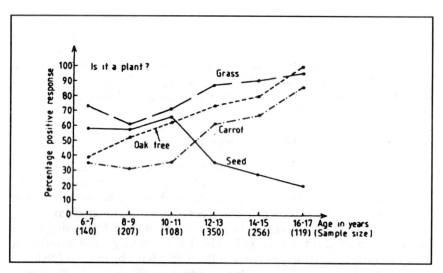

Figure 6   (Osborne and Freyberg, 1985, p. 7)

In similar investigations of children's ideas about what are 'animals' it was found that

Many of the pupils considered only the larger animals, such as those found on a farm, in a zoo, or in the home as pets, as animals. Reasons for categorizing something as an animal, or not doing so, included the number of legs (animals are expected to have four), size (animals are bigger than insects), habitat (animals are found on land), coating (animals have fur), and noise production (animals make a noise).

(Osborne and Freyberg, 1985, p. 30)

It is clear that the everyday usage of words has a considerable effect, which is particularly strong in the case of the concept of 'animal'. Research carried out by Bell and Barker (1982) involving interviews and a survey of children from age 5 to 17 years showed that children's initial idea of what is an animal is restricted to large land mammals. For instance, a high proportion of their sample of 5-year-olds recognized a cow as an animal and the proportion rose to 100 per cent by the age of 7 years. However, creatures such as worms and spiders were not considered to be animals by three-quarters of the 9-year-olds and only a slightly lower proportion of 12-year-olds. Only a fifth of the sample of 5-year-olds considered a human being to be an animal and this proportion rose to just over a half for 9- and 12-year-olds.

Commenting on these findings Osborne (1985) makes the point that signs in shops such as 'No animals allowed' would reinforce a narrow view of the notion of animal. So would the label 'animal house' in a zoo and the distinction between animals and fish that tends to be part of the common usage of the words. These everyday ways of using the word conflict with the 'correct' use, based on the common features shared by all animals. The conflict can have serious consequences in children's misunderstanding if there is any uncertainty as to which meaning of the word is being used in a particular instance. A teacher can do nothing to prevent the word being used loosely in everyday situations but can do something to find out what meaning the word conveys to the children. Bell (1981) suggests that the teacher should help children to form the scientific idea of 'animal' and at the same time make them aware that this is different from the everyday meaning.

Processes of life

A useful summary of research into children's ideas in this area is provided by the SPACE project Research Report (1992). In general it shows that children's ideas develop to make sense of their expanding knowledge of living things around and of their own bodies. For instance, young children become aware of the insides of their bodies, starting with the heart, as separate organs each with a single function. Later they come to perceive connecting channels between the organs which enable them to work together. In the SPACE research children were asked to draw on an outline of the human body what they thought was in their own bodies. It was found that

> children draw those organs or parts which are more easily sensed – the heart which beats, bones which can be felt and the brain because the capacity for self-conscious reflection and awareness has developed by this age. In general, organs such as kidneys, lungs, intestines which are not sensed, are not part of children's knowledge of the body.
>
> (SPACE research report on The Processes of Life, 1992)

A further investigation by the SPACE team of children's ideas about the conditions that a plant needs to grow showed the impact of their everyday experience. Children of six or seven years indicated that the plant needed water or soil or sun, with few mentioning all three. Older pupils tended to replace 'sun' by light and heat and the number of requirements mentioned increased with age. The role of the soil in helping plants to live was regarded as simply being for support; very few children indicated that it would provide 'food' or substances needed by the plant.

Materials

The ideas children have about the use of materials for various purposes are at first circular: we use paper for writing on because paper is good for writing on. There seems to be no explanation needed in terms of properties of the material, just that it is chosen because it serves the purpose. Later the use of materials is recognized as being directly related to the children's experience of the properties required by various objects. For example, chalk is used for writing on the blackboard because it is soft and white, glass is used for windows because you can see through it, wood is used for doors and furniture because it is strong, firm, keeps out the rain and doesn't tear or bend (SPACE research report on Materials, 1990).

In relation to changes in materials, too, there is a stage in which there seems to be no need for explanation. For example, children use their experience of finding rust under bubbles of paint on metal gates or bicycle frames to conclude that rust is already there under the surface of metal, hence there is no need to explain what causes it to form.

Energy

Investigations of children's ideas about light have shown remarkable similarity in relation to the role of the eye in seeing things. Children who are past the stage of believing that objects no longer exist if they are hidden from view or if they close their eyes, nevertheless describe the process of seeing as if it is their eyes that produce the light that makes the objects appear. Figure 7 shows a 10-year-old's drawing of how you see a bottle standing on a table when the light is switched on.

In a class of 26 9–11-year-olds, eight showed arrows from the eye to the bottle, four showed the light rays with arrows from the bottle to the eye and two had them going both ways, as in Figure 8. The remainder (12) showed no connection between the eye and the bottle. Their responses, however, leave one in no doubt that they have worked out their own explanation of experience, which is not the same as the explanation given by physics.

It is perhaps understandable that the eye is seen as an active agent rather than a receiver, for this fits the subjective experience of 'looking'. When we choose to look at something we do feel our eyes turn as if we

Figure 7

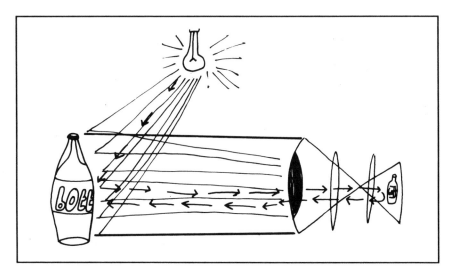

Figure 8

are the active agent in the process, and indeed the arrow from receiver to object does represent the line of sight. A variation on this idea is to regard the presence of light as somehow activating the eye, as described in Figure 9.

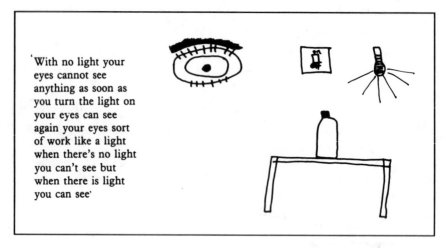

'With no light your
eyes cannot see
anything as soon as
you turn the light on
your eyes can see
again your eyes sort
of work like a light
when there's no light
you can't see but
when there is light
you can see'

Figure 9

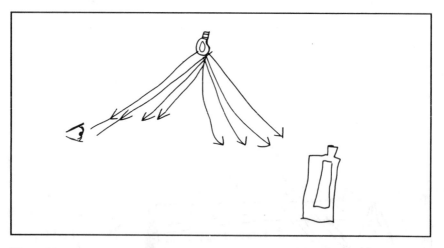

Figure 10

Figure 10 is typical of the responses from a class of younger children (7–9-year-olds). All but four of the 27 in the class showed light spreading to the eye and the bottle but nothing between bottle and eye. The children's interpretation of the situation does not take into account the need for light to fall on the object and to be reflected by it, or to be given out by it, for it to be seen. Piaget showed in his early work that 9- and 10-year-olds did not connect the onset of darkness at night with the lack of sunlight, they 'explained' darkness by describing it *as* night, something that comes because people get tired and need to sleep (Piaget, 1929). Thus the children's grasp of the relation between what is seen and the person seeing it depends on their linking up various ideas about daily experiences and noticing the patterns in them: that the sky goes dark when the sun disappears, that the more light that falls on an object the brighter it appears, that if you want to see something in a dark room you shine a light on it not into your eyes and so on.

These examples serve as a reminder of some points made in the last chapter about the role of process skills in the formation of children's ideas. The experiences needed to grasp the relation between an object and the conditions in which it can be seen can be based on common everyday occurrences. The development of the idea depends on the way the children process these experiences. If they are selective in the evidence they choose to take into account they may find their ideas reinforced. For instance, if they consider only what happens when they look from one object to another and when they close their eyes they may confirm the notion that something must come out of the eyes to see the object. But if they are made to challenge this idea by trying to make sense of the inability of the eyes to see in the dark or the changes that appear in an object if different coloured lights are shone on it, then they may have to consider alternative ideas that fit this evidence better.

The more an apparently simple idea is explored, the less simple it becomes. The first thought might have been that the idea that 'seeing things involves light coming from them into our eyes' is rather trivial and can be taught in a sentence, or even assumed. On further thought this appears to be far from the case. When we try to understand the origin of children's ideas we find a certain 'logic' in them, but only if we accept their selection of the evidence they use and, like them, ignore other possible reasons and reasoning. The appreciation of their 'logic', however, brings a realization of the difficulty of changing children's ideas. It is not just a matter of broadening their range of experience; they have to be willing and prepared to give attention to evidence which does not fit their view, to reflect on it and to relate one piece of experience to another (for instance, that the effect of the sun going down and a torch being switched off in a dark room are both connected with being able to see things).

Quite a number of different activities can be suggested as relevant to this one relational concept. Children can explore the conditions in which objects can be seen, try to explain what is happening in each case, try to predict the effect of changes in the surrounding light, of the object's position, of putting a screen in various positions. They can turn attention to the eyes that see; how they move when a person looks in different directions, what happens when they are covered with different materials: opaque, translucent and transparent but coloured. Once they begin to realize that the eye is a receiver it might be appropriate for them to find out about its structure in human beings and other animals, but the purpose being to consolidate and refine the idea that seeing involves light coming into the eye not to learn the names of the parts: lens, retina, cornea, etc.

Ideas about the ear's role as a receiver in hearing sound are formed more readily than the equivalent ideas about the eye. This may be because the sources of sounds are more obvious than the source of light from objects which are seen by reflecting rather than emitting light. However, children have different ideas about the transmission of sound and the part played by 'vibrations'. Often vibrations are linked with the source when they are directly observable but not otherwise. For example, a 7-year-old wrote:

> I stretched a rubber band between my finger and thumb and plucked it with my other hand. I noticed it doesn't make very much noise, it vibrates and hurts my hand. I plucked a rubber band that was on a box. I noticed it makes a loud noise and it doesn't vibrate. I can play a tune.
>
> (SPACE research report on Sound, 1990, p. 50)

There is also a distinction in many children's minds between sound and vibration. Describing how a 'string telephone' made with yoghurt pots and string works, a 10-year-old wrote:

> The voices went to the string and were then transfered into vibrations which went down the string and when it got to the other yoghart pot and were then transfered back into a voice.
>
> (unpublished SPACE research)

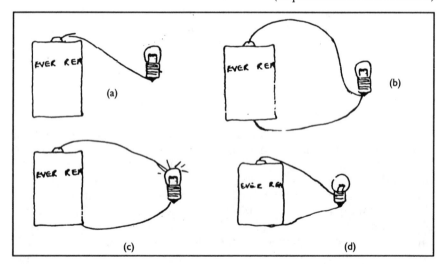

Figure 11

Inquiries into children's ideas about simple electric circuits have shown that the representation of a single connection between battery and bulb, as in Figure 11(a) is persistent and indeed is produced by pupils who have had experience that it does not work in practice (SPACE research report on Electricity, 1991). The representation in Figure 11(b) is arguably a more sophisticated view, but one which fails to recognize that there are two different connections to complete the circuit within the bulb, while Figure 11(c) does this but in a way which would not work. The SPACE team reports a marked increase in the correct connections depicted following activities in which the children were asked to discuss and draw how they would make connections, then to try out their plan and when they achieved success to compare what they did in practice with what they first thought.

Forces and movement

The relationship of forces acting on an object to its movement is a difficult area for primary science because so often the accepted scientific view is counter-intuitive. For example, it is a matter of everyday experience that a moving object such as a ball rolling along the ground stops moving apparently 'by itself' without any agent to stop it. But this ignores the force exerted at the contact with the ground and with the air. Many forces like these are 'hidden', including the important one of gravity, and are ignored by children in making sense of why things stop moving. Thus a ball thrown upwards into the air will be thought to have an upward force on it when it is moving up, zero when it reaches its highest point and a downward force when it is moving down.

Gunstone and Watts (1985) identified some 'intuitive rules' from their review of research into ideas about force: that children identify force with living things – they are a result of some intention; that objects in constant motion need a constant force to keep them moving in the same way; that an object that is not moving has no forces acting on it; that a moving body has a force acting on it in the direction of motion. These are all ideas which have a certain logic in relation to limited everyday experience and are held by many secondary school pupils and not a few adults. Their apparent 'common sense' makes them difficult to change.

Floating is a phenomenon depending on the balance of forces acting on an object in water, but children often consider that other factors are involved, such as the speed of movement of the object and the depth of water. In addition the concept of what is 'floating' is problematic. Some research in New Zealand (Biddulph and Osborne, 1984) explored what children understood floating to mean by using cards showing pictures of various objects in water, some floating and some not. The children ranged in age from 7 to 14 years and over 100 were interviewed individually. The results from the interviews were backed up by a survey of a larger number of children which served to confirm the main findings and establish where there appeared to be a trend with age in the children's ideas.

When discussing the pictures showing objects floating with part above the water surface and part below (a person floating in a life-jacket for instance) the children's decision as to whether or not it was floating appeared to be influenced by how much of the object was above the water and how much below the surface. If a large proportion was above the surface there was general agreement that it was floating, but if only a small part was above the surface (as in the case of a bottle floating with only the neck above water) there were many (42% in the survey) who said it was partly floating and partly sinking. A 9-year-old was reported as saying in an interview that 'It's floating and not floating. The top is floating and the bottom's not.'

The inferred movement of an object also affected judgement as to whether or not it was floating. Half of the pupils thought that the yacht in Figure 12(a) was not floating, and several of the younger children also claimed that the speed boat in Figure 12(b) was not floating because it was moving. An 8-year-old said 'It's going fast, and floating is staying still and floating around.' With objects totally submerged (such as a person snorkelling) just under a half described them as not floating.

Figure 12   Floating: **(a)**, yacht in trouble; **(b)**, speed boat going fast (from Biddulph and Osborne, 1984)

The children were also asked about a range of possible variables that might affect floating, such as the size of the object or the depth of water. The results show a definite trend with age. Only 10% of the 8-year-olds thought that a whole candle would float at the same level as a short piece of the candle. This proportion was 30% for 10-year-olds and 65% for 12-year-olds. Even at the age of 12 years, however, a quarter of the children thought the full-length candle would float lower than the short piece. To investigate the effect of changing the depth of water the children were shown the picture in Figure 13 and asked to compare the level of floating of the launch in the deep and shallow water. Half of the 8-year-olds said it would float lower in the deeper water, but only about a fifth of 10- and 12-year-olds gave this answer. About two-thirds of the 10- and 12-year-olds said the level of floating was unaffected by the depth but only 40% of the 8-year-olds said this was so.

The results of this research could be readily tested by teachers by discussing examples of floating with their own pupils in an informal way. Those who have done this have been surprised at how similar their findings are to the ones of the New Zealand researchers. They realize, too, how easy it is not to notice the children's different interpretation of what floating means.

Figure 13   Floating launch on lake (from Biddulph and Osborne, 1984)

The Earth and its place in the Universe

Children's early ideas about the movement of the Sun and Moon derive from their perceptions of rapid movements of the positions of these bodies caused by the children's own movement from one place to another. If they stand in the shadow of a tree the sun appears to be behind the tree; if they move out of the shadow the sun no longer appears to be behind the tree; the fact that they can see the sun wherever they are gives them the idea that it follows them around. Older children can distinguish this apparent rapid and irregular movement from the regular patterns of movement day by day, although these will inevitably be interpreted as the Sun moving round the Earth.

Other objects in the sky include clouds, which feature in the development of children's ideas about the weather. Attempts to help children understand the water cycle can cause confusion if they do not take into account the ideas the children may have about evaporation and about clouds. Young children do not see the need to explain why water dries up – 'it just goes by itself' (SPACE research report on Condensation and Evaporation). Later some recognize the effect of the Sun, but give it a very active role, such as in Figure 14.

Some even included what looked like a drinking straw reaching from the sun to the water! In the views of some children the clouds have this active role, being permanent features ready to receive evaporated water:

> When the water evaporates it goes on a cloud and then the cloud goes in any place and later it will go out as rain. In will keep going until it is all gone and then it will go to another place with water and do the same. The cloud is like a magnet so the water does through the cracks and goes up, that is what I think.
>
> (SPACE research report on Condensation and Evaporation, 1990, p. 30)

General characteristics of children's ideas

These examples have not been presented as a formal review of research but they do represent ideas which have been found by different researchers working in different contexts. These similarities in themselves

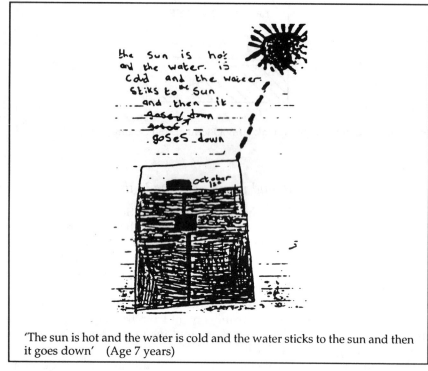

'The sun is hot and the water is cold and the water sticks to the sun and then it goes down'   (Age 7 years)

Figure 14 (SPACE research report on Condensation and Evaporation, 1990, p 29)

point to the ideas as being the product of reasoning rather than of childish imagination. This view is supported by studying the ideas and noting that, once children see the need for an explanation of things, they base their ideas on their experiences of them. However, there are several shortcomings in their ideas arising from one or more of the following:

- their experiences are necessarily limited and therefore the evidence is partial – so they may well consider rust to be within metals if they have only paid attention to it when it appears under paint or flaking chrome plate
- children pay attention to what they perceive through their senses rather than the logic which may suggest a different interpretation – so if the sun appears to move around and follow them, then this is what they think
- younger children particularly focus on one feature as cause for a particular effect rather than the possibility of several factors – as in the conditions needed for living things to grow healthily
- the reasoning they use may not stand comparison with scientific reasoning – if they used their ideas genuinely predictively they would be

disproved, but instead they may 'predict' what they know to fit the idea

• they may use words without a grasp of their meaning – we have seen that this can happen with 'floating', 'vibration' and 'evaporation' but many more examples could be cited

• they may hold on to earlier ideas even though contrary evidence is available because they have no access to an alternative view that makes sense to them – in such cases they may adjust their idea to fit new evidence rather than give it up, as in the idea that 'light turns the eye on'.

Implications for teaching

The clear evidence that children have worked out these ideas for themselves and that they make sense to them, within the confines of their limited experience and their limited ways of reasoning, means that the ideas cannot be ignored in teaching. To do so, research suggests, is likely to leave these ideas untouched with pupils learning 'the right' ideas by rote for the purposes of meeting the demands of school and examinations (Osborne and Freyberg, 1985). The main implication for teaching is, then, that these ideas which seem rational to the pupils must be taken as the starting point. The task of the teacher when setting out to introduce a topic having in mind the development of certain main ideas is, first and foremost, to find out the existing ideas of the pupils about this topic. This can be done by including specific activities in the 'scene setting' or by introducing activities that would be a normal part of starting a topic but are designed to reveal the pupils' ideas. Specific techniques are proposed in a later chapter (Chapter 9) but already some indications have been given about what this may mean in the examples earlier in this chapter; for example, asking pupils to draw what they think is the reason for something happening, or to write about it, or, most often, to talk about it in structured small groups or a whole class discussion.

The next step, having revealed the ideas, is to find an appropriate way of responding to them. There is no one method for this, but a set of strategies from which the most suitable for a particular situation can be chosen. The choice will depend upon the diagnosis of which may influence the children's thinking. For example:

• if an idea could be challenged by testing a prediction based on it then the pupils should be helped to make such a prediction and to plan a 'fair' test of it. This is likely to involve helping pupils to develop their use of process skills since it is likely to be failure to apply rigorous process skills that led to the pupils forming the idea in the first place

• if an idea is derived from a narrow range of evidence (as in the case of the rust within the body of the metal) then the strategy would be to provide more evidence

- if the use of words is suspect, then the pupils can be asked to give examples and non-examples of what they understand the word to mean.

These strategies, discussed in more detail in Chapter 7, are not mutualiy exclusive. The first – helping pupils to test their ideas – is likely to be the most powerful and so most frequently used, but within it there will be occasions when discussion of words and extension of experience (in seeking more evidence) have a role.

In planning how to help pupils develop their ideas it is useful to keep in mind that

- it was most probably their direct experience, through their senses, that led them to the interpretation they have made, so it is likely that this is also the best route to take to convince them to change or revise their ideas. So, while there is a place for introducing alternative ideas from books and other secondary sources, first-hand experience should be provided wherever possible
- younger children may have ideas which seem more 'correct' than those of older pupils. This is not backward progress but the result of earlier ideas becoming confused by the greater complexity of experience as they grow older. For example, a young child may well refer to all animals (s)he knows as animals, but it is later, when introduced to the words 'insect', 'mammal', and so on, that there is confusion about what is an animal
- children may have a 'locally correct' idea about a phenomenon in one context but not recognize that the same explanation holds in a different context. For example, the evaporation of water from clothes blowing on a line may be explained in terms of water 'going into the air' while puddles on the ground may be thought to disappear only because the water seeps into the ground.

All these points underline the message that encouraging the development of the main ideas identified in Figure 5 requires, for each one, an extensive list of experiences. These would probably be best not tackled all at one time but taken in two or three sets spread over a year or two or perhaps incorporated into other topics, for evidently there are many other ideas embraced by the kinds of activities that have just been outlined. Revisiting ideas and progressively developing them is often preferable to trying to focus on them for a single prolonged period of time. The interconnections between one idea and another mean it is better to make small advances in several and return to each later than to try to press one forward at a time. It is rather like trying to raise a heavy platform on a number of supporting jacks: each one must be raised by a small amount at a time to maintain stability. This analogy is quite apt, for it reminds us that we should not be in too much of a hurry to force the development of children's ideas and skills. It is a slow process and important that there is a reasonable equilibrium between a child's ideas and his experience; this provides the confidence that he can make sense of the world around and the motivation to do so. Then as experience expands, as it must do, he will strive to relate his ideas to new challenges and change them as found necessary.

A further theme emerging is the importance of the way children think and reason about their experiences. They will develop scientific ideas only in so far as they develop scientific process skills, the matter to which we turn in the next chapter.

4

Children's Ways of Thinking

The skills and attitudes involved in learning with understanding are the subject of this chapter. When learners use existing ideas to attempt to make sense of new experience and when their ideas change as a consequence, the outcome – the learning – depends on the way in which they process the information, how they select, gather and use it. The term process skills is used here for the mental and physical skills involved. In what follows these skills will be identified and defined, not as a dictionary definition, but in terms of actions of children at various points in development. Although it is useful to discuss them separately, in practice process skills are not so easily separable in what children do. The investigation described in Chapter 2 has made the point that children plan, do, observe and interpret in close succession and in almost any order. It is just for convenience that the skills are discussed here separately.

The application of ideas and process skills is influenced by attitudes. If a child, or an adult for that matter, is not willing to try to make sense of observations or to carry out an investigation, it is immaterial that (s)he is capable of doing so. Attitudes therefore have an important influence on learning, as they do on the rest of people's lives: in their reactions to people, to objects and events. However, there is no reason to regard them as inborn and immutable, but rather every reason to consider attitudes as learned from experience. They develop in children gradually as a result of encouragement and example to act and react in certain ways. By their nature, as generalized aspects of behaviour, they cannot be taught in the way that specific facts and skills can be; they are transferred in subtle and often unsuspected ways.

In this chapter we discuss some attitudes particularly relevant to science education. Matters relating to how to encourage development of both process skills and attitudes are taken up in Chapter 7.

Identifying scientific process skills

Component skills of enquiry or investigation are difficult to disentangle; rarely is a particular skill used in isolation – little happens, for example, without observation and communication being a part of it. So different groupings of skills have been identified by different authors of curricula and curriculum materials. The 1991 National Curriculum in Science (DES, 1991a) identified three strands within the attainment target Scientific Investigation: 1. ask questions, predict and hypothesize; 2. observe, measure and manipulate variables; 3. interpret their results and evaluate evidence. The Scottish *5–14 Curriculum Guidelines* for Environmental Studies identified five components of Investigating: planning; finding out; recording; interpreting; reporting, and an additional outcome: positive attitudes to the environment (SOED, 1991).

In both of these UK curricula the strands are followed across all developmental levels and given different meanings at each level. In some curricula, however, different sets of skills are identified at various levels with no explicit links between components at different levels. The New Zealand draft *Science in the National Curriculum* (New Zealand Ministry of Education, 1992), which has eight levels covering the whole of primary and secondary education, is of this kind. It does not use the word 'hypothesis' until levels 5 and 6, although statements at earlier ages could be regarded as relating to early stages of hypothesizing (for instance 'developing explanations', at levels 1 and 2).

The explicit or implicit description of development of process skills, which appears in almost every curriculum document relating to science, has *de facto* decided the matter of whether process skills *do* develop. This has been a bone of contention among science educators. What has called progression into question is the interaction of processes and the content on which they are used. A 9-year-old, for example, may be quite capable of successfully investigating the relationship between how a paper aeroplane flies and the shape of its wings, while failing to investigate the relationship between the concentration of a solution and its osmotic pressure. Ideas that a child may have about the content play a central role in the way skills are used and it has been suggested that it is not the skills that change, but rather that development is the ability to deploy them in relation to more complex content. Evidence from research (APU, 1988, and the STAR project, Russell and Harlen, 1990) challenges this position, however, suggesting that, at least in the primary years, there are differences among children's use of process skills when dealing with content within their grasp which suggest a hierarchy of development.

It seems that there are preferences for expressing skills in various ways just as there are for using different headings in identifying areas of conceptual development. In general these are differences in communicating the same overall range of ideas and skills rather than fundamental differences in the goals of science education. At the primary level, communication is helped by choosing headings which have become familiar and this is part of the reason for deciding to discuss process skills here under the following six headings:

observing
hypothesizing
predicting
investigating
drawing conclusions
communicating

In the next section we discuss what is meant by each of these with some indication of how this varies for children at different points in development. No sequence in performing or combining skills is implied in the order in which these are listed and discussed. All are seen as contributing to the mental and physical activity required to develop ideas about the world around through collection and use of appropriate evidence.

The process skills in action

Observing

Although observation involves the use of the senses to gather information, it is essentially concerned with more than merely 'taking in'. It is a mental activity, not just the response of sense organs to stimuli. Chapter 2 has already mentioned the part that existing ideas and expectations play in this mental activity and the role of these ideas in observation is important in discussing its development.

The purpose of developing children's skill of observation is so that they will be able to use all their senses (appropriately and safely) to gather relevant information for their investigations of things around them. A significant part of this statement is the gradual development towards distinguishing the relevant from the irrelevant in the context of a particular investigation or problem. Children will not be able to make this distinction, and they may miss significant information, if they narrow the focus of their observations too soon. Thus in their early development children should be encouraged to make as many observations as they can, giving attention to detail and not just gross features.

Many young children are well able to do this in relation to objects which interest and intrigue them. For instance, in one infants class two goldfish were named and recognized by the children, though they were apparently indistinguishable to a visiting adult. The children were clearly capable of noticing small details of difference and their ability to do so in other situations could be encouraged until it develops into a generalized skill. 'What is different about these things?' can be the start of a game with young children or of more serious enquiries for older ones. But it is important that the question 'What is the same about them?' should also be asked. There are many differences between these two objects (see below) but it is the things that are the same which help to identify them. Thus it is important for children to make wide-ranging observations of similarities and differences and to pay attention to details as well as gross features.

Observations are, however, usually made for a purpose. Looking for similarities and differences for no particular reason except to see how many one can find soon palls. It is best pursued when the similarities or differences are needed for some reason. A contrived reason can be to group or classify. Children's classifying activities often start with their collections of objects. The collection itself is a set of objects with something in common and the children should be encouraged to identify the common features before subdividing them. Various alternative criteria to be used in subdividing should also be developed and discussed so that the children's attention is focused separately on different observable features of the objects.

Ordering objects or events is also a way of focusing attention on to particular features of difference between one and another. Encouraging children to make observations of events and objects which change in a set sequence, in the sky and seasonal changes for example, helps them to pick out from all the features that can be observed those which relate things in a sequence. This can also encourage them to observe a process carefully during its course and not just at its beginning and end. For example, if children can watch bubbles rising when they put water into a jar half full of soil, or see worms burrowing and making casts, their observations will help them not just to know what happens but something about how it happens.

Relating one observation to another and finding patterns or sequences in them is part of interpreting observations. This has to be included in the skill of observation, mainly because it cannot be left out. What is observed is selected by expectations and hence interpretation is built in from the start. Patterns are not found by first making all possible observations and then seeing what relation can be found. Rather there is a to-ing and fro-ing between observations and possible patterns while the observations are being made. This is why we often see or hear something more clearly a second time, not because we take in more information, but because we focus on selected parts and cut out the 'noise'.

The ability to interpret observations and select relevant information is indeed an important and advanced feature of observation. But at the same time as encouraging it in children it is essential to help them to be conscious of the selection they are making and to be aware that there is other information to be used. If this is not done there is a danger of present ideas and ways of looking at things acting as blinkers which prevent us from ever seeing beyond what we expect. The level of development at which a person can reflect on the process of his observation and can consciously and spontaneously go beyond the limits of the framework of existing ideas is something to be aimed for throughout education.

Hypothesizing

It is a pity that this word is avoided by many teachers and pupils, probably because it sounds 'too scientific' or, perhaps, in the case of children, because it is difficult to pronounce and spell. It describes concisely an important process in children's scientific activity which otherwise needs a clumsy phrase such as 'suggesting tentative explanations'. To use the word 'explaining' implies a certainty which is rarely justified. If we want children to realize that scientific knowledge is tentative and always subject to disproof or change in the light of further evidence then it is useful to introduce the word 'hypothesis' more frequently.

The process of hypothesizing is attempting to explain observations or relations, or making predictions in terms of a principle or concept. Sometimes the principle or concept is one that has been established from previous experience, in which case the process is one of applying something learned in one situation to a new situation. (If the situation is the same as a previous one, it is a matter of recall rather than application.) In other cases the process may be closer to generating a new principle or trying out a hunch. The word 'new' should be qualified, though, since it is new to the individual concerned and not necessarily new in any absolute sense. However, the distinction between generating and applying is less clear than it is sometimes thought to be. The process of applying a principle or concept is part of its development in a child (or an adult). It will be better understood, and so have a slightly different meaning, as a result of being applied. Thus applying it is part of the development of a concept. Similarly, a 'new' idea is seldom created out of nothing, it may be an inspired guess that some relationship exists but there are usually clues relating past and present experience to spark off this creativity.

To apply concepts or knowledge from one situation to another the child has to recognize some similarity between these two situations or events. The clues may be fruitful and lead to suggested explanations which stand up well to checking. For instance, in Chapter 2 the children's explanation that the floating of the same-sized wooden blocks depended on their mass was tested by 'weighing' the blocks in their hands as well as by using the spring balance, but the idea came to them before weighing of any kind was done and was presumably based on earlier ideas and experience about floating objects.

Sometimes less fruitful clues are used and the 'explanation' is soon found to be faulty. The explanation of the sticking of the wet wooden blocks to each other by the girls who said 'They're magnetic' is an example. It would not be long before someone challenged them to show that the wood was magnetic using some of the usual tests of magnetism, which would inevitably have failed. However, the girls did not fail in respect of attempting to apply knowledge to explain what they saw, but they may have needed more experience to distinguish useful clues from false clues.

As the examples in Chapter 3 have shown, young children often see no need for an explanation in terms of a relationship or mechanism of why something happens. That the situation exists seems to be sufficient for them – 'plants grow best by the window', 'I hear because I listen hard', 'the truck stops when it can't move any more'. When some cause-effect reasoning comes in, it takes different forms, best explained with the help of an example. A group of children were using a 'fast wheels' car track, making measurements of how far the cars went along a horizontal piece of track after starting at various points on a sloping part. One of the girls asked 'What makes it go further when you start it from here?' The explanation given by one of the group was 'because it starts higher'. For him, this statement of the circumstances was explanation enough. He did not appear to understand that there was need to enquire further. Another child said, 'It's energy. It's got more energy.' She appeared to be satisfied to put a label on the problem. She may have been able to work out in her own mind why 'energy' explained the observations, but she certainly did not attempt to convey it to others. Eventually, the girl who posed the question in the beginning answered it herself. 'I know,' she said, 'it's my hand that gives it more energy when I lift it higher up to start with.' Here was a principle not just stated, but applied.

It is not difficult to agree that the child who stated only 'energy' is unlikely to have developed her understanding of the concept in this example, while the one who described how it applied may well have added to her grasp of the meaning and usefulness of the concept of energy. The interplay of concepts and process is very clear here; it is obviously to the advantage of children's understanding that they develop the ability to apply ideas beyond the levels of identifying circumstances or naming concepts towards describing how a general principle applies to a certain problem. Some ways of providing opportunities for this development and the teacher's role in it are discussed in Chapter 7.

Predicting

Predicting plays an important part in the model of learning described in Chapter 3 and for that reason alone it is necessary that its meaning is made clear. A central aim here is to distinguish it from the meaning of hypothesizing and from guessing.

Predicting often has a close relationship with hypothesizing but this is not always the case. A prediction may be based on a hypothesis *or* it may be based on a pattern detected in observations. When it is based on a hypothesis it may be expressed as if it precedes the hypothesis although logically it follows from it. For example, the prediction that 'this cup will be better than that one for keeping coffee hot because it is thicker' includes the hypothesis that thick cups retain heat better than thin ones and the prediction as to which will be best then follows from it, even though it is stated first.

When a prediction arises as a result of finding a pattern in the association of one variable with another there may not be a hypothesis for explaining this association. For example, a child finds that a clockwork toy goes 1 m 20 cm when the key is turned round three times, 1 m 50 cm for four turns and 2 m 20 cm for six turns. This could be the outcome of an investigation leading to the conclusion that 'the more turns the further the toy goes'. It could also be the basis for a prediction about how far the car will go with two, five, seven turns, leading to further testing of the relationship.

Neither hypotheses nor predictions are the same as guesses. As we have seen, they both have a rational basis in an idea or in observations and a guess does not have this property. Guessing is exemplified in the actions of a teacher with a group of reception children while cutting open fruits of various kinds to see what was inside. There was one of each kind of fruit and before the grapefruit was cut, the children were asked to 'guess' how many pips there would be in it. Their answers were random guesses, for even if they had used existing knowledge of grapefruit to suggest a number of the right order, there was no way of estimating how many would be in that particular fruit. This was not a prediction, it was indeed a guess and the teacher was using it to add excitement to the activity.

But young children tend to use the word 'guess' to describe what they think will happen even though there is some basis of experience for it. Asked to predict how many more marbles would be needed to just sink his plasticine boat, an 8-year-old said that his suggestion of two more was just a guess. However, on probing, it was clear that he had used observation of the effect of putting different numbers of marbles into the boat and he thought 'it will go down too far with three more, but one might not be enough, so I'll say two'. So he was reasoning from experience rather than guessing. Was the fact that he was not sure that it would be two that made him describe it as a guess? Children often 'predict' what they already know to be true, so they may think that there has to be some certainty about a prediction. They need to be helped to realize that while both a prediction and a guess are unsure, the important distinction lies in having a reason for a prediction. Questions such as 'why do you think that?' when a prediction/guess is made may provide this help. If there is a reason (which need not be 'right' but must be consistent with the prediction) then acknowledging that this is a prediction and not just guessing will help children to make this distinction for themselves.

Investigating

All of the process skills could be regarded as part of investigation so it is necessary to delimit what is meant by considering it as a separate skill. An investigation can begin with the identification of an investigable question:

> Which is the strongest of these materials?
> What differences are there between the places where the roses grow healthily and where they do not?
> What will happen if you shine light on the woodlice?

Investigations are also carried out to test predictions but these too have to be in investigable form and can be expressed as questions. So the prediction that 'the ice cube will melt more slowly outside than inside the classroom' is tested by answering the question:

> Does the ice cube melt more slowly outside than inside?

In other words, all investigations can be regarded as starting from an investigable question or a problem which can be expressed in such a form. The importance of encouraging children to raise questions – and then handling the questions effectively when they do – is a matter to be taken up in Chapter 5. In discussing investigations here we are concerned with what happens after an investigable question has been raised, that is, with the planning and carrying out of an investigation rather than with finding something to investigate.

Although planning can be considered a theoretical process, different from carrying out the plan, in practice it need not precede or take place separately from the investigation. It is a characteristic of young children that they think out what to do in the course of doing it; they do not anticipate in thought the result of actions, unless the actions are already very familiar to them. For young children planning and performing an investigation are interwoven; they may plan no further than the first step and from the result of this think what to do next.

More extended planning becomes possible with maturity and experience. For instance, 9- and 10-year-olds who are used to devising fair tests can plan beforehand how to compare the hardness of tap water and spring water using soapflakes. Others of the same age with little experience of fair testing would be less likely to produce effective plans and would have to find out what is involved by trying something and probably making mistakes. At all ages, including adulthood, the process of planning an investigation will be more difficult with unfamiliar types of problem, but the more experience and understanding we have of the general principles of investigation the more widely we are likely to be able to apply them.

Investigations vary in their complexity. The simplest ones are those where it is possible to separate the things that can vary and to change one independently of the others so that the effect of changing it can be judged in an 'all things being equal' way. These are the kinds of investigation to which primary children should be introduced so that they can develop understanding of making fair comparisons. However, not all scientific problems are of this kind. Often changing one condition inevitably affects another, for example, if you deprive a plant of water you inevitably also deprive it of the minerals dissolved in the water and may well raise its temperature since it will not be cooled by the evaporation of water. However, where such considerations do not arise the steps to be taken to carry out a 'fair' investigation (discussed in more detail below) are:

- define the problem in operational terms
- identify what is to change in the investigation (the independent variable)
- identify what should be kept the same so that the effect of the independent variable can be observed or measured (the variables to be controlled)
- identify what is to be measured or compared or what circumstances are to be observed when the independent variable is changed (the dependent variable)
- consider how the measurements, comparisons or observations are to be used to solve the original problem.

The steps to be taken in a particular investigation vary according to the subject matter but the same principles apply. This can be illustrated by considering two apparently quite different types of question; ones which concern the effect of making some changes and seeing what happens and ones which concern the effect of things not under our control. Examples of the first type are 'What happens if we put soap flakes into the tap water and the spring water?', 'What happens if we use different strengths of liquid fertilizer on our plants?', 'Does salt dissolve in other liquids as well as it does in water?'

These questions can be investigated experimentally because the things which can vary (the variables) can be changed at will. This is not possible in the other main type of investigation which concerns relations between variables which are not susceptible to experimental control in classroom activities. Questions such as 'Does the moon's phase affect the weather?', 'Are the trees whose leaves open early in the spring the first ones to drop their leaves in the autumn?' In these cases there is no control over the independent variable (the moon or the opening of leaves on the trees) and the investigation has to be devised so that the information is gathered from situations which arise naturally rather than those which are created experimentally.

Although other parts of planning may be carried out as the action proceeds, the first step has to be to define the question under investigation operationally. This means making clear what effects are to be measured or compared. For instance, 'Does salt dissolve better in cold or hot water?' is not investigable until 'better' is defined. It could mean: 'Can more salt be dissolved?' or 'Does the salt dissolve more quickly?' Again, 'Which is the best wood for making a bow for shooting an arrow?' can be defined operationally as which wood is lightest, strongest, most bendy, stiffest, shoots the arrow furthest for the same effort or, even, cheapest.

Once the problem has been defined operationally there are two levels at which the planning of an investigation may take place, the general and the specific. The general level involves identifying the variables to be changed, controlled and measured, but their values are not decided. For example, to investigate whether salt dissolves in other liquids as well as in water, the planning at the general level would be:

What to change (independent variable)?	The kind of liquid
What to keep the same for a fair test (the variables to be controlled)?	The mass and temperature of the liquids
What to measure or compare (the dependent variable)?	How much salt will dissolve in each one
How will the result be found?	By comparing the amount of salt for each liquid

To take the planning to the specific level it is necessary to decide which liquids to use, how much of each, how the amount of salt dissolving will be measured. Before becoming enmeshed in detail, however, it is worth completing the plan at the general level as it helps children to keep their problem in mind and to see how the separate parts of what they are doing relate to the whole investigation. If planning starts with the details not only is this more difficult but it is almost impossible for children to realize the similarities in the approach to devising different investigations.

When the plan progresses from the general to the specific level of planning procedures for fair testing, matters of practicality have to be considered. 'Can we obtain all the different liquids?' 'Are they all safe to handle?' 'Is there enough salt?' 'Do we have a balance on which to weigh the liquids before and after adding the salt?' If the answer to any of these questions is 'No' then the specific planning may have to be reconsidered. By taking a small mass of each liquid we can reduce the amount of salt needed but it may introduce a problem of accurate measurement. If there is no appropriate balance available it will be necessary to reconsider how the 'amount' of salt needed in each case can be compared. Instead of weighing, a measure of volume could be used: the number of spoonfuls added, for instance.

It can be seen that throughout these steps between the general and the specific planning the original problem has to be kept clearly in mind. Otherwise it is easy to end up answering a different question from the one posed. This is all part of the thinking which is essential to science education. Activity (doing things) is important but if children only do, without thinking about why they are doing certain things, the value of the activity is likely to be much reduced.

In some investigations the order of events must also be taken into account. Children quite often learn this through making mistakes. For example, they may fail to record initial conditions before making changes, seeing whether baking changes the weight of the dough by weighing only after the bread has been baked or looking at the effect on the fish in the aquarium of changing the water by changing the water first and then observing how the fish behave. A certain amount of learning by mistakes is a good thing but development is probably slower than need be if children keep repeating mistakes which could be avoided by some thinking and planning.

The importance of planning procedures carefully is greater for those investigations where the independent variable is not under experimental control. For example, to find out if the bulbs that are planted first also flower first, it is too late at flowering time to remember that the time of planting for each one was not recorded: the growth cannot be rerun. The same applies to other procedures for making fair comparisons or tests about subjects which cannot, or should not, be experimentally manipulated. One might investigate the effect on the populations of wild flowers in an area where a wood is cut down, but not cut down a wood to do this. Therefore, such an investigation would need very careful planning so that a fair comparison could be made before and afterwards. The planning skills which children can develop in other investigations, where mistakes can be made and put right more easily, have particular value in the investigation of natural events. When they are not applied there is little opportunity for investigation in such contexts and the activity is confined to making observations.

Drawing conclusions

This process skill logically comes into play when data have been collected, although there is always some anticipation before the end point is reached. When carried out systematically and carefully it means putting various pieces of information or observations together and deducing something from them. For example, that if the level of water in a jar with a plant in it goes down more quickly than the level in a jar without a plant, then the plant has something to do with the disappearance of the water. Putting this together with a further observation that stems placed in a soluble red dye become red enables the conclusion to be drawn that the missing water passes up the stems. This is different, however, from 'concluding' from this evidence alone that water passes up into all plants and all parts of plants. Premature generalization has to be avoided; jumping to conclusions is not the same as drawing conclusions.

Children all too readily jump to conclusions on limited evidence. For instance, one of the boys in Chapter 2 (p. 16) confidently affirmed 'all wood floats' (presumably he had never tried ebony or lignum vitae). To help them become more critical about the justification for their conclusions it is useful to distinguish between evidence which is available and inferences which go beyond it.

Beginning with conclusions which keep close to the evidence, these often involve finding patterns in the results – the extent that changes in one thing tend to go with changes in another. This is central to drawing conclusions from investigations of the kind discussed in the last section, where one variable is changed at a time. As a start it is helpful to encourage the process skill of looking for patterns in cases where a clear pattern is there to be found. The distance a toy car rolls before it stops when started on a ramp at different heights, the pitch of a stretched string changed in length, the pitch of the notes made by striking bottles with different amounts of water in them, the lengths of shadows at different times of the day, all these will give patterns of clear regularity. Opportunities should be taken to use such patterns to help children make predictions which they can then check. How long a string is needed to give a certain note? How high should the ramp be to make the car reach a particular spot? Predictions that stay within the range of the original information are interpolations, whereas those that go beyond it are extrapolations. By using the patterns they find, children will realize the purpose and value of finding them. They will also have ways of systematically summing up their findings which are more reliable than jumping to conclusions.

Not all patterns are regular, of course. A great deal of scientists' work is concerned with distinguishing trends or relations in numbers from total randomness (e.g. is the number of deaths among people given a certain drug greater than those not given it?). Young children cannot be expected to make precise tests of trends but they should be introduced to the idea that many patterns are not exact, for any of a variety of reasons. What is important in this elaboration of the process skill is that they do not just ignore data which do not fit an exact pattern. They can query it, repeat a measurement if possible, but if it still does not fit they must accept the pattern as an approximation. They should also be helped to realize that even when all their data do fit a pattern the relation is still a tentative one since they can never be sure that, if they found more information, some of it might not fit the pattern.

Ensuring that all the data are taken into account in a pattern is part of the skill of interpreting which becomes increasingly important as more complex data are encountered. In simple cases it is possible to 'get away' with taking note of only the extreme cases. This is what the girls did with the wooden blocks (see p. 22). 'The lightest floats the best and the darkest doesn't float so well' was to them a pattern, though they had not checked whether the colour and floating of the other pieces of wood fitted in with it. If in these simple cases children are helped to check that a pattern fits all the information then they will be in a better position later to deal with more complex patterns.

The process of inference takes the interpretation further than looking for patterns in numbers or other data to suggesting relations which account for the existence of the patterns. An inference goes beyond the data in a different way from a prediction, for it would require not more of the same kind of evidence to check it, but rather information of a separate kind or a separate enquiry. An inference is more like a hypothesis, but stated as part of a conclusion rather than an idea to be tested.

In a simple case, suppose a young child is rolling two tins, one half full of sand and one with a heavy weight attached to one side inside the tin. She finds that one tin will roll evenly and then stop whereas one moves in jerks and will oscillate before it stops. After playing with these for a while she may well be able to predict something about their movement: where they will come to rest or which side of the tin will be uppermost at rest. This can be tested by rolling them again. She may also infer that one has a solid lump stuck on the inside and the other has not. This inference will not be checked by more rolling; it can only be checked by doing something different: looking inside.

Drawing conclusions is more than 'rounding off' a practical activity. It should be regarded as the most important part, involving comparing initial ideas with new evidence and deciding whether the ideas fit or need to be changed or whether other ideas need to be tried. It is at the heart of active learning, where mental and practical activity come together and should be given plenty of planned time.

Communicating

Communication is an outward extension of thought. It helps in the process of rearranging thought, linking one idea to another and so filling in some of the gaps in a person's network of ideas. Often communication gives access to information or alternative ideas which help understanding, as in a discussion, in listening to someone else or in reading a book. At other times the act of communication helps one over a difficulty of understanding without any apparent input as a result of communicating. The enlightenment that can come from writing is an example; a more striking one, commonly experienced by teachers, is of the child who comes to them with a problem and while explaining it, finds the way out of the difficulty with no help except a receptive ear on their part.

As thought is such an important part of learning science and communication essential to thought, both as a process and as a means to an end, so development of skill in communication is central to education in science. This same claim could, of course, be made for education in any area of the curriculum and we shall have to restrict discussion here to communication particularly relevant to science. It includes both verbal communication, that is, language in written and spoken form, and non-verbal communication, by using conventional symbols and ways of representation through drawings and diagrams, tables and graphs. There is also a formal and an informal side to communication, both of which have to be considered in developing the related skills.

The formal side of discussion is the class discussion involving all the children and the teacher. The aim may be to share ideas, stimulate interest, put forward possible explanations, decide how to test them or check them out in other ways: from books, for example. Such an exchange needs a structure or it may become a free-for-all with little achieved. In discussions people have to speak one at a time, listen to each other and keep to the topic. It is for the teacher to provide this guidance on structure, but without dominating the content of the discussion. 'Keeping to the subject' must not be used as an excuse to censor the discussion; if a comment is made which cannot be followed up in the context of the subject in hand, the teacher must remember to return to it later. The aim is to ensure that everyone who wishes to has a say and each is given a chance to rearrange his or her ideas through expressing them or asking questions.

Informal discussion, by its nature, is quite different. It is characterized by the exchanges children have in groups at playtime and out of school. They interrupt each other, sentences rarely get finished, they challenge and contradict others' views. In the context of group work in the classroom the exchanges are toned down, rather more formal, but still unstructured. Through these discussions the children learn that others' ideas are different from their own, have access to a wider range of ideas and can try out their own at an early stage in their formation. (There is more about the value of group discussion in Chapter 5, p. 83). The children's discussions recorded in Chapter 2 provide some examples: the difference in the floating of the blocks is explained in terms of the air in them, bubbles of air, their weight, their being made of wood, all from one group in about 30 seconds. Later, several alternative reasons for one block floating lopsided are put forward and this leads to some of these being checked. It is not always the person who first voices the suggestion who follows it up. Thus the discussion advances the ideas and the activity of all the members of the group. Again, the teacher's role is largely one of ensuring that this happens. When it does happen the teacher can join in as an equal and unobtrusively inject ideas which the children may not have considered.

The formal side of making records of work is dreaded by children if it involves them in an apparently meaningless drudgery. Science work 'written up' only for the teacher (who already knows all about it anyway) hardly comes under the heading of communication. The purpose of writing should be clear to everyone involved so that it can be undertaken with this purpose in mind. It is easiest to begin by considering the purpose of recording informal notes, for it is often forgotten that children need help in how to do this to appreciate its value from experience.

Informal notes are a personal record of jottings and drawings which act as an extension of memory. They are put down in an individual manner for they are meant only for the individual, no other audience. If children are allowed and encouraged to do this they will realize the value of making records for themselves and this will lead them to understand the value of making more formal records as well. 'Being allowed' to keep personal notes means just this, that they are what the child, not the teacher, wants to record. The teacher can, however, make suggestions about what should go into the informal notes: observations and particularly measurements which may be quickly forgotten. Informal notes should never be 'marked' by a teacher, but it is useful to discuss them with the child for they are an important source of information about his progress. If the teacher can pick up points where the child can be helped (perhaps just in supplying a new word) then the notebook becomes a valuable means of communication between child and teacher as well as a personal record for the child himself.

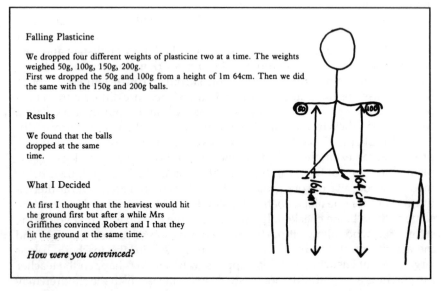

Falling Plasticine

We dropped four different weights of plasticine two at a time. The weights weighed 50g, 100g, 150g, 200g.
First we dropped the 50g and 100g from a height of 1m 64cm. Then we did the same with the 150g and 200g balls.

Results

We found that the balls dropped at the same time.

What I Decided

At first I thought that the heaviest would hit the ground first but after a while Mrs Griffithes convinced Robert and I that they hit the ground at the same time.

How were you convinced?

Figure 15

More formal records of work can also become a medium for genuine communication between teacher and pupil. For example, Andrea's account of dropping balls of Plasticine of different weights (in Figure 15) seemed to leave some ambiguity in the mind of her teacher. The question 'How were you convinced?' was written to remind both of them to clear this up.

In other parts of Andrea's work there are several examples of the teacher's question being answered in writing. At the end of the piece about the switch in Figure 16 the teacher wrote 'Connected it to what?' Before writing anything else in her notebook, Andrea answered this question.

Alarms
For our first experiment we made an ordinary switch. We needed a thin piece of balsa wood, six crocodile clips with plastic covered wire, a bulb, a bulb holder and a battery.
We nailed two paper fasteners through the copper strips and through the wood.

Then we connected the wire

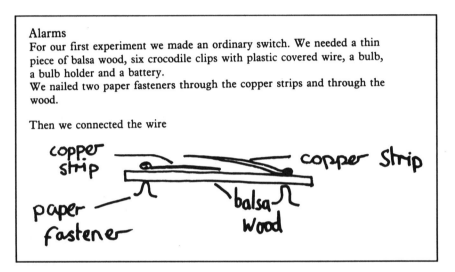

Figure 16

Later Andrea tested several materials in a simple circuit. The final section of her report is shown in Figure 17, including the teacher's question and Andrea's answer.

We found that all the metal like things allowed electricity to pass through to the bulb and all the things that didn't have any metal in didn't allow electricity to pass thou through to the bulb.
What general names do we give these two groups of things? Conductors and insulators

Figure 17

As children grow in experience the information which they have to record becomes more complex and they need to use graphs, tables and other conventions to help them communicate. These should be introduced as skills to use as opportunities arise. Bar charts are a popular method of recording since they can be used while gathering simple information where the range and organization can be anticipated, forming a cumulative record (e.g. the number of children of different heights). For more complex data it is necessary to collect and tabulate it before deciding on the best graphical form to use to reveal the patterns, or whether a graph is needed at all.

Other means of arranging findings and displaying them should be introduced as and when they can be used. Making a plan of an area with symbols showing where various types of plant or building are found, drawing a cross-section, keeping a weather chart, creating a flow diagram to show changes in sequence, showing directions on a map: all these are activities in which children can be introduced to a range of ways of representing and communicating information. At first they will be used only when suggested by the teacher, but the children will gradually be able to take over the decision as to the most appropriate form to use in a particular case. This change will be helped by examples, from information displayed in different ways in the classroom and from seeing the teacher use appropriate representational forms during class discussions.

When there is a range of ways of communicating available to the children, formal reporting becomes more of a challenge and less of a dull routine. The purpose, whether it be a formal reporting from groups to the whole class or a display for the class, or an exhibition for a wider audience in the school, will be part of the decision as to appropriate forms of communication. With the audience in mind and the tools (the knowledge of different ways of presenting information) available, formal reporting can then have value both as a process and as a product.

Identifying scientific attitudes

Attitudes have been defined in different ways. Here we taken them to describe the state of being prepared or predisposed to react in a certain way to particular objects, persons or situations. The term 'scientific attitude' is sometimes used to describe children's reactions to science as a subject and to the activities of scientists. It would seem, however, better to describe these as 'attitudes to science', reserving the term 'scientific attitudes' for the attitudes *of* science, the ones with which we are concerned here. These are predispositions towards the activities involved in science, such as the use of evidence, creating ideas and treating the natural and man-made environment in certain ways.

Describing a person as having a certain attitude is a generalization about his or her behaviour. An attitude can only be said to exist if certain behaviour is displayed in a range of similar situations. It cannot be assumed from an isolated instance of behaviour that this is part of a general pattern, but once a pattern has been established, and an attitude can be said to exist, it predicts to some extent the likely reactions in a related situation. A person who listens with interest to others' ideas on one occasion may or may not do so as a regular thing. If such behaviour is known to be a regular feature then this justifies the generalization that he or she is open-minded. Describing someone as open-minded is a succinct way of making a general statement about how he or she has reacted in the past and is likely to react in the future in certain situations.

There are many attitudes of value to all kinds of learning, but we have picked out for consideration here five that are of particular relevance to science. As with the process skills, various titles could be given; the ones chosen here and the attitudes subsumed within them are:

- *curiosity* (questioning, wanting to know)
- *respect for evidence* (open-mindedness, willingness to consider conflicting evidence)
- *flexibility* (willingness to reconsider ideas, recognition that ideas are tentative)
- *critical reflection* (willingness to reconsider methods used, wanting to improve ideas and performance)
- *sensitivity to living things and to the environment*

Curiosity

A child with curiosity wants to know, to try new experience, to explore, to find out about things around him. It is obvious that this is an attitude that will help learning of all kinds and especially learning by inquiry. Curiosity often shows in the form of questioning, but asking questions is not the only sign of curiosity nor the only symptom to be encouraged. Inviting children to ask questions is indeed one way of showing that curiosity is valued and the attitude can be fostered this way *if* the result is satisfying and interesting to the child. There is a danger, however, of asking children to verbalize their questions too early. Something new, on first encounter, may elicit questions which are no more than expressions of interest. Time has to be allowed for a child to take in what is there and relate it in his or her mind to what is already known. Then will come the questions that help him make sense of it.

On first seeing black swans in a bird park a group of 8- and 9-year-olds were full of questions such as 'Why are they black?', 'Why do they have red eyes?', 'Are they the same as white swans?' If their teacher had tried to answer these questions, the children would not have listened to the answers. It was as if they had said 'Look, they're black', 'Look, they've got red eyes' and so on. Only later, when they had watched them for a while and answered some of their own questions by observation, did they put the questions that they really wanted to have answered, such as 'Do they mate with white swans?', 'Are there other colours of swans besides black and white?'

Young children and those with a limited attention span may get no further than asking the superficial question that expresses interest before they turn to another topic. Questioning brings satisfaction if it helps them to share their pleasure and excitement with others. This is part of a natural course of development and to discourage it by disapproval will risk a decline in curiosity. On the other hand, the satisfaction that comes from expressing curiosity will help children reach a more mature stage where interest is sustained for longer and questions are more thoughtful. There may be fewer questions, indeed curiosity can be expressed in other ways, but there will be more interest in finding the answers, for the questions will be designed to help relate what is already known to the new experience.

Then curiosity appears not so much as a flow of questions but as a wanting to know. This desire to find out stimulates effort to find out, perhaps by investigation, perhaps by using a library or making a special visit. The questions need not have been asked of anyone else, the motivation comes of having asked them of oneself. When children have reached this stage, putting new experiences in their way is more likely to lead to learning through their own effort.

Respect for evidence

Science concerns both the process of describing how things behave and the product of this endeavour. The process is essentially one of gathering and using evidence to test or develop ideas. Although a theory may have its beginning in an imaginative guess, it has no status until it has been shown to fit evidence or make sense of what is known. Thus the use of evidence is central to scientific activity; this is true at school level as much as at the level of the work of scientists, so attitudes towards it are of great importance in science education.

Children talking among themselves have a keen sense that an unsupported statement is not necessarily to be believed. 'How do you know that's true?', 'Prove it' feature in their private arguments in one form or another. (There is an example in Chapter 2, p. 14, where Cheryl challenges with: 'How do you know it's the varnish when we haven't even looked at it?') It is when they are in the company of adults who expect children to accept statements because of the force of the authority behind them that the desire to ask for evidence often has to be suppressed. If an adult appears to accept statements without evidence, or at least offers none in passing on the statements, the attitude transmitted can be the opposite of what is educationally desired. Thus the part of respect for evidence which appears as a desire to know the evidence behind statements is something which has to be preserved and developed by presenting evidence whenever possible or at least indicating that supporting evidence does exist.

To obtain really convincing evidence may well take some perseverance and it is sometimes this quality which determines whether or not an initial idea leads to a useful concept. There are splendid examples of perseverance in the work of famous scientists, such as Charles Darwin and Marie Curie, who persisted against difficulties of various kinds to gather the information required to give their ideas a thorough test before feeling sure enough of them in their own minds to advance them in public.

In their own way children can extend their ideas further with a little perseverance; what may at first appear beyond their grasp may come within it if their tendency is to continue rather than give up when faced with difficulties. Perseverance is not merely persistence; this may be part of it, but persistence in an unrewarding line of action or argument is not rewarding. The willingness to try again has to be accompanied by learning from the earlier failure so that later attempts or ideas are modified by experience.

Even young children can respect evidence in the sense so far discussed but it takes rather more maturity to extend this respect to situations where other evidence or other ideas may conflict with the evidence and ideas so far taken into consideration. A prerequisite here is open-mindedness or a readiness to listen to, or attend to, different points of view. In the activity with the blocks of wood the girls quoted in Chapter 2 were not the only group to discover what they called the 'magnetic' attraction between the blocks. Another group did so as well but they considered an alternative idea that the air and water caused the force rather as in a suction pad. They argued the pros and cons for some time and showed open-mindedness in changing their original view. One might say that the girls quoted showed less open-mindedness since they were ignoring the evidence that pointed against the force being magnetic.

The willingness to consider conflicting evidence is another facet of this attitude. Take the example of three children timing the bobbing of a weight on a spring. John wanted to time only one bob, up and down once, while Gary said it was better to see how many times it went up and down in a minute and Maria wanted to time 20 bobs. John argued that it would gradually slow down after the first bob, so his idea was best; Gary's point was that it would be easier to compare with different weights if you kept the time the same; Maria's reason was that you should time complete bobs but more than one. They all listened to each other, and to that extent showed open-mindedness, but they each decided to do it in their own way and did not use the result to consider the pros and cons of each approach.

In these cases, however, there is not enough in one example to make a judgement. In any single instance many other circumstances may affect the outcome; it is only when a pattern of similar response is noted across several instances that comment on the attitudes of the children could be worthwhile.

Flexibility

Flexibility of mind bears a similar relation to the product of scientific activity as respect for evidence does to the process. The concepts that we form to help our understanding of the world around change as experience adds more evidence to develop or contradict them. Sometimes it is a gradual refinement, as when the idea of energy develops from being related to what people can do, to being associated with moving things, to being possessed by things which can move other things and existing in a variety of forms. In other cases there has to be a sudden change, as in conceiving of light as behaving both as wave motion and as particles. The changes are most rapid in children's early years since their limited experience means that their first ideas are often quite different from what they need to understand wider experience later. Unless there is flexibility, each experience that conflicts with existing ideas would cause confusion and create a rival idea instead of modification and a growth of an existing one. Flexibility is needed to adapt existing frameworks to fit increased experience.

Since even young children manage this adaptation quite readily they show willingness to reconsider ideas though they may not realize how much their ideas have changed. For instance, 5- or 6-year-olds tend to have views about whether things sink or float which relate to size. Soon size is found not to be important and weight takes over: 'heavy things sink, light ones float'. Then children find light coins sinking and heavy logs of wood floating and their ideas have to change again, and so on it goes.

As children become older and their ideas closer to those of adults they change less often. There is a danger that flexibility of mind may decrease and the idea creep in that at last they now have the 'right' ideas. This is disastrous to continued scientific development. Instead the aim should be for flexibility to mature and extend to the recognition that ideas are tentative. An understanding of scientific activity can be reached, eventually, only through realizing that all its products (concepts, knowledge, principles and theories) are valid as long as they fit the evidence we have, but as we never have all the evidence there is no certainty about their validity. Although children of the age we are considering may be some way from this realization, their path towards it can be kept clear, and not blocked off, by the attitudes they develop at this earlier stage. It is worthwhile developing the habit of prefacing conclusions with 'As far as we can see . . .', 'On the basis of this investigation . . .' or words to the same effect. It also helps to discuss with children at times just how their ideas have changed, how they used to think that all wood floated (until they tried ebony and lignum vitae) and that metal sank (until they tried hollow metal objects). Fostering this attitude also helps children to feel that they can participate in developing ideas rather than receiving 'the right ideas' from others.

Critical reflection

In the context of science activities this means looking back over what has been done, deliberately to see if procedures could have been improved or ideas better applied. It is an attitude that is related to respect for evidence and flexibility but relates to making a more conscious effort to consider alternatives to what has been done. In practice it may be manifest in self-critical comments, in repeating part of an investigation or even starting again in another way. On the other hand, there may be no critical comment to make; the recognition of having taken a useful course of action is also evidence of having reviewed what has been done. In any event the attitude shows in reflecting on what has been done, using it as something to learn from; pausing instead of dashing off without a second thought to another activity.

Such indications of critical reflection are not often part of young children's spontaneous behaviour. The encouragement of this attitude demands positive action and good examples. Action is best begun in small groups, where the group activity is reviewed and there is no danger of an individual child being put in a defensive position. A teacher might well ask the group at the end of an investigation to consider what changes might have improved their work and leave them to do this alone. Their experience of trying in the way they did is then likely to help them learn the pitfalls to be avoided in future activities. Once they embark on their own critical review and find some benefit from it they are more likely to do this for themselves more generally and so to develop willingness to reconsider methods and ideas.

The value of developing this attitude is clearly that it increases the potential learning, of the processes and ideas of science, from each activity. But if children are to indulge willingly in a critical review which may indicate flaws in methods and thinking there must be some perceived benefit.

Part of this can be the satisfaction of finding better ways of investigating and more powerful ideas, but this intrinsic reward may not be enough; support and approval from the teacher is also needed. It may not be easy in many cases to respond positively when children find that they could have improved what they have done without giving the impression that they should have done better to begin with. But encouragement to reflect critically can be so effective that it is worth the effort to praise and to show an example by ensuring that suggestions made by the teacher, too, are reviewed. Eventually, children will not only be willing to join in but will take the initiative in wanting to improve on past ideas and performance. This commitment represents a higher level of maturity in developing the attitude, which may become evident in reviewing previous experience and possibilities before embarking on an investigation as well as afterwards.

Sensitivity to living things and the environment

In science education children are encouraged to investigate and explore their environment to understand it and to develop skills for further understanding. Unless investigation and exploration are governed by an attitude of respect for the environment and a willingness to care appropriately for the living things in it, such activities could result in unnecessary interference or even unpleasant harm. So it is important that growth in skills of enquiry and concepts should be accompanied by a development of sensitivity towards living things and responsibility towards the environment.

These attitudes are ones that are more obviously linked to particular concepts and understanding than those we have considered so far, though one of our main themes is that all attitudes, concepts and skills are interrelated to some degree. It is more likely that someone with an understanding of, say, the effect on wild flowers of over-picking, will look and not pick than someone without such understanding who may pick the flowers innocently. There is no certainty about this; the knowledge helps but it is not enough to create the attitude. The converse is also true, fortunately, that lack of understanding is not an inevitable barrier to forming these attitudes. Thus, although many of the concepts relating to care of the environment are too complex for very young children to grasp (air pollution and ozone depletion, for instance), and some are controversial (the need to preserve endangered species, seal-culling, even fox-hunting), it is still possible to begin the development of attitudes towards the environment by example and rules of conduct.

Young children soon pick up the signs that certain living things have to be treated differently from non-living things. The analogy is with themselves and their own need for food, rest, etc. As their understanding of 'living things' extends from being confined in the early primary years to furry mammals to a wider range, including things such as spiders, worms and plants (see p. 43) it is worth making an effort to ensure that their caring attitude is also extended to these things. Keeping ants, snails, a wormery, etc. in the classroom is certain to help children appreciate these as interesting creatures with fascinating and complex behaviour patterns. Such animals can be brought into the classroom for a while to be studied and then carefully replaced in their natural environment. Helping their teacher do this is a significant step towards adopting such caring behaviour themselves.

The mature form of this attitude shows in responsible behaviour to the street as much as to the countryside environment, to animals of all kinds as much as to pets. This requires commitment, and a degree of understanding, not reached by many children in the primary years. In the meantime it is necessary to ensure that children are willing to obey simple rules designed to prevent thoughtless harm to the environment. At first rules will have to be imposed by the teacher and discussed with the children so that they appreciate that there are reasons behind them. But an aim should be to involve children in deciding on rules and procedures as soon as possible; the preparation for a trip, nature walk or starting a school garden patch gives opportunity for this experience. It is useful to introduce and discuss the guidance issued by organizations such as the Nature Conservancy Council (ASE and Nature Conservancy Council, 1990).

The pressing nature of environmental issues is so great that it is tempting to force too much onto children too early. There is a delicate balance to be drawn. On the one hand, it has to be remembered that

> Children do not pollute the environment. They do not spray insecticides, or weed killers. They do not impregnate the atmosphere with sulphur dioxide. They never hide toluene and benzene in the ground beneath new living areas. They do not defile the surface water with phosphates and oildumps, or the deep sea with nuclear waste. Yes, they may throw away sweet papers and the like but these do not pollute the Earth; they do not even begin to pollute it . . .
>
> The general issues of environment are important and we do not wish to negate this when we state that they have to be tackled in primary education through children's interaction with it at their own level, not through handed-down adult concepts. The experience of the environment is unique for every child. Getting to know the environment and learning to understand relationships within it is a very personal experience for the child, who is at the centre of it.
>
> (Elstgeest and Harlen, 1990, pp. viii and ix)

On the other hand, it has to be remembered that attitudes which will shape later adult behaviour develop early. The discussion of the consequences of actions with which children are familiar, from avoiding litter to recycling paper and metal, should aim to engender responsibility for their actions within their personal experience. Then, as their experience and understanding grow, so will their responsibility.

5

Language and Scientific Development

This chapter is mainly concerned with spoken language, one of the two 'major means by which children in schools formulate knowledge and relate it to their own purposes' (Barnes, 1976, p. 19), the other means being writing. These words of Barnes indicate his view that the importance of language in learning is more than as a means of communication but as having a significant part in the development of thought. A brief summary of various theories on this matter forms the first section of the chapter.

Subsequent sections are concerned with more practical aspects of speech. First there is discussion both between pupil and teacher and between pupil and pupil, which Douglas Barnes has done so much to elucidate. Then we come to the form of verbal interaction which is a prominent part of everyday classroom exchanges – questioning, by pupils and by teachers. The value of questioning by pupils depends, however, on teachers being able to deal with the questions in a way which both satisfies the pupils and encourages further questioning; various strategies for handling questions are proposed with this aim in mind. The final section takes up the issues surrounding the introduction and use of 'scientific' words at the primary level.

Words and thought

Since the product of our thinking so often emerges in words, language has an obvious relationship to thought. Thus this relationship is addressed in the theories of cognitive psychologists and others who have concerned themselves with describing mental development. While not denying other forms in which thinking and knowledge may be expressed – in drawings, artefacts, actions and manipulations – language and other symbolic means of communication (such as mathematics) clearly have a prominent and probably dominant role.

Two different schools of thought exist about the relationship between language and thought. On the one hand is the view that speaking is a means of communicating thoughts which have been developed through actions and interaction with things in the world around. On the other hand is the view that thinking and speaking are virtually the same, that language has a key function in developing ideas not just in communicating them.

Piaget's view of intellectual development lays less emphasis on the verbal interaction between child and adult than do the views of Bruner, Vygotsky and Ausubel. For Piaget, the development of knowledge is tied to physiological development of the brain and learning is brought about by direct physical activity with things around. Thoughts are internalized *actions* not words, and language a means of sharing thoughts, not of developing them. Until the child reaches the stage of formal operations (Piaget, 1964), usually after the age of 13, the role of the teacher is seen mainly as facilitating first-hand activity and social interaction with peers.

Bruner emphasizes the role of language in translating experiences into a *symbolic* form in the mind. The development of language in the child opens up the possibility of direct input into a child's thinking through language and the reordering by the child of experience by using language 'as a cognitive instrument' (Bruner, 1964b). Vygotsky shares this view that language is a means of reinterpreting the world: 'Speech . . . does not merely accompany the child's activity; it serves mental orientation, conscious understanding; it helps in overcoming difficulties' (Vygotsky, 1962).

In Ausubel's theory of 'meaningful learning', the role of first-hand activity is subordinated to the role of giving meaning to verbal statements. Ausubel, like Bruner, believes that any scientific idea can be made accessible to children in some form. He does not believe that learners invent ideas but learn them from others. What is needed is that the idea or theory to be learned is broken down and expressed in language appropriate to the learner, then illustrated by practical activity. The significant point is that he regards verbal statements as the source of knowledge and the role of practical activity as giving meaning to them (Ausubel, 1968).

There is no intention to delve into these theories of cognitive development and learning, but rather to show that verbal language, and particularly speech, features significantly in them. Whether the belief is, as Barnes claims, that pupils come to their own understanding of experience through talking about it, or that direct verbal instruction is necessary, there is no disagreement that both verbal and practical activity have important roles in science education. It is possible that by following the ideas of Piaget, mediated through educators who have translated his views of learning into classroom experiences, there has been an overemphasis in primary classrooms on activity at the expense of discussion. Moving from one activity to another without pause for thinking and reflection is not an effective learning experience. The alternative is not direct verbal instruction but planning time for discussion into practical work.

Before turning to the subject of discussion more directly, the relationship between language and thought should not be left without reference to learning contexts where there is a difference between a child's language of instruction and the language used in the home. This situation arises not only in the case of immigrants but also in those countries where science textbooks are only found in European languages or where there is a change from the indigenous language to an official language used in the school, often from about the third year of the primary school.

Studies of learning in countries where the home language differs from the language of instruction have produced varying findings. Where the teachers are themselves less competent in the second language (of instruction) than in the home language, it appears that children learn best in the latter. This is providing the language is rich enough to express the scientific ideas and the essential tentativeness of scientific knowledge. If children can form ideas with understanding in one language, these ideas are not damaged by later translation, but if subtle ideas cannot be formed, then learning clearly suffers. This can be either because the home language is limited or because of uncertain knowledge of the official language.

The role of discussion

In the section on communicating in the last chapter there has been some reference to formal and informal discussion between teacher and pupils, with the focus on sharing ideas. Here the focus is on the role of discussion in helping the construction of ideas by learners. Douglas Barnes has provided some telling evidence and arguments to support his contention that 'The more a learner controls his own language strategies, and the more he is enabled to think aloud, the more he can take responsibility for formulating explanatory hypotheses and evaluating them' (Barnes, 1976, p. 29).

By studying children's speech when involved in group tasks, Barnes showed how individuals contribute to an understanding of an event (or process, or situation). An idea of one child is taken up and elaborated by another, perhaps challenged by someone else's idea and leads them back to check with the evidence or to predict and see which idea stands up best to a test. With several minds at work there is less chance of ideas being tested in a superficial manner than there is if one child does so with no one to challenge it. The challenge can only be made if the thinking is made open and public through the use of language. Thus Barnes argues that talking is essential to learning. By 'talking' he does not, however, mean the formal reporting or answering of teachers' questions which in some classrooms is the only speech officially sanctioned. Barnes lays particular emphasis on the value of talk among children with no adult authority present. In such situations children with a problem to solve use non-formal speech: they interrupt each other, hesitate, rephrase and repeat themselves. Barnes sees this hesitant or 'exploratory' talk as signifying the openness of the situation and constituting an invitation to all involved to throw in ideas.

The opportunity for exploratory talk of this kind comes only when the children are in charge of the situation. Generally, this does not happen when the teacher is present, for his or her presence provides an authority which children expect to be greater than their own views. As Barnes (1976) says:

> the teacher's absence removes from their work the usual source of authority; they cannot turn to him to solve dilemmas. Thus . . . the children not only formulate hypotheses, but are compelled to evaluate them for themselves. This they can do in only two ways: by testing them against their existing view of 'how things go in the world', and by going back to 'the evidence'.
>
> (Barnes, 1976, p. 29)

It is not difficult to see that learning through talking is exposing children not only to different ideas from others but compelling them to think about how those ideas relate to previous and new experiences. In other words they are finding better ways of dealing with ideas and checking them against evidence; they are developing the mental process skills. Hence what Barnes has to say, while relevant to all learning, is particularly significant for science. In making this point, he goes further in proposing a role for language in helping children to reflect on the way in which they have processed the ideas and information available to them:

> Much learning may go on while children manipulate science apparatus, or during a visit, or while they are struggling to persuade someone else to do what they want. But learning of this kind may never progress beyond manual skills accompanied by slippery intuitions, unless the learners themselves have an opportunity to go back over such experience and represent it to themselves. There seems every reason for group practical work in science, for example, normally to be followed by discussion of the implications of what has been done and observed, since without this what has been half understood may soon slip away. Talk and writing provide means by which children are able to reflect upon the bases upon which they are interpreting reality, and thereby change them.
>
> (Barnes, 1976, pp. 30-1)

Questioning

Asking questions is a powerful way of attracting a response from someone. Children ask questions in class in order to expand their knowledge, as well as for other reasons (see below, pp. 88 and 90); teachers ask questions of children to provoke their thinking, to check up on learning and also for other purposes such as to control behaviour and to monitor and regulate activities. The concern here is with questions relating to understanding rather than to classroom routine and control, and with both asking and answering such questions.

Teachers' questions

Teachers are able to plan, design and monitor their questioning in a way which is not expected of children. There are three aspects of questioning to be considered which contribute to its effectiveness for particular purposes: form, timing and content. These are not independent dimensions but all need to be considered in framing questions to achieve the intended kind of response.

Form refers to the way in which the question is expressed. Two of the important ways in which questions can vary in form are: open or closed, and person-centred or subject-centred.

Open questions leave many more options for answering than closed ones. For example:

> Open: What do you notice when the soil is put into the jar of water?
> Closed: Do you see the bubbles rising from the soil in the water?

It is easy to see that the open version is more likely to provoke a range of responses, while the closed one focuses on one particular feature. The former is useful when interest is in all the observations children might make but the latter has a place when there is a significant feature not to be missed.

Person-centred questions are expressed in a form which invites whatever ideas the person may have, with no implication that one is more 'correct' than another. Subject-centred questions, by contrast, ask about the content in a way which suggests that there is a right answer. For example:

> Person-centred: What do you think the bubbles might be?
> Subject-centred: What's inside the bubbles?

It is much less easy to give a tentative or speculative answer to the second of these questions than to the first. If a teacher is interested in children's ideas then the person-centred and open form is the way to express the question. Closed and subject-centred questions are much less useful for this purpose but may have value for other purposes such as probing what children have found in their practical activities, that is, when information is being sought from children. However, in practice the balance of different kinds of question is probably too much on the closed side, judging from the research of Galton, Simon and Croll (1980), who found that only 5% of teachers' questions were classified as 'open'.

Attention has been drawn to the timing of questions by Jos Elstgeest (1985 and 1992), who has pointed out that even a well-framed question can be ineffective if it comes at an inappropriate point in children's activity. Teachers often ask a question at the wrong time because of their eagerness to press ahead too quickly, he suggests. As an example he cites asking children who were listening carefully to the range of sounds around, 'how are these sounds produced?' The question strangled the very inquiry that the teacher hoped to provoke. The same question would have been the right one to ask at a much later stage, but what was needed at the time was more along the lines of 'how could you make a sound like . . . the rustling leaves . . . or the car horn . . . or the church bell . . ., etc.?'

It is important to keep the timing of questions in mind as we turn to consider their content. At the start of a topic, the purpose of questions may well be to find out the ideas that children have about the subject matter. So, when embarking on a topic about rocks and minerals the teacher would provide a display of stones, rocks and minerals, inviting children to add to it, and encouraging them to handle, scratch, sniff, put pieces in water and generally explore them. During this time these kinds of questions might be used to explore the children's ideas:

Where do you think these are found?
Why do you think some are smoother than others?
What do you think makes them different colours?
Can you think of why the colour changes when they are wet?

After initial exploratory activities, children can be encouraged to investigate their ideas by questions of the following kind:

How could you find out if your idea works?
According to your ideas, what would happen if . . . How could you find out if this does happen?
Can you find a way to . . .?
Can you find a way to stop this happening?

This last question is an example of what Elstgeest has called 'odd questions' which are useful when used occasionally to stimulate enquiry. The odd question, 'the opposite of what you may be thinking of, may turn out to be the right at the right time' (Elstgeest, 1992). He provides the following as examples:

• In how many ways can you upset the equilibrium of a balance?
• How would you stop a magnet from attracting a piece of iron?
• How would you grow a plant without soil?
• How would you drop an egg without breaking it?

At the stage when investigations are under way, questions can be phrased to encourage the use and development of specific process skills. The timing has to be right, of course, so that the question is not an interruption but a stimulus to action and to thought. The following examples (taken from Harlen, 1992) relate to the six process skills discussed in Chapter 4. The content is the germination and growth of various kinds of seeds. The setting might be where children have begun by looking at various kinds of dry seeds, and proceed to plant them and follow the growth of the seedlings. Suggestions for questions relating to each process skill are as follows:

Observing
- What do you notice that is the same about these seeds?
- What differences do you notice between seeds of the same kinds?
- Could you tell the difference between them with your eyes closed?
- What happens when you look at them using a lens?

Hypothesizing
- Why do you think the seeds are not growing now?
- What do you think will make them grow?
- Why do you think (the soil) helps them to grow?
- Why do you think these seedlings are growing taller than those?

Predicting
- What do you think the seeds will grow into?
- What could we do to make them grow faster?
- What do you think will happen if we give them more (or less) water/ light/warmth?

Investigating
- What will you need to do to find out . . . (if the seeds need soil to grow)?
- How will you make it fair (i.e. make sure that it is the soil and not something else which is making the seed grow)?
- What equipment will you need?
- What will you look for to find out the result?

Drawing conclusions
- Did you find any connection between . . . (how fast the plant grew and the amount of water/light/warmth it had)?
- Is there any connection between the size of the seed planted and the size of the plant that grows from it?
- What things made a difference to how fast the seeds began to grow?

Communicating
- How are you going to keep a record of what you did in the investigation and what happened?
- How can you explain to the others what you did and found?
- What kind of chart/graph/drawing would be the best way to show the results?

Children's questions

It is not difficult to encourage children to raise questions, unless, that is, their natural inclinations to do so have been discouraged by thoughtless treatment from adults. In school, children who ask questions are sometimes made to feel foolish; at home, they may have been told directly by a busy parent to 'stop asking so many questions'. But a little encouragement on a teacher's part can usually revive children's questioning, especially if all questions are accepted as worth answering and not just those the teacher feels to be important.

It is particularly relevant to begin by reaffirming the value of children raising questions of all kinds when discussing one particular kind of question, the investigable kind, for it is not intended to give the impression that these are the only kind of question worth asking. Raising a variety of questions, including poorly expressed and vague ones, is important to children's learning, for questioning is the means by which a child can fill in some links between one experience and another and can make his own sense of the world. Such learning is helped, however, if teachers, and eventually pupils, recognize the distinction between the kinds of question that science is concerned with and questions which cannot be settled by scientific activity. Science addresses questions about what there is in the world and how it behaves. In answer to such questions assertions can be made which can be tested; for instance, 'Does wood float?' and 'Do you find trees on top of mountains?' The answers 'Yes, wood floats' and 'There are no trees on the top of mountains' can be tested by investigation or by consulting someone who has found out. These are science-related questions.

The situation is very different, though, for questions such as 'Is happiness the only real aim in life?' or 'What is knowledge?' These are philosophical questions and are not answered from observation or logical argument. Nor can science address questions of value or aesthetic judgement. It can tackle 'Which watch keeps better time?' but not 'Which watch is more attractive?' or 'Which is worth more money?'

Within the range of questions which science attempts to answer we are particularly concerned in education at the primary and lower secondary levels with a small subset of questions. These are the questions to which children can find answers through their own activity. So they have to be not only empirical questions but questions to which the children can find answers or about which they can make and test assertions.

Questions that children ask range over all kinds and the children themselves are not aware that they are asking quite different sorts of questions and that some cannot be answered by science. To develop this awareness is a significant part of their education, but it will come only very slowly and through realizing the kinds of questions that can be answered by their own investigations.

The first step is to encourage children to raise questions of any sort. Putting collections of new things in the classroom, taking children out for walks or visits, ensuring variety in the materials they handle, are useful for this. The following list contains some of the questions that children asked after handling a range of different pieces of rock (Osborne *et al.*, 1982):

What are rocks made of?
How do they get their colour?

Why are they hard?
How do rocks get their shape?
Why do rocks have holes in them?
Why are some rocks different weights than others?
Why are rocks sometimes smooth and flat?
Is gold a rock?
Why is diamond the most valuable rock?

Similar sorts of lists of questions were reported by the same researchers on a variety of other topics. Not many of the questions seem capable of leading to investigations by the children. Faced with such a mixture of questions which have few straightforward answers, a teacher might well prefer not to encourage children to raise questions!

But a more positive response can be made after studying the questions carefully and trying to understand the children's intention in asking them. Often the exact words used are not carefully chosen and so we should not read too much into them. 'How do rocks get their shape?' could easily be expressed as 'Why are rocks different shapes?' Indeed, the researchers who reported this list collected questions from separate classes of children and found 'Why are they different colours?' sometimes and 'How do they get their colours?' in other cases. Questions such as these do not seem to ask for specific information but rather are an expression of interest, a way of saying 'Look at all the different shapes' or 'I've just realized that rocks are not all the same colour'. An appropriate response to such questions is therefore to share the children's interest and perhaps take it further: 'Let's see how many different shapes/colours there are'. A teacher will be able to judge from the children's reaction whether there is particular interest in the shapes and colours or whether these were passing comments expressed as questions.

Children's questions always include some of a second kind, asking for straight information: 'Is gold a rock?', 'Why is diamond the most valuable rock?' or perhaps one that well might have been in the list 'Where did all these rocks come from?' The answers to these can be given directly, if the teacher knows, or the children can be referred to a source of the information. They are facts, some a matter of definition; they add to children's knowledge, which is important to their understanding of the world but is by no means all of it.

Questions of a third type are more likely to lead to investigations. They are the ones that often give teachers most difficulty because they require complex, not mere factual, answers. Many teachers may not know the answers and those who do will realize that the children's existing concepts are not sufficient to enable them to understand the answer. 'Why are they hard?', 'Why do they have holes in them?', 'Why are rocks sometimes smooth and flat?' are examples of these. They ask for an explanation, but in fact if the children were to be given the explanation they would probably not understand it, and might well be deterred from asking such questions in future. So teachers should *not* feel inadequate at not answering such questions from their own knowledge; in most cases it would be the worst thing to attempt.

Instead of presenting a problem to the teacher these questions actually present the opportunity to help children define investigable questions, that is questions which they can answer from investigations. 'Why are rocks sometimes smooth and flat?' could be used to lead to an investigable question by asking:

Where do you find rocks that are smooth and flat?
What is the same about places where smooth flat rocks are found?
What is different about places where rocks are not smooth and flat?
Could these differences account for the shapes of the rocks?
Could we make a rough rock into a smooth one?

So the end point may be a series of questions such as 'Does rubbing one rock against another make them smooth?', 'Does putting them in water make any difference?', 'Do you need a harder rock to rub against a softer one to make it smooth?' Once children embark on answering any of these questions, inevitably others will occur. And since the further questions are generated in the context of activity, it is likely that many of them will be framed by the children in terms of things they can do themselves. Thus once begun the process of defining questions is self-generating.

Children soon realize from experience what kinds of questions they can and cannot answer from investigation and what kinds require a different approach. Ten-year-old Stephen, looking at a giant African land snail, wanted to know why it grew bigger than other snails he had seen, how long it was and what it could eat. He set about answering the last two questions for himself and when asked how he thought he could find out the answer to the first said 'I suppose I'd have to read a lot of books'. Knowing how to answer different kinds of questions is more important to children than knowing the answers, but it comes only through experience of raising questions and discussing the process of answering them. While not suggesting that we should never answer children's questions, if we do this all the time we prevent them from learning how to set about answering them for ourselves.

Handling children's questions

There is hardly any aspect more directly related to teachers' confidence in teaching science than the ability to handle children's questions. Anxiety that children may ask questions which they cannot answer leads many teachers to organize the children's work so that opportunities for asking questions are minimized. Using work cards which keep children busy following instructions and which provide the answers has this advantage, while for others, doing all the talking and asking all the questions themselves serves the purpose of preventing children from asking questions. Developing techniques of handling, rather than answering, questions is the key to loosening these tight strategies. Providing more opportunities for children to do their own reasoning inevitably means that they will be asking questions as they strive towards understanding. Thus handling the questions is a prerequisite for working in this way.

Although investigable questions have to be identified as the basis for scientific activity, if children are to be encouraged to ask these kinds of questions it is necessary to encourage all questioning and so to be prepared to handle the questions that result. It is also necessary to remember that children sometimes ask questions for motives other than curiosity. Sometimes they are seeking attention and sometimes seeking approval or hints about what the teacher expects. Handling questions in a way which indicates preference for investigable ones over unnecessary procedural ones will provide the necessary deterrent.

A first step in responding to a question is to identify it as one of the four types which have been discussed. Next is to be aware of techniques of handling each type, some of which have been hinted at in discussing children's questions. These techniques can be summarized as follows:

1. *Questions which are comments or expressions of interest.* (e.g. Why is it raining today?) Children do not pause for an answer when they ask questions of this kind. They require only sharing of interest. There may be an opportunity to develop this interest into an investigable question, by asking, for instance, 'How many days this week has it rained?' 'How can we keep a record of the weather?'

2. *Questions asking for information.* (e.g. Does it rain more often in England or in Wales?) Here an answer is expected and if it requires only factual information, the teacher may supply it directly, or suggest a source where the child may find it or undertake to find out at a later time. Factual information is useful in testing ideas and there is no reason to withhold it or to insist that children must find out everything for themselves. Learning to use sources of information helps children to expand the evidence on which their ideas are based.

3. *Questions which are investigable by the children.* (e.g. What happens if we plant the bean seeds the other way up?) Children's questions of this kind are not often expressed in a form which is already investigable, but can readily be made so. There may be a difficult decision for teachers as to whether to supply the simple answer or whether to devote the time needed for children to investigate the question for themselves, in which case they will learn more than the simple answer. The opportunity to find the answer from the things themselves by their own actions gives children valuable experience of scientific activity

and not just the information about whether the bean will or will not grow upside down.

4. *Questions which require a complex answer* beyond the comprehension of the children. (e.g. Why is the soil brown?) These require some clarification in discussion with the child. They may be philosophical questions, if, for example, the intention was 'Who made the soil brown?' These kinds cannot be answered and are best treated as questions which are expressions of interest. Taken at face value, however, it is possible to answer the question as to why soil is brown, in terms of how we see colour, the composition of white light and what happens to light reflected from objects that we see. However, all of this, even if familiar to a teacher, would be incomprehensible to most primary pupils and to try to explain it would give the message that science is something they can't understand. They would hesitate to ask further questions for fear of another dose of indigestible information!

So, giving complex answers should be avoided, but the questions should not be left unheeded. It may be necessary to say that 'the reason is too complicated for me to explain, but we can find out more about it'. The first thing may be to find out if all soils really are brown. What different colours can be found? Where are they found? What is the same and different about soils which vary in colour? Soon this leads to several investigable questions from which the children may find the answers at the level which satisfies their interest for the moment. This way of 'turning' a complex question into one or a series of investigable questions is an important skill for teachers to develop. It has been usefully described by Sheila Jelly as follows:

> The teaching skill involved is the ability to 'turn' the questions. Consider, for example, a situation in which children are exploring the properties of fabrics. They have dropped water on different types and become fascinated by the fact that water stays 'like a little ball' on felt. They tilt the felt, rolling the ball around, and someone asks 'Why is it like a ball?' How might the question be turned by applying the 'doing more to understand' approach? We need to analyse the situation quickly and use what I call a 'variables scan'. The explanation must relate to something 'going on' between the water and the felt surface so causing the ball. That being so, ideas for children's activities will come if we consider ways in which the situation could be varied to better understand the making of the ball. We could explore surfaces, keeping the drop the same, and explore drops, keeping the surface the same. These thoughts can prompt others that bring ideas nearer to what children might do.
>
> (Sheila Jelly, 1985, p. 55)

Introducing scientific vocabulary

When should teachers introduce the technical language of science and expect children to use it correctly? Should this be done, as it were, from the beginning? Or should we allow children to describe things in their own words even though more precise terms are available? What do we do about those words which have both an 'everyday' and a 'technical' meaning, such as 'work', 'force', 'power', 'condensation'? These are not separate but interconnected problems and opinions differ as to how to deal with them.

Many of the words used in science label a related set of ideas or characteristics. The word 'solution' is a useful example. For the scientist it means a system in which one substance is distributed at the molecular level in another without being chemically combined with it. It includes the solution of solids in solids as well as in liquids, liquids in liquids and gases in liquids. For the secondary-school pupil the meaning will be much less extensive, probably being restricted to solids in liquids but still bringing with it the notion that there is a limited amount of solute that will dissolve in a given amount of a solvent, that solutions are clear but may be coloured and are different from suspensions. Younger children will use the word 'solution', however, as if it had an even more restricted meaning. It may not include a coloured solution or a solution in which some solid remains undissolved. As their experience increases the meaning they have for the word changes; if they study science in the sixth form it may approach the meaning of the scientist; if not it may stay at the level of their 13-year-old experience, or it may become a word they only use for the answer to a crossword puzzle!

It would be unreasonable to insist that the word 'solution' should only be used with its full scientific meaning (indeed it would never accumulate this meaning without being used in a more restricted sense first). But it is equally unreasonable for the word to be used the first time a child experiences a solid disappearing into a liquid. A good argument for this point of view has been put forward by Brenda Prestt (ASE, 1980). She compares a word to the wrapping of a parcel, which obscures its contents (its meaning).

> Words introduced too soon are part of that 'verbal wrapping paper' of science. . . . Many teachers say that children 'like' to use technical words even though their understanding of them is very limited. I would suggest that wrapping paper can be very gaudy and attractive but it still covers and obscures the contents of the parcel.
>
> (ASE, 1980, p. 79)

If the 'right' word is not to be introduced too soon but in time to help children begin to attach to it the package of ideas it stands for, how can the best time be judged? Brenda Prestt suggests that the answers to the following questions will help in this judgement:

> Does the word matter?
> Does it add to the child's understanding if he uses it?
> Does he have to know the word *now*?
> Would insisting on the use of the word be useful to the child?

There is probably no single guideline that can be used for all children and all words. Reflecting on these questions could certainly help in specific cases. When the answer to most or all of them is 'yes' then the child must have had experience relating to the ideas it represents and may be already expressing its meaning in his own words. This really is the 'right' point to introduce the word, when it fills a gap and fits into the child's vocabulary with meaning. A simple example is of supplying the word 'sinking' to a young child who is describing an object as 'falling to the bottom' of the bowl of water. The word 'solution' might be offered to the older child with plenty of experience of putting various solids in water who wanted to describe how the liquids 'that you can see through' are different from the liquid before any solid was put in.

The most persuasive argument for waiting until the child seems to need the word before introducing it is that there is then more chance that the 'package of ideas' that it represents to the child will be not too far away from what it represents for the teacher or the author of the books the child might read or other people with whom the child may communicate. It does children no service to provide words which they cannot use to convey meaning because they do not realize what meaning the word has. Of course we cannot prevent children collecting words, like stamps, and showing off their trophies by talking about black holes, radioactivity, cloning and such. But we accept this for what it is, mere imitation of adult language, not intended for communication.

The same argument can be the guideline for the words that are used not only in science but have a more precise meaning when used as a scientific term than when used in everyday life. It is pointless to try to prevent the word 'work' being used for occupations, like thinking, which involve no 'work' in the physicist's understanding of the word. When the word is required in its scientific meaning, that is, when children have some notion of the concept, then is the time to say 'the word "work" is used for this in science and not for other things that are called work.' The everyday use of the word can be discussed as well as the scientific use to clarify the distinction (cf. the suggestion about the meaning of 'animal' on p. 43). Thereafter, the teacher should be careful to notice how the children are using the words, by listening and reading what they write, so as to find out the concept that is conveyed by the children in the words they use.

Concern about the special vocabulary of science should not take all the attention. Normal non-scientific words can also present a barrier to communication if they are put together in complex structures. When we say warm air is 'rising' (instead of going up), light is 'travelling' (when we could say that it is going from one place to another), a balloon is 'expanding' (rather than getting bigger), we should stop to ask ourselves: Do we really need to use these words? Do they help the children's understanding or are they just another layer of verbal wrapping paper?

So we are brought back to the discussion of language and thought with which we began this chapter. When a new word is introduced it will be necessary to spend some time discussing with children their view of where it fits their experience. Asking for examples and non-examples is a useful way to approach this. For instance, in the context of introducing the word 'dissolve' where children had been using 'melt', can they give examples of things dissolving and examples of things becoming liquid which are not dissolving? Children need time and encouragement to reflect on earlier ideas and to ask themselves, for example, 'is this, that I used to call melting, what I now know to be dissolving?' Reflection to revisit existing ideas is necessary so that earlier experience is taken into ideas as they expand and so that ideas called forth by words bring with them all the relevant experience.

6

Opportunities for Learning for All Pupils

The model of learning discussed in Chapter 2, forming the main theme of this book, leads to a particular meaning of the term 'opportunity to learn'. When new experiences are within the reach of existing ideas and where process skills enable the development of ideas for understanding the new experience, then learning can take place. So the provision of activities at the right level of demand and setting appropriate expectations is one prerequisite for learning. This 'getting in the right ball-park' is an important part of planning class activities, which has been called 'macro-matching' (Harlen, 1992).

Children are individuals, however, and have different existing ideas and skills. So for each to have opportunity to learn there needs to be a closer match at the individual level. This 'micro-matching' is a second prerequisite to be considered. It depends upon teachers' knowledge of individual children's ideas and skills and upon appropriate expectations and support.

Further, at both macro and micro levels of matching, differences which follow from gender, ethnic background and learning difficulties have to be taken into account. If *all* children are to have opportunities to learn then activities are needed which engage their different interests and methods of teaching used which enable equal participation of all children in their own learning.

Matching at the general level

At this macro level we are concerned with identifying the broad bounds of the activities that provide opportunities for learning for primary school children (aged 5 to 12 years). We leave to the next section consideration of the 'fine-tuning' needed to provide individual children with experiences which are genuine 'opportunities for learning' for each one. The guidelines for identifying the kinds of activities likely to match children at different stages come from studying the characteristics of children at different stages: their interests, the nature of the ideas, the skills they can deploy. Despite individual differences, there are clear patterns in children's development, revealed by research and by observation of practitioners. The research of the SPACE project (see Chapter 3) has identified patterns in children's ideas about things around them, as did Piaget's extensive research of conceptual development. From these sources come descriptions of the progression in children's thinking. We have already considered the ideas, skills and attitudes we want children to develop, but what kinds of experiences help this development? This is the question which has to be kept in mind in proposing learning activities.

Criteria for selection of activities

Two important dimensions of activities which deserve consideration are their content (subject matter) and the way in which children engage with the content.

Content is closely related to development of ideas, for clearly activities with snails lead to ideas about living things, not about magnets, for instance. The relationship between the development of skills and content is different; activities with both snails and magnets can develop skills of observing and interpreting. The content must provide the interest and motivation for children to become involved in an activity that is going to challenge and develop ideas. The method of engaging with the content is the main determinant of opportunities for development of process skills and attitudes. Included in this is the influence of the kind of equipment that is used. There are issues relating to these aspects of activities which need to be considered in a little more detail before arriving at a summary of the criteria for selection of activities.

Children's interests

Interest for children is an important consideration, but a goal to pursue rather than a condition to be ascertained. Much valuable time has been used less productively for learning than it might have been by following too slavishly the dogma of 'following children's interests'. The effect has often been to narrow children's range of experiences by seizing too early on things in which they have already shown interest instead of attempting to expand their interests. The readiness with which children are intrigued by new things, or new ways of looking at familiar things, shows that interest can be created. It is perfectly possible for children to become completely absorbed in activities that they did not themselves suggest, but this does not mean that their interest can be captured by *any* activity. The criterion of interest should be applied after there has been chance for children to encounter new phenomena. This makes the question of starting points for topics particularly important.

What makes an activity interesting? It is generally because there is something puzzling about it, something that we have an urge to settle in our own minds. If I've always wondered how they make plastic bottles without a seam showing, then I am interested to visit the factory where such bottles are made. If someone shows me a new material that I've never seen before ('Potty putty', for instance) then I am interested to touch it, play with it and perhaps investigate its properties in a more ordered way. Each person's puzzles are slightly different, of course, and so what interests me will not necessarily interest another. It will depend on their previous experience and whether the links between this and new experiences raise problems to be solved. To some extent the outcome of this process is unpredictable for any individual. It is more predictable for children than for adults, however, for their experience is more limited and the possibility of puzzle-raising consequently greater. But it is not just the new and unexpected that can puzzle children. The familiar has puzzles in it and these are often the most intriguing to them. Who would have thought that four blocks of wood floating in a tank of water would keep children busily investigating literally for hours? This is what happened to the children quoted in Chapter 2, and not just those; the same activity invariably creates similar intense interest in children. There was nothing apparently new except that the materials were selected to make them puzzle about floating in a way that they may not have done before and offered the chance of working on this puzzle. So in seeking to create interest we should have in mind links with previous experience when presenting either novel phenomena or familiar ones in a new light.

Relevance to things around

The potential interest in activities concerning familiar things leads to another criterion for choice, that the content should be related to things around children. At one level this means using the environment as the source of content; the idea of the variety of different living things can be developed on the shore, at the zoo, in the park, in the wood, according to the location of the school. At another level, however, it means ensuring a link between real phenomena and the activities in the classroom. Fine, if the study of a swinging pendulum really does have some function in helping to understand things in the world around, but not if the link is theoretical and obvious only to the scientist.

The degree to which problems should be simplified for children is a complex issue. One approach is to suggest that children should tackle the problems they find in their exploration of the world around. These problems are inevitably complex, for reality is not simple. The complexity can indeed be so confusing that the underlying basic ideas may not be apparent. The understanding of what makes winds blow in certain directions at a particular speed is a case in point. An alternative approach is to simplify the real situation and take it apart to study its component ideas separately. So we look at one time at how air moves upwards over a source of heat, at other times at how it moves towards places where the pressure is reduced and so on. The danger here is of creating activities which may not seem to have much relevance, in the eyes of a child, to what is happening in the world around and which they cannot combine in puzzling over the real problem. Science activities then become things that the children do in science lessons rather than means of increasing their understanding of things around them.

There is no easy solution to this dilemma; in some cases the better course of action may be to accept the complexity of the problem and in others to break it down into simpler component problems. It may help in deciding which is better in a particular case to recall two points: first, that the children's ideas at any time need not be the ones that remain with them for ever; secondly, that they will form some ideas about the things around them even if we, as educators, consider them too complex. If we want children eventually to understand that wind is moving air and how its movement is created we can discuss and investigate the children's ideas about the wind so that they realize their ideas don't fit all the evidence and they will keep puzzling about it. Or, we can ignore the children's ideas and attempt to create the 'right' ones about how air is made to move through activities designed to illustrate relations, such as heat causing air to rise, and which 'work'. Experience at the secondary level, where the latter approach has been tried for years (and with children who might be more able to abstract the relevant ideas), suggests that it is not very successful. Many pupils do not see the point of the activities they do and are far from making a connection with the world around. (Much evidence of this is summarized in Osborne and Freyberg, 1985.)

It seems, then, that there is a strong case for interpreting the criterion of relevance of content to things around as 'relevance perceived by children', not as relevance perceived by teachers, scientists or other adults. Once the children are investigating a relevant problem it may well be possible to separate out one aspect for study, to test out an idea or hypothesis. This does no harm, as the connection with the real problem is already established. For example, some of the children working on the problem of how to keep an ice-cube from melting (without putting it in the freezer) wondered whether the same materials they used to surround the ice to stop the 'cold' getting out would or would not keep heat getting out of a warm object. They ended up using food cans filled with hot water and covered by jackets of various materials. This is a fairly common activity, suggested in books both at primary and secondary levels, and can mean little to those undertaking it if it comes 'out of the blue'. For the children who came to it via the ice-cube problem, however, it had a great deal of meaning and marked a considerable advance in their ideas about heat and changes of temperature.

Opportunity to use process skills
Although the link between concepts and content is particularly important, since the content of activities largely determines the opportunities for concepts and ideas to be developed, the interrelation of concepts and process skills means that opportunities for using and developing process

skills have also to be considered in the selection of content. This opportunity is mainly a matter for the *way* in which the content is encountered in the activity, but it may also influence the range of content selected. Stirring of sugar, salt and other things into water is particularly 'rich' for the development of the meaning of 'dissolving'; similarly, other examples of content could be found that would be included in most lists aiming to cover the ideas on p. 40. But some content can be chosen because it is 'rich' in opportunities for process-skill development rather than for concept development. Examples include content that helps patterns to be detected (adding marbles to a pan on the end of a spring), that helps children to separate variables and test their effect separately (the simple pendulum, for instance), that requires the devising of fair tests (finding which paper is best for backing a book). The content of these activities is linked, tenuously, to the basic ideas (movement and properties of materials) but they are justified not by these links but by the process skills they involve. In some programmes of science activities (e.g. Science, a Process Approach, 1966–1976) the content was deliberately chosen to have no link with science concepts to focus more sharply on the process skills being used. So, for instance, children make inferences about the contents of black boxes and seek for patterns in the colour changes that occur when unknown liquids are mixed.

The issue of the process dimension in relation to content is somewhat parallel with the issue discussed in relation to the concepts. Should the content be simplified, made trivial, so that it does not interfere with the smooth application of a scientific approach to gathering and processing information, or should the content be 'real', but messy, and not necessarily easy to handle with a scientific approach? The danger of the former is that the process skills may be developed but not seen to be relevant when real problems are encountered. The danger of the latter is that scientific processes are carried out only superficially and children fall back on everyday ways of thinking.

There is no clear cut rule to be followed and the only viable approach is to weigh the pros and cons in particular cases. It can be wasteful on two counts to select content that is trivial. In the first place, learning the skill has then to be followed by learning to apply it. Secondly, the chance to develop concepts while learning the skill has been missed. The arguments based on children's learning lead to the conclusion that if we wish children to come to understand the world around by their own reasoning and trying out their own and others' ideas then they must be using this reasoning and testing it out in their investigation of real things and problems. The ideal is that while solving a problem or checking an idea they also become aware of better ways of solving problems and testing ideas. If this awareness does not come about, for one reason or another, there may be a case for introducing some special activities with simplified content, but these should not become the only or even the main content encountered.

In selecting or designing an activity it is evident that there is more to be taken into account than the content. It is not difficult to imagine rather different outcomes from contrasting ways of dealing with the same content. Take, for instance, an activity commonly included in a topic on 'Ourselves', whether taller people generally have larger feet than shorter people. (The concepts to which this can contribute concern the variation among individual living things and any patterns in these variations.) The children could be set to plan for themselves how to carry out this investigation, deciding on what information they will need and how they will gather it, bring it together and interpret it. They might also be asked to report to others what they find out. They would be involved in using skills of planning, in thinking about variables to be controlled and variables to be measured and in coming to their conclusions they would check their findings against the evidence to present a convincing case. Alternatively, the same children could be given a set of instructions:

• take 20 people and measure their height
• measure the length of their feet
• make sure you do all the measuring in the same way (all without shoes on)
• put your results in this table (given)
• etc. etc.

The subject matter as far as content is concerned is the same, but in the second case the amount of thinking that the children do is much less and indeed they could complete the activity and do very little working out for themselves about the reasons for what they were doing. Clearly, the opportunities for process skill and attitude development are much less in this second activity than in the first. It could be speculated also that the information and relation (if any) that the children obtain would mean more in the first activity since they would have a much clearer idea of the reason for taking and interpreting the measurements.

Decisions about the nature of the activity, as opposed to only its content, also determine the extent to which scientific attitudes can be developed. Opportunities for fostering attitudes depend only marginally on content but heavily on the way the content is handled. With almost any content children can develop the habits of not accepting the first idea to be suggested, of listening to others' ideas, of checking all possibilities against evidence, of suspending judgement if there is insufficient evidence, of critically reviewing their approach to solving a particular problem. So criteria for devising or selecting activities must include opportunities for development of such attitudes.

Equipment
A further consideration in relation to ways of engaging with content is that of equipment. In many schools the problem is not usually one of choice (should we use jam jars or laboratory flasks?, saucers or Petri dishes?) because there are usually only jam jars and saucers available anyway, but rather of feeling that the lack of specialized equipment is a

disadvantage to primary science. If, instead of modelling what is done in the primary school on the image of secondary science, we consider the learning we want to bring about, then the use of everyday equipment has strong positive advantages.

Use of things that are familiar to children to help them explore and understand their surroundings emphasizes that they can do it through their own actions and thinking. They are not prevented from observing the diffusion of colour from a coloured dissolving crystal by lack of a glass beaker, a bunsen burner or the right chemicals; they can use things very readily available in the classroom or at home. The directness of the use of simple equipment emphasizes the point that answers can be found in the objects or situations themselves. The use of specialized equipment too early interrupts this message, makes science something distant and mysterious. When more precision is appropriate, later in the secondary school, then the equipment used has to allow this. If by then the pupils have formed the basic ideas and are building on them there may be no disadvantage in separating problems from their context. When these basic ideas are still being formed, however, they must be seen to be relevant to the understanding of phenomena in everyday life. Unfamiliar equipment can present a barrier to this relevance. For further discussion, see Chapter 10, p. 173).

Summary

Bringing these points together, the criteria for selection of activities are that they should:

- give opportunity for developing basic ideas about the world around (as described in Chapter 3)
- be interesting and intriguing to the children
- relate to their everyday experience and help them understand it
- give opportunity for developing the process skills (as listed and discussed in Chapter 4)
- give opportunity for fostering scientific attitudes (as indicated in Chapter 4)
- involve the use of simple and familiar equipment that does not constitute an obstacle to involvement with the phenomenon being investigated (see Chapter 10).

These criteria are now used in considering activities for pupils in three overlapping age ranges: infants (5–7 years), lower juniors (7–9 years) and upper juniors (9–12 years).

Learning opportunities for infants (5–7 years)

Children in this age group have characteristics relevant to their learning which have been described by researchers and confirmed by teachers' experience. The main ones of relevance are:

- The need to carry out actions to see their result rather than 'think through' them. Whereas, for instance, older children could work out that if they increase their size of stride they will take fewer strides to cross the room, the 5- or 6-year-old will have to get up and do it, with small strides and then with longer ones.
- They look at things from only one point of view, their own. They may not realize that a different point of view makes things look different unless they physically move to the other position. Even then they may not realize that it is a different view of the same thing.
- They focus on one aspect of an object or situation at a time. For example, the youngest children identified either sun or water or air as needed to keep plants alive, but not a combination of these, as did older children (Chapter 3, p. 44).
- Their idea of the cause of a particular effect rests in the presence of some feature or object and does not extend to a mechanism. So the drum makes a sound 'because it is very loud', the candle burns 'because someone lit it', the washing dries 'because of the sun'. So-called explanations are often tautologous and merely express an observation in a different way: 'the car went because of the wheels'.
- They tend not to relate one event to another when they encounter an unfamiliar sequence of events. They are likely to remember the first and last stages in the sequence, but not the ones in between. For example, a 6-year-old, after watching sand run through a timer, was reported as being able to draw the timer and its contents at the beginning and end, but not in between. Given five drawings of the timer as the sand was running out he could not arrange them in sequence (Match and Mismatch, 1977).

There are clear consequences of these points for the sorts of activities the children will be able to learn from. The children's limitations are obvious. It will be no use expecting them to see patterns in events until they have begun to connect events in a sequence; the notion of a cause being related to an effect is still developing, so the idea of separating two or more variables to test the effect of each separately is still a long way off; their limited experience will mean that their ideas tend to be based on few very specific instances, selectively observed, having little explanatory power as far as new experience is concerned.

Equally clear are the indications for the kinds of experience that are appropriate at this age. Action and thinking are closely related to each other, reflecting their even closer identification at an earlier, preschool, stage. Thus infants need to be able to act on things, to explore, manipulate, describe, sort and group them. First-hand experience and exploration of objects in their immediate environment is the chief aim of teaching science to infants.

The content of the activities is therefore found in what is around the children and suitable topics start from everyday events. Common topics, encompassing activities across the curriculum including science, include

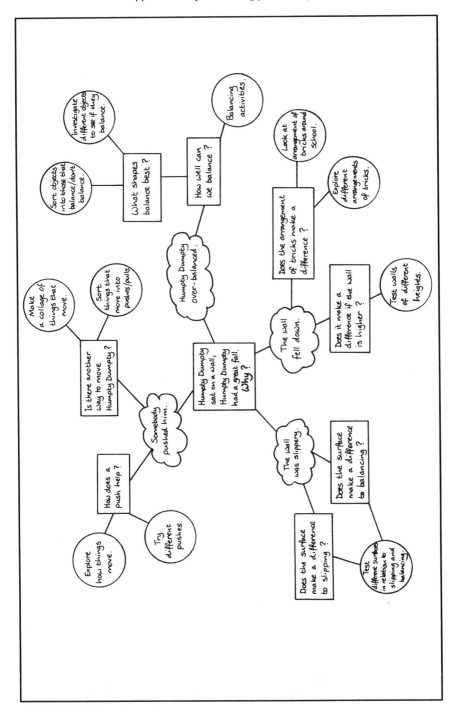

Figure 18   Developing children's ideas through a context

cooking, shopping, travelling, pets, holidays, Christmas and other re-
ligious festivals, toys, the park/shore/street, etc. Ways in which activities
within a topic can arise from children's ideas are proposed in the Nuffield
Primary Science teachers' guides, based on the SPACE project research.
Figure 18 shows a summary of activities about forces and movement
starting from the nursery rhyme Humpty Dumpty.

We shall deal with the teacher's role in the planning and execution of
activities in the next chapter; our concern here is with the overall nature
of activities and their goals. Starting from the familiar the content should
gradually introduce new experiences to the children (making a periscope
with mirrors, for example). Though the main emphasis in terms of process skills used will be on observation, raising questions and discussion,
there should be a gradually increasing demand in the use of these and
development of other skills. When the children have had plenty of experience of acting on things and using the skills they already have with
success, they will become able to replace some action by thought and they
are then on the way to rational thinking and the development of higher-
level process skills.

The children's activities should therefore include plenty of:

● looking, handling, using other senses on material collected and displayed in the classroom
● watching, standing and staring at things in their natural state in the
  immediate neighbourhood
● collecting things and sorting them
● trying things out
● making things, particularly models, that in some way 'work'
● taking things apart and reconstructing them
● talking about what they have observed and sometimes recording it in
  pictures and models and in words when they can
● discussing their ideas and trying to think of explanations for things
  they have noticed.

Learning opportunities for lower juniors (7–9 years)

On the assumption that children have had the kinds of experience indicated in the infant-school years, they will reach the lower-junior stage
having already made some advances in their thinking. A major advance is
the ability to use thought instead of action, to think things through, in
certain circumstances. The ability to do this develops gradually
throughout the junior and middle years. It is very limited at first, restricted to those actions with which children are very familiar and which
necessarily involve the real concrete objects they have been exploring.
The main characteristics of children's thinking at these ages follow from
the limited ability to carry out actions in thought. The advances over the
previous thinking are that:

- they begin to see a simple process as a whole, relating the individual parts to each other so that a process of change can be grasped and events put in sequence
- they can think through a simple process in reverse, which brings awareness of the conservation of some physical quantities during changes in which there appears to be an increase or decrease
- they may realize that two effects may need to be taken into account in deciding the result of an action, not just one (for instance, that heat *and* moving air help wet things to dry more quickly)
- there is some progress towards being able to envisage things from another's point of view, as long as this point of view is one that they have experienced for themselves at some time
- they can relate a physical cause to its effect and are less likely than before to say that, for instance, the leaves fall to the ground because the tree wants to get rid of them.

The limitations are:

- these kinds of thinking are carried out only on the familiar; they are no substitute for action and first-hand experience when new things are encountered
- thought about whether changes have really happened or are only apparent depends on how strong the visual impression is; thus apparent changes in volume of the same amount of liquid in different containers (which can confuse adults, after all) are less easily challenged by thought alone than changes where reasoning can more easily contradict perception
- the quantities that can be manipulated in the mind are those that can be seen and easily represented mentally, such as length and area; mass, weight and temperature are less easily grasped
- as might be expected, the complexity of a problem or situation influences the ability of children to approach it using rational thinking; they may be able to investigate the effect of one variable but if there are two operating together it is unlikely that their effects can be separated.

The implications for children's activities are that they should expand in two main ways. The range of content should be increased beyond the immediately familiar. The way in which the children interact with this new content might well be similar to their activity in the earlier phase, mainly finding out by observing, discussing, questioning and recording. In this way their experience of the variety of living things may be increased, through visits, books, films; their knowledge of different materials may be extended by making and handling collections of plastics, rocks, various kinds of wood, metal, fabric, building materials; their awareness of the way different things work may be expanded by investigating simple machines and mechanisms.

The second type of expansion in activities is a change in the way of finding out more about the already familiar things around them. The children can be helped to realize that some of the questions they ask can be answered by doing more than just observing things closely. They can see what happens when they do something to make a change and do this in such a way that they are sure that the effect they find *is* the effect of their action and not of something else. The idea of 'fairness' that is involved here is an important step towards investigation in a controlled manner. They also begin to make fair comparisons between things: to find out which toy car goes furthest, which paper towel soaks up water best, which paper dart is the best flyer, etc.

Again, the provision of activities should be such that opportunity is given for children to use the skills and ideas they have already developed and to extend them. Giving them more of the kinds of activities they learned from as infants is not sufficient; there has to be more challenge in the form of:

- a wider range of objects and events to observe and to relate to their existing experience
- tasks that require close observation of detail and sequence of events
- investigations of the effect on some object or system of changing a variable systematically, keeping other things the same
- tasks that require a search for patterns or relations in observations
- problems that demand fair comparisons between objects or materials
- encouragement to try to explain how things work
- expectation that they find answers to their own questions by systematic and controlled investigation rather than just 'do something and see what happens'.

A good example of the kind of activity described in the last of these points is the basis of a work card from the Learning Through Science (1982) Schools Council project's materials. As part of an investigation of containers (bottles, boxes and bags) it is suggested that the strength of plastic bottles is investigated as in Figure 19.

Here the children are being asked to do something they will certainly enjoy, banging and squashing bottles until they break, but to do it in a controlled way. A quantitative element is introduced but this is in terms of counting rather than measuring. Careful measurement is best left until a little later, when it is more obviously needed. At this point the physical difficulties of making measurements are likely to obscure understanding of what is being judged or compared.

Learning opportunities for upper juniors (9–12 years)

The progression in children's thinking in the upper junior years is towards both more widely applicable ideas and more structured and rigorous thinking. Given continued encouragement to think about a series of actions or changes as a whole they become able to deal with more complex phenomena and can entertain the idea that more than one variable may be influencing a particular outcome. This has a significant impact on the activities that the children can tackle at this time. Investigations can be carried out and problems solved in a more controlled manner than before. Children respond to the need for measurement in their investigations, the need for accuracy in observation and precision in the use of words and in recording.

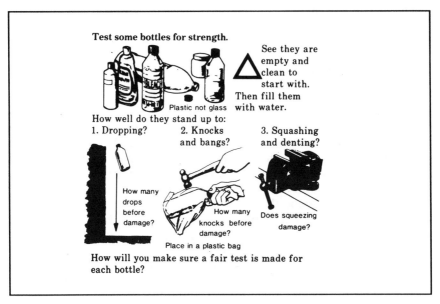

Figure 19   Reproduced with the permission of Schools Council Publications from 'Materials' (Learning Through Science) Macdonald & Co. (Publishers) Ltd., 1982. (Original in colour)

So the strengths of the thinking of the upper-junior-school child are that:

• they can to some extent handle problems which involve more than one variable
• they can use a wider range of logical relations and so mentally manipulate more things
• they show less tendency to jump to conclusions and a greater appreciation that ideas should be checked against evidence
• they can use measurement and recording as part of a more systematic and accurate approach to problems
• they can think through possible steps in an investigation and produce a plan of necessary actions.

However, the limitations of the thinking are still considerable:

- The ability to separate and manipulate variables is confined to simple cases where the variables are obvious and can be physically separated. It may not extend to situations where combinations of variables have to be chosen such that one variable only is changed, as for instance in finding the effect of thickness on the noise made by a lathe of wood when it is held at one end and flicked at the other. Here different thickness but the same widths and lengths have to be compared.
- The things that can be manipulated mentally are restricted to those that have a concrete reality for the child. These are things the child can perceive as real and so represent in his/her mind; (s)/he does not have actually to have touched them for them to have this reality. The reality can be conveyed through books, pictures, television as well as first-hand perception of distant things such as the sun, moon and stars.

As long as these limitations are kept in mind there is a great deal that children of these ages are capable of doing to help their growing understanding of the world around them. They will not be able to think in terms of abstractions and theories. Their focus will be on how things behave rather than on why they behave as they do. Their conclusions will be limited and they should not be encouraged to generalize prematurely. 'All the kinds of wood I have tried float' is a more suitable, and accurate, conclusion than 'all wood floats'.

A very wide range of activities is now available for these children and the main challenge in providing learning opportunities is to make sure that the full range of kinds of learning are covered. Investigations must extend beyond busily devising tests to find the best colour for a car to be easily seen, the best polish for shoes, the strongest carrier bag, etc. The range of activities should include:

- problems that can be tackled by detailed observation carried out for a recognized purpose and involving the use of instruments to extend the senses, such as magnifiers and a microscope, where appropriate and available
- discussions in which children raise questions about phenomena or objects in the surroundings, suggest how the answers to various types of question could be found and so begin to realize that science can answer only certain types of question
- practical problem-solving
- production of plans for investigations before they are carried out
- discussion of how problems have been tackled in practice, how to tackle new ones, how observations and results of investigations might be interpreted, how to report work to others
- the creation and testing of possible explanations of phenomena
- extension of knowledge through use of books or other sources of information.

The emphasis that there was in the infant and early-junior years on *doing* gradually gives way in the later junior years to a shared emphasis on doing, planning, discussing and recording.

Measurement plays an increasingly important part in investigations as these begin to demand that more accurate observation and careful distinctions are made than previously. Measurement has to be refined and the use of new techniques and instruments introduced and practised. Repetition of measurements and regard to accuracy should become part of a more careful quantitative approach by the end of the primary years.

Progress in the skills and attitudes may well depend on children being allowed to try their skills in gradually more demanding and complex problems. So it is understood that the list of activities above indicates what the children should be doing for themselves, through their own thinking, not following instructions for actions devised by others. It is through trying, and sometimes failing, that, at this point as before, development takes place. A child who tackles a problem requiring the separation of variables, but who fails to keep other variables constant while varying one, will get results that do not make much sense. In the discussion of what (s)he did (s)he may realize the mistake and take a step towards a new way of thinking about such problems. Without being allowed to make the mistake (s)he may well not have learned so much.

Matching at the individual level

We now turn to the matter of matching at the micro level, the fine-tuning of activities to the individual child. When the challenge of an activity and the support in tackling it are such that a child can use existing ideas to try to understand it and through doing so develops his/her ideas, then the activity is truly a learning experience.

Matching at the individual level has been an enduring ideal of education which takes account of the learner's activity. The Plowden Report endorsed it as follows:

> The teacher's task is to provide an environment and opportunities which are sufficiently challenging for children and yet not so difficult as to be outside their reach. There has to be the right mixture of the familiar and the novel, the right match to the stage of learning the child has reached.
>
> (CACE, 1967, para. 533)

Ten years later the HMI survey of primary schools presented the first attempt ever made to quantify the extent of matching for 7-, 9- and 11-year-olds. There were clear trends in their findings (DES, 1978) that were presented for different areas of the curriculum and for children in three broad ability bands (as judged by their teachers). The greatest degree of matching was found in reading, mathematics, writing and physical education; the least was found in art and craft, history, geography and science, the last taking the lowest position in every table. The less-able groups were better matched in all subjects than the children of average ability who in turn were better matched than the more-able groups.

A subsequent study by Bennett and co-workers reported on matching in infants' classes where they found that 'More than half of the observed tasks were mismatched . . . Mismatching appeared to have important consequences in terms of lost opportunities and limiting experiences for high attainers and confusion for low attainers' (Bennett *et al.*, 1984). This study found a much lower level of matching than the earlier HMI survey, much of it arising from children being given tasks judged to be too easy. They also reported a difference between their own judgements and those of the teachers as to the degree of match. Half of the activities judged by teachers to be a match were thought too easy by the researchers. If indeed the HMI, like the teachers in Bennett's study, overestimated the matching (by as much as 50–60%), then the results for science begin to look even worse. In less than one in five classes would there have been science activities which matched the average and more able children, with only a slightly higher proportion for the less-able groups.

Matching is not giving children more of what they can already do. Therefore it is not valid to take success on an activity as an indication of matching. A child can have completed the activity successfully without having advanced his ideas or done more than used skills already prac- tised. The reason why matching is more common with less-able children may well be that the mismatch is usually one of overestimation and so the signs of mismatch are visible in failure or inadequate performance. When performance is satisfactory it is not easy to distinguish a match from a mismatch due to underchallenging the child.

The essence of matching is progress; the child makes some advance in his ideas, skills, attitudes. This advance may only be made by experien- cing some initial failure: a first idea that does not work and is replaced by another that fits better, some observations that have to be made more carefully, plans that have to be reconsidered and so on. If these initial difficulties are overcome, resulting in learning, then the activity did pro- vide the opportunity for some advance in thinking. Matching means challenging children to take a step forward. But of course the step has to be of the right order; not too big so that they stumble and not too small so that they are marking time. Just what is the right size depends on many features particular to the individual child and to the activity; it can never be accurately predicted.

Uncertainty exists about all aspects of matching. It is not possible to know exactly the existing point of development of any child's ideas, process skills and attitudes. These are things that are changing all the time in the dynamics of learning and living. Further, too little is known about the sequence of learning to be sure of the next step which is the 'right' one to take at any particular time; there is no certainty about particular activities providing the right challenge for particular children. But this does not mean that we cannot attempt anything. The key factors which help towards matching are

- letting the children help, by using their ideas as the lead in identifying appropriate goals
- monitoring ideas to ascertain whether progress is being made towards the goal
- varying the degree of help for individual children.

What this means is not as demanding as it may seem at first. Monitoring ideas does not require formal assessment, but takes place during the usual teacher-pupil interaction (see Chapter 9), particularly through open and person-centred questioning by the teacher (Chapter 5, p. 84).

An important aspect of matching is the amount of help given to a pupil. For example, in planning an investigation, some children may be given, either orally or in writing, the support of a framework of questions (what is it that you're going to change/keep the same/measure?), while others may be able to plan without the support of this framework. All will, hopefully, achieve a plan for an investigation and through the process will advance certain aspects of their skill of investigating. This illustrates an important point about matching, that it does *not* mean pupils working individually on different tasks, supposedly tailored to their individual needs. As already mentioned, any attempt to do this would be invalid, since neither the 'need' nor the appropriate 'treatment' could be diagnosed accurately. Besides, imposing individual working would deny the benefits of discussion and the opportunity to develop ideas co-operatively.

For matching to take place, however, certain classroom features are required. There must be the flexibility for differentiation to take place, that is, for pupils to work:

- *either* in different ways on broadly similar tasks
- *or* on different tasks within a shared topic
- *or* with varying degrees of support.

Which of these is the appropriate structure for differentiation will depend on the subject matter of the particular activities and the goals the teacher has in mind.

The grouping of children for practical work depends on more than their ability in science. However, it is important to note that children with different ideas can be of particular help to each other, not in the same way as in a teacher-pupil relationship, but simply by extending the range of ideas available to a group. This has been confirmed by research in which the progress of pupils in groups formed in different ways was assessed. One set of groups was formed of children whose ideas about the activity varied widely (the differing groups) and the other set was formed of children whose ideas were similar. The results were quite clear cut:

> Looking at the change from the pre-tests to those post-tests that were administered several weeks after the group tasks, it is clear that on five of the six comparisons the children from the differing groups progressed

more than the children from the similar groups. Moreover, when the differing groups contained children whose level of understanding varied, the more advanced children progressed as much as the less. This being the case, we felt our results provide reasonably consistent evidence for the task being more effective with differing groups.

(Christine Howe, 1990, p. 27)

An important feature of these results is that the differences showed later rather than at the time or immediately after the activities. From this the researchers concluded that 'interaction when concepts differ is a catalyst for development and not the locus of it.' (op. cit.)

Opportunities for all

While all children vary in their response to science activities, these variations are overlaid by differences which are related to gender, cultural background and learning difficulties. Thus the notion of matching learning activities to pupils' interests, ideas, skills and attitudes must include consideration of these factors if the activities are to provide equal opportunities for learning.

Where discrimination against particular pupils exists it is generally unconscious. In a busy classroom it is not necessarily seen as a problem that certain children seem reluctant to take part in practical work or that ideas are rarely offered by certain groups. Thus the first task is to become aware of what is happening. Thereafter, conscious steps can be taken to prevent discrimination and to monitor the effectiveness of the steps taken.

Following this same order of events, we shall first consider the problems that certain groups can encounter in relation to science, then come to the possible preventative measures that might be taken.

Gender differences

At the primary level there are few large differences in performance in science between girls and boys. The Assessment of Performance Unit (APU) national surveys found that there were small differences either way:

> In particular, there is definite evidence that boys are on the whole more competent than girls in handling co-ordinate graphs and explaining scientific observations (usually in physical science), with girls performing equally well or slightly better than boys on questions involving other forms of data representation (pie charts, bar charts, etc.) and on questions requiring similarities and differences between objects and specimens to be noted.
> (APU, 1988, p. 30)

The main consistent difference was in performance on applying science concepts, particularly physical science concepts.

This relative weakness on the part of the girls in physical science is marked and very general; it applies across the range of concepts included in the assessment framework and persists in the data for 13- and 15-year-olds. It has been suggested that differences in the out-of-school activities of boys and girls . . . must be relevant in explaining this phenomenon.

(ibid.)

This difference in physical science concepts has been found in other countries and confirmed in international surveys (Comber and Keeves, 1973; IEA, 1988; Lapointe, Mead and Askew, 1992). However, what is perhaps more important for their later scientific development is that girls were consistently given a lower rating than boys in their willingness to undertake an investigation. This is a tendency that many teachers can confirm from observations of their own children. Girls' participation in group practical work frequently takes the form of watching boys and/or writing down the results.

Cultural differences

Science is about the world around, which for young children means their immediate environment, their family, their food, what is in their home, their neighbourhood. If science investigations only concern what is found in the immediate environment of a typical white British child then those with different experiences are likely to feel excluded. Children of other backgrounds should be able to investigate *their* food, *their* customs, *their* musical instruments, plants from the countries of their parents and grandparents, etc. Otherwise they are likely to regard science as something which does not relate to them and they will progressively distance themselves from it.

Learning difficulties

Children with learning difficulties are generally so described because of difficulties in learning in other areas of the curriculum, usually language. They may or may not have difficulties in science. There may well be children who have difficulties in gaining access to the same direct experience as others, through sensory disorders or limited mobility. There will also be others whose difficulties are in communication or in behaviour so that they lack experience of working in groups, discussing observations or drawing conclusions from their observations. Such children may have become regarded as having no ideas of their own and so left out of discussions, thus extending the distance between themselves and others.

Taking action

Although they arise for different reasons, the situations that result in discrimination (albeit unconscious) reduce the participation of pupils in direct handling and investigation of objects in the world around them. In the case of girls, participation may be increased by including a balance of topics of interest to girls and boys and, where possible, ones which are gender-neutral. But this may not be sufficient if boys tend to dominate practical work whatever the topic. Where teacher intervention does not succeed in preventing boys from 'elbowing-out' the girls from the action, it may be useful to have single-sex groups for practical work. Some teachers have also found that having small group discussions at the reporting stage provides girls with opportunity for reflection and restructuring their ideas which they shy away from in whole-class discussions.

To provide learning opportunities for children from all cultural backgrounds, activities should be designed to include materials and events of relevance to all their homes and customs. Children of Asian ethnic origin may also need encouragement to express their ideas and to ask questions, if by tradition they expect school to provide information from an authority. A gradual approach is necessary, enabling them to see other children expressing ideas and to realize the role this has in the activities. Also, work in small groups may help children to voice their ideas and so begin to engage in activities which develop them.

Children with learning difficulties are likely to need to spend longer in handling and playing with materials and in observing events more than once. Often, because of the extra time needed for most things, the reality is that they have less time for these important experiences which are basic to science. Thus the main aim will be to enable the children to spend more time in direct experience of concrete materials. It will also be important for these children to use the full range of techniques for expressing their ideas – talking, drawing, building models, pointing and showing – so that children with writing or other communication difficulties are not disadvantaged when it comes to contributing ideas. Some may discuss or show their ideas more willingly in a one-to-one situation, while others may be more responsive in small groups.

Bringing these suggestions together show that most apply to all children, but special attention needs to be given to those in the groups discussed, who may benefit particularly from

- the inclusion of materials and events which are familiar and of interest to them
- ensuring that they have plenty of time to spend in direct contact with objects and materials to be investigated
- establishing a classroom climate which values and responds to all ideas expressed by children
- encouraging a wide range of ways of expressing and sharing ideas
- providing opportunities for children to work and discuss in small groups where there is a supportive rather than a competitive atmosphere.

Having taken some action it is important to keep it under review. This may be facilitated by teachers in a school asking themselves collectively and individually questions such as these, suggested in the draft guidelines for Scottish *Environmental Studies 5–14*:

- In what ways can teachers ensure access to studies in the environment for all pupils, including those with special educational needs?

- In what ways does your programme stress
  - the interdependence of different cultures?
  - their contribution to society?
  - struggles for justice and equality?

- What steps does the school take to promote positive attitudes to other people and to address instances of discrimination and racism?

- In what ways does the school policy avoid stereotyping of pupils'
  - participation in activities?
  - resources for learning?
  - choice of courses?

(SOED, 1991, p. 75)

7

The Teacher's Role

Teachers' interventions during activities have a central influence on children's learning. But productive interventions don't just happen by accident; they take place in a classroom organization designed to bring children into contact with materials, with problems to solve, with information, with others' ideas to compare with their own; where time and space have been organized to allow teacher and children to talk and listen to each other. It is the intention in this chapter to look at the teacher's role, not just in helping children during their activities, but in planning, organizing and setting up the conditions for various activities to take place and for help to be given when needed.

It is not profitable, however, to discuss how teachers might plan their lessons without reviewing what it is they want to plan for. The kind of learning we want to encourage has been discussed in some detail in earlier chapters.

The purpose here is to consider what role the teacher should take if the intended learning is to take place. What sorts of things will pupils be doing to use and extend their ideas, process skills and attitudes? What will the teachers be doing to encourage progress and development? These are the questions considered first before discussing some implications for planning to translate the answers into practice.

The teacher's role in helping children to develop their ideas

In Chapter 3 some characteristics of children's ideas were identified and from these, it was suggested, there follow various implications for attempting to help children to change or modify their ideas and so to progress towards the more widely held and applicable scientific view of things. The relevant characteristics which need to be kept in mind, drawn together in full on pp. 51, 52, are that children's own ideas appear to emerge from their own reasoning (which is often not logical and rigorous in the way typical of scientific reasoning), are based on inevitably limited experience, may be expressed using scientific words but without a grasp of the accepted meaning of these words, and may be retained longer than really necessary if there are no alternative ideas which are more convincing to the children. Consideration of these characteristics leads almost automatically to the action that a teacher may take to help the development of their understanding: helping children to test their ideas more rigorously (which implies the development of process skills); extending experience; discussing words; providing alternative, more scientific, ideas; enabling children to review past experience in the light of any change made in their ideas. We shall consider the teacher's role in relation to each of these.

Helping children to test their ideas

If we think about how children arrive at their ideas it is often the case that they have taken account only of certain evidence and ignored anything that is contradictory, or that they have not compared like with like. For example, as mentioned on p. 46, the idea that the eye is the active agent in seeing by sending out beams to what is seen is only tenable in relation to a limited range of experiences; it will not easily explain how the brightness and colour of things can be changed in different lighting conditions. Or, the idea that wooden blocks can be magnetic would hardly stand up to testing a prediction that, if magnetic, they should be able to attract metal materials that magnets attract.

An important part of a teacher's role in science is to set up the expectation that *all* ideas have to be tested, not just the children's but any the teacher proposes or ones found in books. If this becomes routine, then there will be no implied criticism in asking children to 'find a way to see if your idea works'. Once accepted, the teacher can help children to express their ideas in a way which can be tested and to gather and interpret evidence with the necessary care. In other words, the focus is then on the way in which they use process skills and attitudes, as discussed later in this chapter.

Not all tests of children's ideas will be of the kind suggested in books of scientific activities and the teacher should be prepared to be as imaginative as the children in devising ways to address unexpected ideas. For example, children who suggested that mice drinking water from their tank left out at night (to explore ideas about evaporation) were responsible for the lowering of the level of the water, decided to test this idea by leaving some cheese beside the tank. Evidence of nibbling of the cheese, they said, would be a test of their idea about the participation of the mice. Untouched cheese, but continued loss of water, forced them to consider an alternative explanation.

Extending children's experience

It is not always the case that children have ignored evidence; often evidence that they might have used is just not available to them, as it is to adults. For example, it is reasonable to hold the hypothesis that rust may originate inside the body of a metal if a child has only ever seen the exposed surfaces of metal objects. Cutting through a rusted nail may be all that is needed to show that this is not the case. (This could be interpreted as testing the prediction that rust is found inside the metal; indeed all ways of extending children's ideas could be regarded as ways of testing ideas.)

The teacher's role is to provide gradually extended experience as a matter of routine. This can be through classroom displays, which are added to as a topic proceeds; through posters and photographs mounted on the walls, information books at the right level, for reference in the book corner; through visits, visitors and full use of the school buildings as resources for observation and activity. Against this background of regularly varied experience, specific information and activities can be introduced in response to the ideas that children are found to have. Thus a teacher who introduced 'fast growing plants' into the classroom did so as a result of children expressing the belief that plants do not grow during the day but only at night. These plants not only grow so quickly that a difference can be detected during a school day, but their life-cycle takes only a few weeks and so the change from buds to flowers and the setting of seeds can be experienced in a time-scale that has an impact on children's understanding of cycles of growth and reproduction.

Discussing words

We have considered in Chapter 5 the judgements to be made about introducing scientific words to pupils. It was implied that the teacher's role is to judge the right time to introduce an appropriate word to describe events or objects that children have already experienced and need to name. However, children pick up words from other sources and take some delight in trying them out. When children use scientific words, from any source, it is necessary to find out what meaning they have in mind rather than to assume that it is the same as the accepted meaning. A useful way of doing this is to ask the children to show some examples of what the word means: 'tell me about something that is melting . . . vibrating . . . evaporating . . ., etc.'. If the example is of something rather different from the meaning of the word (as when evaporating is confused with condensing, for instance) then the correct word can be introduced and the children should become involved in thinking up and demonstrating examples of both condensing and evaporating – or whatever words were confused. Encouraging children to challenge each other's use of words can sharpen their thinking at times when the teacher is not present.

Providing alternative, more scientific ideas

This is perhaps the approach which needs the most careful judgement even though it may seem the most obvious role for the teacher to take. The delicacy of judgement is required because it is all too easy to destroy children's confidence in their own thinking and reasoning if their ideas are swept aside by premature presentation of the 'right' ones. The best way of avoiding this is to ensure that more scientific ideas are introduced, not as being 'correct' but as alternatives worth considering, *and* that these are tested in terms of the evidence available so that everyone can judge the extent to which they 'work' in practice. For example, the teacher whose class proposed that thirsty mice were responsible for water disappearing from the tank (p. 117) introduced the notion of water evaporating, after the children's own ideas had failed the test. She turned the children's thinking to water disappearing from clothes hung out to dry, asking the children to think about the similarities between the two events and about whether the same thing could be happening to the water in the tank. Further experimenting with similar dishes of water covered and uncovered provided evidence for the children to see that this was a possible explanation – although only after the demise of the hypothesis about mice, since this, too, would have explained the difference!

As children progress in ways of thinking and experience they can be encouraged to consider alternatives, by argument and information from secondary sources and not only from what they can experience directly. Thus, for example, models of the solar system can be used to introduce explanations of the apparent movement of the sun and moon which can override the naive interpretations of direct observations.

Enabling children to review earlier experience in terms of new ideas

When early ideas that children have used to explain things to themselves are changed by the impact of investigating and thinking about new experience, it is important for there to be some review of their understanding of earlier experience. Without this there may be a residue of naive ideas which are still used to explain previous experience. For example, we can all probably recall believing in something like 'the man in the moon', but recognize that this belief was overtaken by more rational views. It would be illogical to believe in a man in the moon and the moon as understood more scientifically. To avoid the equivalent in children's growing ideas the teacher should help them to reflect on previous experience in terms of new ideas. It is helpful to be quite explicit about 'how your ideas about . . . have changed' for this legitimizes changing ways of understanding things, which is essential for the continued development of ideas.

The teacher's role in helping children to develop process skills

In describing the course of development of the process skills in Chapter 4 reference to the teacher's role could not be avoided. So some of the points to bring out here have already been made. We can therefore be brief in reviewing the opportunities required for process-skill development; indeed, it soon becomes apparent that there are patterns emerging which apply to all skills.

Observing

It may be recalled that the 'purpose of developing children's skill of observation is so that they will be able to use all their senses (appropriately and safely) to gather relevant information from their investigations of things around them' (p. 58). This describes what we hope will happen as a result of development. But of course children start by being unable to make a distinction between what we adults may see as relevant and irrelevant to an investigation. The focusing on relevant observations should not be forced, for it may end in children trying to see what they think they ought to see rather than what seems really relevant to them.

At the beginning of the development of observation the teacher's role is to provide opportunities for children to make wide-ranging observations. There are four main aspects of this opportunity:

- interesting materials or objects to observe and appropriate aids to observation (such as magnifiers)
- sufficient time to observe them
- invitations to observe
- discussion of what is observed

Materials that can potentially interest children abound in their surroundings and can be brought into the classroom for closer inspection and for display. A little thought to what is displayed can, however, increase the information children can gather from their observations. Shells and pebbles might be displayed not only dry, but in water, so that their colours show more clearly. Snail shells of different sizes but of the same type provide a chance for children to find out through observation how the shell 'grows'. Children can also get some idea of mechanisms from observation of objects that can be taken apart, like a bicycle bell, torch or clock (preferably one made for this purpose!)

Classroom displays give children the chance to use odd moments for observing things and can provide fruitful starting points for activities without taking up formal class time. A headteacher noted the characteristics of a good display that attracts children in the following comment:

> At the moment one of my staff has set up a display of edible fungi – tastefully laid out on a multi-level, fabric-covered background – and with them are lenses, cards bearing single questions and two colourful and attractive books on fungi. Children are drawn to it, and whenever I pass there are children examining the fungi, comparing them and suggesting answers to the questions. The display is a way of directing children's learning, encouraging involvement and creating a meaningful environment.
>
> (Ian Bennett, personal communication)

If children have not had time to observe displayed material at their leisure it is essential, when new material is gathered or provided at the beginning of an activity, to allow a period of time for them just to look, touch, smell and perhaps listen, before suggesting a task. Time is also an important element at later stages in an investigation, so that observations can be checked, refined and extended. By watching a group of children with new materials it is interesting to see how they often appear to observe very superficially at first. This may well be just a first quick run through, however; given time and encouragement they start again, more carefully, sometimes using measurement to decide whether or not differences they think they have seen are real. If the teacher stops the activity after their quick tour of what there is to see, then the only observations they make are the superficial ones and they are prevented from going into depth. So providing time is an important part of the teacher's organization.

Some children need few 'invitations to observe' but others are more reluctant and may be easily distracted after a superficial glance. There can be many reasons for this; likely ones include the effective discouragement of detailed observation by allowing insufficient time, or the teacher plying them with questions too soon. Reluctant observers can be helped by a teacher making a comment that might encourage observation rather than a question, which can seem threatening. For example, 'Look what happens to the pebbles when you put them in water' is more of an invitation than 'What happens to the colour of the pebbles when you put them in water?'

Discussion plays a major part in encouraging observation at all stages. In the early stages of development, talking about his own observations and hearing about what others have observed helps a child to make some sense of what he has found, to fit it into his understanding of the things just observed and of the others like them which he may have encountered previously. He may find that what others report differs from his own view, so he will return to observe more carefully, focusing on the particular feature that will decide the issue.

The move towards focusing is a sign of progress in developing observation skill. It is then appropriate to help this development with questions: Do the snail shells all have the same number of turns? Is there any connection between the size and the number of turns? These questions encourage the children to focus the observations for themselves. Problems in which objects or events have to be placed in some sequence are useful for this purpose, for they demand that the children find and focus on the feature that determines the sequence.

The narrowing effect of focused questions should be moderated by more open ones: What else is different about the shells of the same type of snail? What things are the same about shells of different types? Answering these questions helps children to realize that their focused selective observation uses only part of the information that is available. It can prevent them becoming blinkered by existing ideas which lead them to observe only what they expect.

Discussion can provide a teacher with important information about whether children have observed what was there to find. It is otherwise difficult to know what has been registered by children. Just because certain features can be observed and may be noticed by the teacher does not mean that they are observed by children. The reverse may also be true, of course, the children noticing things unobserved by the teacher who may have a different focus. It is important for the teacher to know what has been observed and what has been considered by the children to be relevant to the purpose of the observations. Since she cannot be with children throughout their activity, she may not even know what features were observable. So when she comes to discuss with children what they have found it is important to begin from what they observed, before considering their results. If there is any doubt about the basis of their evidence an 'action replay' can be called for. Take the example of the teacher who left a group of 11-year-olds swinging pendulums to decide whether the weight on the end really did make a difference to how fast they swung (they were sure it must). On return she found them confidently reporting that the larger mass made the pendulum swing faster. Mystified, the teacher asked them to show her that they were right. They set two pendulums swinging and waited until one stopped. 'You see, this one stops first, but the other one goes on longer: it takes longer to stop 'cos it's faster.' The pendulums had in fact been swinging at the same rate but the children took no notice of this. The influence of the children's ideas on the focus of their observations is very obvious here.

In summary, the teacher helps the development of observation skill by:

• providing opportunity (materials and time) and encouragement for children to make wide-ranging *and* focused observations (by comments and questions)
• enabling children to talk informally about their observations, to each other and to the teacher (discussion)
• finding out what they took notice of and what interpretation they made of it (by listening)
• arranging for observations made in small groups to be shared in a whole-class discussion.

Hypothesizing

As defined in Chapter 4, this process skill includes the application of concepts and knowledge in the attempt to explain things. The difference between application of something already learned to explain a new phenomenon and generation of an explanation from hunch or imagination, is not as great as it may at first seem. Both ways of attempting to explain should be encouraged. For, although it is important to help children to use information or ideas learned previously in making sense of new experience, it could give them a closed 'right answer' view of science if this were the only approach used. The question put to children in asking for an explanation should more often be 'What could be the reason?' than 'What is the reason?' For instance, what could be the reason for:

- some pieces of wood floating higher in the water than others?
- apples turning red when they ripen?
- pigeons sometimes puffing out their feathers?
- snow melting on the footpath before it does on the grass?
- Julie's salt dissolving more quickly than David's?

To all of these questions there could be more than one answer. Thinking of all the possible ones they can is a worthwhile task for children to undertake in small groups, where their combined ideas will be richer than those of any individual. Furthermore, in groups the children are less worried about contradicting each other and turning down far-fetched ideas or ones that would not explain the phenomenon. For example (about the snow melting on the path):

John: People walk on the path and not on the grass, so that took it away.
Peter: But it was on the path as well at the start and went before anyone walked on it, didn't you see? Can't be that. I reckon the path was wet – wet sort of dissolves the snow . . .
Mary: They put salt on roads . . .
John: Yes, that's it.

Peter's idea, too, was later challenged but he stuck to it because there was no convincing evidence against it so it went down on their list of possibilities. It was noteworthy that as this discussion went on the children began to talk in terms of what might be happening instead of the more certain earlier claims of what was happening. Another feature of the situation was that what they were trying to explain was a shared experience and one which provided the chance for them to check some of their hypotheses. Other ideas needed information from further observations or tests, depending in this case on the co-operation of the weather. The important thing was that they were not trying to advance grand theories to explain a whole range of phenomena (e.g. energy is needed to cause a change of state), but making sense of particular things in their immediate experience. Success and enjoyment in doing this would help the development of the ability to hypothesize which might well serve them well later when they might have to entertain alternative grand theories.

As well as the ideas generated within a group the children should have access to ideas from others outside the group. Listening to what other groups have proposed is one way, but they should also be able to consult books and other information sources. Part of the teacher's role is to make relevant books, posters and pictures available, selected so that the children can easily find ideas in them. For lower juniors it helps to place appropriate books next to the aquarium or the display or have them ready when a particular topic is to be discussed. Older children might be expected to find books for themselves.

The provision for development of hypothesizing therefore involves the teacher in:

- selecting or setting up phenomena which children can try to explain from their past experience
- organizing groups to discuss possible explanations
- encouraging the checking of possibilities against evidence to reject those suggestions which are inconsistent with it
- providing access to ideas for children to add to their own, from books and other sources (including the teacher and other children).

Predicting

As mentioned on p. 62, predictions can be based on hypotheses or on patterns in observations where there is not necessarily an explanation of the associated variables. In either case, using hypotheses or patterns predictively is important to testing them. The question 'does this idea really explain what is happening?' is answered in science by first predicting a so far unknown event from the explanation and then seeing whether there is evidence of the predicted event taking place. For children the explanation may be in terms of associated circumstances rather than mechanisms, but the same applies. For example, the appearance of a misty patch after breathing on a window pane may be explained 'because my breath is warm and the window is cold'. Although there is much more to the explanation than this, it is still possible to use this idea to make a prediction about what will happen if the window is warm and not cold. Investigation of 'breathing' on surfaces of difference temperatures would test predictions based on this hypothesis. In the case of patterns, take the observation that in salt water a hard-boiled egg will float, a raw one sink and a soft-boiled one stay suspended. The pattern here may be used to predict the state of the inside of an unknown egg without there being an explanation of how cooking affects the density of the egg.

It is not easy to encourage children to make genuine predictions, as opposed to guesses, on the one hand, or a mere statement of what is already known, on the other. At first it is useful to take them through the reasoning which connects the making of a prediction to the testing of an idea: 'according to our idea, what will happen if . . .?' and so 'if that happens, then we'll know our idea is working so far. Let's see.' It is also important to check whether 'we already know what will happen'; only if the answer is not already known is it a real prediction and a genuine test of the hypothesis or pattern.

The prerequisite for this kind of interaction is that the children are engaged on activities where they can generate hypotheses to test or observe patterns. Such activities include those where an explanation can arise from the observations, as in the behaviour of a 'cartesian diver', why footsteps echo in some places but not others, why moisture forms on the outside of cold containers taken from the fridge into a warm room. So the teacher's role includes:

- providing opportunities where children can investigate their ideas through making and testing predictions
- discussing with them how to make a prediction and test it
- helping them to recognize the difference between a prediction and a guess by asking them to explain how they arrived at their prediction
- expecting them to make predictions of something that is not already known in order to test their ideas.

Investigating

As with other process skills, the basic prerequisite for development is opportunity to use the skill. At the outset, however, it must be recognized that practical work is not the same as investigating; following instructions is not investigating; mere physical activity is not the same as investigating and trying to understand what is happening. Unless children sometimes take a problem and work out for themselves all the steps in solving it (listed on p. 64) they have little chance of developing skills of planning and carrying out investigations. They may not even realize that planning by someone has gone into the activities that they carry out by following instructions. When they come to plan for themselves for the first time they may have little idea of what to think about and put into their plan.

Planning is, however, a complex skill and to do it well takes a great deal of time. Two things follow. First, that planning should begin with simple problems, with no greater demand than just 'tell me what you're going to do'. Gradually, more can be expected, such as the planning of a fair comparison, followed later by discussion of variables and eventually the notion of control at a more sophisticated level. The second point is that children do not have to plan out every activity for themselves, though they should have the chance to do so quite frequently. It is particularly useful to provide guidance in planning in those investigations where they have only one chance to make the observations and mistakes cannot be easily rectified by starting again (such as in gathering information during visits or using materials that are strictly limited in availability).

The kind of help which children require changes as their skill develops. The supporting structure the teacher provides can be gradually reduced as children grasp what is involved in investigating. At first they may need to be reminded to go through the steps of planning, at both a general and a specific level, that have been outlined in Chapter 4 (p. 65). Development of this skill can be aided by reviewing the steps after the investigation has been carried out, whether or not the children planned the investigation for themselves. This is best done during discussion when the equipment is still at hand. Questions which probe how decisions were made, whether fair comparisons were made, how measurements or observations could have been made more accurately, etc., can be asked without implying criticism. Children will gradually be able to take over responsibility for reviewing their work if the teacher introduces it as a regular part of the discussion that should follow any practical activity.

The role the teacher takes in developing skill in planning and carrying out investigations therefore consists of:

• providing problems but not instructions for solving them, thus giving children the opportunity to do the planning
• supplying a structure for the planning appropriate to the children's experience (questions to take them through the steps of thinking about variables to change, to control and to measure)
• sometimes reviewing what is being done during an investigation in relation to what was planned, recognizing that not everything can be anticipated beforehand
• always discussing activities at the end to consider how the method of investigation could have been improved with hindsight.

Drawing conclusions

One of the important aspects of this process skill is looking for patterns which relate together observations or data which might otherwise remain unconnected. The ability to do this enables children to make sense of a mass of information which would be difficult to grasp as isolated events or observations. But not all patterns are easily detected, they may be obscured by features which vary unsystematically. So it is useful in helping children to search for patterns to provide some activities where the patterns can be easily picked out (as suggested on p. 67). Those who have difficulty will be helped by discussion and hearing what others have found, so arranging for children to talk about the patterns they find in their results is important.

There is some evidence that children may grasp patterns intuitively before they can find the way to express them in words. The APU results showed this in examples of children making accurate predictions but without articulating the basis for them (DES, 1981, 1983a, 1984). For example, children often describe the relation between the length and pitch of a plucked string in these ways:

The longer the string the lower the note.
The longest string gives the lowest and the shortest the highest.
A long string gives a low note.
If you change the length the note changes.

Each is correct, but the last three give less information than the first. The teacher's problem is to find out whether children who give an incomplete account of the pattern have actually grasped it as a whole but cannot express it as a whole, or whether they do not see the pattern that links all the information, as done in the first statement. There have to be opportunities therefore for a great deal of talking about patterns and about different ways of describing them. Generally, much too little time is used in this way.

Checking predictions against evidence is an important part of 'pattern finding' work, as well as contributing to an attitude of respect for evidence. So the organization of this work has to allow for to-ing and fro-ing between making observations or finding information and discussing it. Children might also be encouraged to speculate about the patterns they expect to find, before gathering data and checking carefully to see if there is evidence to support their ideas.

As children's ability to detect and express straightforward patterns becomes established their experience can be widened, taking in situations where the relation between two quantities is not an exact pattern. For example, there may well be a general relation between the size of people's feet and their height but there will be people who have larger feet than others who are shorter than they are. Discussion of these cases is useful in encouraging caution in drawing conclusions from patterns. Clearly, with foot size and height there is no cause–effect relation; the pattern shows only that these are features which tend to go together, though not invariably. This is probably because they are both related to other features, ones which determine growth. It often happens that a pattern is found between two things which both relate to a third variable, or a string of other variables, but have themselves no direct cause–effect relation. (Success in school and month of birth is an example, winter-born children tending to be more successful than summer-born children. There is nothing about the time of year that itself makes any difference; it may be related to time in school which in turn is related to measured success in school.)

This digression has been made to show that there are good reasons for resisting the temptation to draw conclusions about cause and effect from observed relations. Causes have to be established through controlled experimentation. Children cannot be expected to realize this but when interpreting findings or information they can, and should be expected to, make statements which keep to the evidence.

It requires a delicate touch on the part of the teacher to encourage children, on the one hand, to try to relate together different pieces of information but on the other hand not to assume a type of relation for which there is no evidence. We also want children to try to explain the patterns and associations they find but to realize that when they do this they are going beyond the interpretation of evidence and making use of previous knowledge, or imagination, in their hypotheses. Summing up, the teacher's role in encouraging children to draw conclusions with caution involves:

• providing opportunities in the form of activities where simple patterns or more general trends can be found (practical work)
• enabling children to talk about their findings and how they interpret them (by questioning and listening)
• expecting them to check interpretations carefully and to draw only those conclusions for which they have evidence (discussion and practical work)
• organizing for interpretations of findings to be shared and discussed critically.

Communicating

The dual role of communicating, as a means of giving or gaining information and as an aid to thought, makes it a particularly important skill. But
the fact that communication may be going on all the time may mean that
no special effort is made to promote it. However, if teachers take seriously
the role of talk in clarifying thinking and giving new slants to ideas and
recognize the value of becoming more explicit to oneself as a result of
being explicit to others (ASE, 1980), then it is important to make sure that
opportunities for free informal talk as well as more formal occasions for
reporting occur frequently. The implications for class organization extend
not just to ensuring that children work and discuss in groups, but that
groups have something in common to communicate to each other. A
teacher of top infants described what she finds a satisfactory organization
for practical activities:

> I have tried a number of ways of organizing practical science in the class-
> room – with varying success. For many activities the class is split into
> groups. One possibility would be to have one group of 4 to 6 children
> doing some practical science while the rest of the class are involved in other
> things. I find that this does not work well. Children are often very stimulat-
> ed by practical science and discuss their observations excitedly with their
> co-workers. I certainly do not want to discourage this enthusiasm and the
> exchange of ideas, but the noise can be distracting for another child in-
> volved in a piece of creative writing! Another disadvantage of small group
> work is that the time for teacher/group interaction is limited, particularly
> for the important initial discussion and the discussion of results at the end
> of the session.
>   A second possibility is to have all the class doing practical science, but to
> keep the group system and give each group its own set of experiments.
> This can work well, particularly if the separate investigations are all dif-
> ferent aspects of a single theme – group results can be pooled, and dis-
> cussed by the class at the end of the session.
>
>   (Jane Glover, 1985)

Equally strong arguments are made for the value of writing to learning.
But, as with talking, the fact that some kind goes on all the time does not
necessarily mean that children have opportunities for the kind of writing
that is most useful for their learning in science. The use of a personal
notebook, which was mentioned in Chapter 4 (p. 70), and keeping a diary,
are devices for encouraging children to use writing to aid their memory
and to help sort out their thoughts. Teachers who wish children to use
these things have to arrange to supply not just the materials, but the
incentive and the time to use them.

More formal written communication in science often involves use of
non-verbal forms: graphs, charts and tabulated numbers. The techniques
of using these are usually not difficult to learn; what is more difficult and
more important is the selection of the appropriate form to suit particular
purposes and types of information. Skill in selecting among possible
symbolic representations comes with experience, but experience is more

likely to bring development if it is discussed. The critical review of activities could, with advantage, include discussion of the form of presentation of findings. The teacher can also help in this matter by displaying in the classroom good examples of information appropriately and clearly presented.

From these points the teacher's role in developing communication skills can be summarized as:

- organizing the class so that children can work and discuss in groups
- providing a structure in the children's tasks that encourages group discussion and the keeping of informal notes
- introducing a range of techniques for recording information and communicating results using conventional forms and symbols
- discussing the appropriateness of ways of organizing and presenting information to suit particular purposes.

Common factors

Looking back now over what has been said about the role of the teacher in regard to the development of process skills a great deal of repetition is apparent. There are certain things the teacher has to do to enable children to use and develop all the process skills: provide opportunity for children to encounter materials and phenomena to explore at first hand; arrange for discussion in small groups and in the whole class; listen to their talk to find out what processes of thinking have been used in forming their ideas; encourage them through comment and questioning to check that their ideas are consistent with the evidence available; encourage critical review of activities and findings as a habit. For many process skills the teacher has, in addition, to provide the children with access to ideas from books, displays and other sources, and to teach them techniques of using equipment, measuring instruments and conventional symbols.

The common factors in the approach to teaching for development of all the process skills constitute both an advantage and a disadvantage. The advantage is that if the teacher does put all these things into practice then the conditions exist for the various skills to be developed in step with each other. Observation advances at the same time as interpretation and communication, for example. Each activity therefore contributes to several areas of development, though to each one only in a small degree. Gradually, the cumulative effect of successive activities builds up the skills. This creates what might be considered by some to be the disadvantage, that opportunities for process-skill development have to be provided frequently, if not continuously. It is no use allocating one or two sessions to developing 'raising questions' or 'planning investigations' and then forgetting about these process skills. Not only will the skill drop out of use but it will probably be actively discouraged if an approach to teaching is adopted which excludes children raising questions and doing their own planning.

Table 1 attempts to bring together the components of the teacher's role in developing process skills and the purposes that each is designed to serve.

Table 1 Components and purpose of the teacher's role in process-skill development

Role	Purposes
Providing the materials, time and physical arrangement for children to study and interact with things from their environment	For children to have the evidence of their own senses, to raise questions, to find answers to them by doing things, to have concrete experience as a basis for their thinking and to be able to check ideas they develop against the behaviour of real things
Designing tasks that encourage discussion among small groups of children	For children to combine their ideas, to listen to others, to argue about differences and to refine their own ideas through explaining them to others
Discussing with children as individuals and in small groups	For children to explain how they arrive at their ideas; for teachers to listen, to find out the evidence children have gathered and how they have interpreted it, to encourage children to check findings and to review their activities and results critically
Organizing whole class discussions	For children to have opportunity to describe their findings and ideas to others, to hear about others' ideas, to comment on alternative views and to defend their own; for teachers to offer ideas and direct children to sources that will extend the children's ideas
Teaching the techniques of using equipment and conventions of using graphs, tables, charts and symbols	For children to have available the means to increase the accuracy of their observations and to choose appropriate forms for communication as the need arises
Providing books, displays, visits, visitors and access to other sources of information	For children to be able to compare their ideas with those of others, to have access to information that may help them to develop and extend their ideas, to raise questions that may lead to further enquiry

Development of scientific attitudes and the teacher's role

Attitudes are more generalized aspects of people's behaviour even than process skills. They can be said to exist only when a general pattern of reacting in certain ways to certain types of situation has been established. One observation of a child spontaneously checking a suggested conclusion by seeking more evidence is not a sufficient basis for assuming that he has the attitude of 'respect for evidence'. But if he did spontaneously check so often that one could confidently predict that he would do so in further instances, then he might well be described as having this attitude.

The nature of attitudes means that there is a great deal that is common in encouraging their development. They cannot be taught, for they are not things that children know or can do; rather they are 'caught', for they exist in the way people behave and are transferred to children by a mixture of example and selective approval of behaviour that reflects the attitude. Indeed, quite frequent reference has already been made to the encouragement of certain attitudes during the discussion of opportunities for process-skill development and it must already be obvious that there is much in common in the approaches required to foster attitudes and skills. Therefore, one example of the teacher's role in developing an attitude is sufficient to establish the approach which would be similar for all. We shall consider flexibility.

Points about the importance of this attitude for scientific development were made in Chapter 4 (p. 76). It was suggested there that young children are often more successful in modifying their ideas than older ones (which is not surprising when many adults are quite inflexible in their thinking). For a continued development of ideas, however, a preparedness to change them in the face of new evidence is essential. This applies to ideas of all kinds, but it is perhaps necessary to stress it particularly in science where it seems rather too easy to give the impression that its principles and concepts exist as correct ideas to be handed on and learned. So somehow we have to find a way of preserving the flexibility that enables young children to develop their thinking.

A useful start to thinking about what can be done is considering why children may become less flexible about their ideas. This may happen because:

- they cling to an idea because it is 'theirs', part of them, and some self-confidence would be lost in relinquishing it
- they may have no better idea to replace the existing one
- they fear being thought to be wrong if they admit the inadequacy of an existing idea
- they need more time to make the mental adjustment required by a possible change.

Teachers can do much to avoid circumstances arising which are unhelpful in encouraging flexibility. Some relevant points have been made in discussing process-skill development. Provision of access to a range of alternative ideas goes part of the way to making sure that there is no shortage of different ideas to consider. As well as making these generally available, however, the teacher also has to consider the children as individuals. What may seem a reasonable alternative idea to one may not appear so to another with different existing ideas and experience. There has therefore to be time for the teacher to talk to, and to listen to, children individually and in small groups.

Individuals also vary in their reaction to group pressures. For some children the small group discussion provides an invitation to 'play' with ideas; they do not feel personally associated with any one and so lose no self-esteem if one idea is changed for another. For others the position may be quite different; they become identified with an idea and so feel a personal rebuff if it is rejected. This situation can be exacerbated by a teacher who reinforces this identification by interventions such as 'Let's try Daniel's idea' or 'Who agrees with Jane?' The deliberate dissociation of ideas from the people who suggest them helps everyone involved to consider them more objectively and more flexibly. This helps, too, in the use of ideas from books (which are not always accurate). Children should be encouraged to consider these on the same footing as any other ideas and not be overawed by the authority behind them.

Children can also be helped by the suggestion of ways of dealing with conflicting views; for example, by drawing up a list and agreeing first of all on what each item really means. Once this is done it might be appropriate to help them to see the difference and to identify the way they can decide which suggestion is 'better'. Alternatively, the best thing may be to leave them to talk and think things through for themselves. It is not always necessary to supply new data to bring about learning. As children become older, particularly, they may learn by reflecting on things they already know about, finding some new significance in them. Encouraging this is encouraging a mature form of flexibility.

Probably the most important role of the teacher, however, is to provide an example of flexible thinking. The teacher can take part in discussion in a way that shows his/her own thinking has changed: 'Yes, I used to think that, too, but then I realized . . .'. The teacher can also deliberately throw in an idea that the children can readily challenge with evidence. But in addition to these contrived examples there should be a genuine readiness to be flexible and to admit mistakes and changes of mind in small matters as well as in scientific explanations. The teacher is the dominating figure in creating the social climate of a classroom. To encourage flexibility this climate has to be one in which differences in views are respected and it is not a matter of shame to have the ideas one suggests disproved by evidence.

The main features of the teacher's role that emerge are:

- showing an example
- creating a classroom climate that gives approval to the behaviour that demonstrates the attitude
- providing opportunity for the attitude to be shown, in the case of flexibility, exposing children to alternative ideas
- making allowances for individual differences
- encouraging children to dissociate ideas from their sources.

If we now look at the other scientific attitudes (p. 73) it is fairly clear that the teacher's role in developing them would have all the features just listed. Opportunity, example, encouragement and a supportive classroom atmosphere are required in all cases. Provision of these should be as much a part of teachers' plans as the selection of content, if we are to take seriously the aim of scientific attitude development.

Planning for learning in science

Now that we have considered what the teacher needs to provide in terms of activities, kinds of intervention and help for children's development of ideas, skills and attitudes, it is appropriate to discuss certain aspects of planning this provision. The discussion is restricted to general organizational issues rather than the planning of specific topics, for which plenty of advice is offered in curriculum materials.

Planning at the class level

Reference has already been made to the value of groups working at the same time on different aspects or questions relating to a class project or topic. If the materials or equipment the children have to use are only sufficient for one or two groups at a time then having all groups working simultaneously will not be possible. The group working will then have to be staggered, some groups working on their science activities while others are involved in other activities. But the whole-class discussions can still be held, being planned to take place when all the groups have completed a particular phase of the group work. Staggering group work may also be necessary if the use of the equipment requires careful supervision for reasons of safety or for the teaching of a particular skill. However, if there are no good reasons for staggering, then having all the groups working together on activities related to the topic has many advantages. Jane Glover mentioned some in the quote on p. 128. Others arise from the value of having a recent experience that is of interest to others and being able to hear what others have done while the work is fresh in everyone's mind. A great deal more learning with understanding is then likely than if each group works on its own topic and has no shared experience to talk about with others.

The discussion the teacher has with groups has also an essential part to play in preparation for a useful whole-class discussion. By taking part in the discussion of each group, and by listening, the teacher can pick up the points of interest and concern, the ideas and the problems, that can usefully be shared between groups. Bringing out these points when the whole class gets together for discussion is then likely to lead to exchanges between pupils which are of interest and benefit to all of them. This helps to avoid the whole-class 'discussion' being of interest only to a few at any time and more a question and answer session between teacher and individuals in turn than a genuine discussion.

The pros and cons of various other possible class organizations are usefully summarized in Table 2. Note that the authors of Table 2 include reference to whole class teaching by 'chalk and talk and demonstration'. Whole class teaching does not necessarily have only this connotation. Research during the 1980s has supported the conclusion that 'whole class teaching is associated with higher-order questioning, explanations and statements, and these in turn correlate with higher levels of pupil performance' (Alexander, Rose and Woodhead, 1992). This defence is not given in order to advocate the wider use of any one organizational form, but to emphasize that 'whole class teaching, group work and one-to-one teaching are particularly suited to certain conditions and objectives' (op. cit., para 101) and a teacher should select which is most suited to the goals of learning at a particular time.

Table 2   Organization of school science

Method of organizing	Advantages	Limitations
Whole class: teaching by 'chalk and talk' and demonstration	Minimum organizational demands. Economical on time and equipment	No first-hand experience. No allowance for individual ability of pupils. Difficult to involve whole class
Class practical: children work in small groups doing similar tasks	Relatively easy to plan ahead. Children can work at own pace if extension work available. Equipment demands known in advance. First-hand experience for pupils	Preparation of extension work. Follow-up lines of enquiry difficult. Quantity and duplication of apparatus. Involves much clearing away
Thematic approach: small groups working independently to contribute to the whole	High in interest and motivation. First-hand experience for pupils. Pupils work at own pace. Builds confidence in communication skills when reporting back	Difficult to arrange balanced cover of science experiences. Difficult to ensure coherence and understanding from report back
Circus of experiments: small group rotating around prescribed activities	Easy to plan ahead, less demanding on apparatus and all can use specialist items. High interest or motivation	Activities cannot be sequential. Occasional pressure on completion time before change-over. Difficult to organise report back on whole circus. Method of briefing essential
Small groups or individuals: areas of study chosen by themselves	Allows variety of interests. High on motivation. Children work at own pace and to own potential	Demanding on teacher. Structured framework necessary. Stretches school's equipment and resources

Reproduced with the permission of Schools Council Publications from 'Learning Through Science: Formulating a School Policy', (Learning through Science), Macdonald & Co. (Publishers) Ltd., 1980.

Planning at the school level

There are some decisions which, in the interests of the pupils, are best taken at the whole school level. These include how continuity in activities from class to class is to be managed, how overlap in topics and gaps in experience are to be avoided. In some systems there is a national or regional syllabus which lays down the skills and concepts to be learned in different years, or the opportunities which have to be provided during certain stages, but there still remain decisions for teachers to make about the organization of these experiences. Chief among these is the extent of integration of science experiences with other learning. General topics (such as 'transport', 'clothing', 'the park', 'festivals') combine objectives of learning science with those of other subjects. Science-focused topics (such as 'water', 'the sky', 'the weather', 'plants to eat', 'stopping and starting'), by contrast, concentrate on the objectives of learning science and are usually labelled as science lessons or science activities. Equally strong cases can be made for the value of both types of curriculum organization. The opportunities offered by general topics are well summed up in the following way by two science advisers:

> An interdisciplinary theme taken by the class for a number of weeks. Groups of children work individually and co-operatively at different aspects guided by the teacher. There are opportunities for the development of class and small group teaching, investigations, visits, and displays. Such an approach encourages children to follow their own interests and design their own investigations. It also allows them to plan their work and share their ideas. The teacher is able to provide a variety of experiences at an appropriate level and to have dialogue with the children, helping where necessary. This way of working avoids severe problems of timing and shortages of equipment, and avoids the artificiality of subject 'boundaries'. Teachers working in this way find it relatively easy to introduce science based on skills and problem-solving.
>
> (Davis and Robards, 1989, p. 8)

The advantages of science topics, on the other hand, are in providing opportunities for in-depth study of particular ideas, explicit attention to skill development in relation to the generation and testing of scientific ideas and the identification by both teacher and pupils of scientific activity as opposed to other kinds of activity. The mixing of science and other experiences has been repeatedly criticized by HMI for superficiality:

> Unfortunately it is seldom that such an approach leads to good science education. The reasons lie in the fragmentation of the subject; the labelling of parts of an activity as science when they may not be scientific at all; and the use of unsuitable science topics because they seem to fit the general topic.
>
> (DES, 1983b)

In a later report HMI stated about general topics:

> Some caution is needed about this approach since the least effective work is often associated with topics where far too much is attempted and – as a consequence – too little is achieved in depth of knowledge, understanding and the acquisition of skills in the constituent subjects.
>
> (DES, 1989, para 74)

A strong defence of subjects in the primary school has been given by Alexander, Rose and Woodhead (1992, para 64), who express the view that it is the teacher's role to give children access to 'some of the most powerful tools for making sense of the world which human beings have ever devised' and not to leave them with only their own ideas and modes of thought.

As well as these differences in educational values there are practical considerations. Indeed HMI have recognized that general topics can lead to good science but require 'outstanding knowledge, expertise and insight from the teacher'. In the past the publication of the work of the few outstanding teachers may have given the impression that this approach to science is much easier than is really the case. The advantages of science topics, on the other hand, are in providing opportunities for in-depth study of particular ideas, explicit attention to skill development in relation to the generation and testing of scientific ideas and the identification by both teacher and pupils of scientific activity as opposed to other kinds of activity. However, the educational benefits of encountering science in real contexts which have meaning for the children must not be forgotten. Retaining the integrity of children's experience of the world is an aim worth preserving as we constantly review our understanding of good science education.

8

Assessment: Purposes, Principles and Approaches

In the context of this book our main concern is with assessment for two purposes, to help inform day-to-day teaching (on-going assessment) and to report learners' progress and achievements (summary assessment). However, assessment for these and other purposes has gained such prominence in education that it is important to consider some theoretical aspects as well as the practical matters of techniques and uses. This present chapter is, therefore, concerned with setting on-going and summary assessment (the subjects of Chapter 9) into the context of other purposes and with discussing the principles which apply to all kinds of assessment.

One of the recent trends in assessment is towards criterion-referencing, and away from norm-referencing. There are obvious implications of this for the identification of agreed criteria. Criteria for this purpose are provided in the National Curriculum of England and Wales, in the 5–14 Development Programme in Scotland and in some other curricula. However, to be consistent with the ideas, skills and attitudes relating to science which were discussed in Chapters 3 and 4, this chapter includes suggestions of some alternative criteria for assessing achievement in relation to them.

The word assessment is used here with a broad meaning and it is important to make clear that we are not assuming that assessing is the same as testing. Assessing is one of the possible ways of gathering information about children; testing is one of the possible ways of assessing. Just as there are many ways of gathering information about children's progress other than assessment (e.g. collecting samples of work, tape recording their spoken language or even videotaping) so there are many ways of assessing other than by testing. Assessment differs from other ways of gathering information in that it involves a description of what children have done rather than a collection of the actual evidence. It replaces the real thing by a summary of it: a comment, a mark, a spoken word; even a smile or a frown or other gesture can be the result of assessment.

Purposes

The range of purposes of assessment can been grouped under various headings. The following five reflect the actual, rather than necessarily the desirable, purposes for which pupil assessment is carried out:

- *On-going*, to help teachers make decisions about the learning of individual pupils; part of the regular day-to-day planning and teaching.
- *Summary*, summarizing the achievement of individuals at a certain time, for reporting to parents, other teachers and the pupils themselves.
- *Selection/certification*, a form of summary assessment used for providing qualifications or allowing progress to a higher level of education.
- *School evaluation*, where assessment constitutes part of the information for monitoring the effectiveness of schools.
- *National monitoring*, for quality assurance at the system level, to keep the performance of the school system under review and monitor trends.

Assessment in each of these categories requires information which fits its purpose and these will now be considered briefly. The requirements in terms of relative emphasis on detail, and on reliability and validity will vary. Reliability is the term used to express the degree of accuracy of the result of assessment, i.e. if the assessment were to be repeated, the extent to which the second result would agree with the first. The reliability of assessment of a child's skill in writing is likely to be less than the reliability of a test of addition and subtraction sums, mainly because it is far easier to mark the latter consistently. Validity refers to the extent to which what is assessed really reflects the behaviour it was intended to assess. For example, a multiple-choice test of knowledge about materials that conduct electricity would not give a valid assessment of understanding of a simple electric circuit, although it would be an assessment of quite high reliability.

On-going

On-going assessment is sometimes described as 'formative' or 'diagnostic'. Its purpose is to help teachers in making decisions about learning experiences of individual pupils and of groups of pupils. It is part of the regular day-to-day planning and teaching. It involves identification of where children are in their learning to inform the action to take. There is an equal emphasis on *using* the information as on finding what has and has not been achieved. Pupils can have a role in assessment for this purpose, through self-assessment and taking part in decisions about improvement.

A wide range of information is needed for this purpose. Indeed, over time it must cover all the skills, ideas, attitudes and other aspects of personal development which are the goals of learning. At any one time the information must be detailed to be useful. There is a high price on validity, less on reliability. The methods used must be ones which can be employed repeatedly and without interfering with the continuity of pupils' activities. The focus is the individual pupil but it is not necessary to assess all pupils at the same time. (See Chapter 9 for examples of methods and procedures.)

Summary

Summary assessment provides information summarizing achievement of individual pupils at a certain point, usually the end of terms and of the school year. The information is meant for those who need it – mainly parents, other teachers and the pupils themselves – and is confidential to them. The range of information in the summary should reflect all the major goals but in less detail than in the case of on-going assessment. The summary may be derived entirely from the record of on-going assessment, but where it is used for selection or streaming or deciding the future placing of the pupils there is a tendency to want to supplement, or even replace, assessments derived from teachers' on-going records with some kind of test or standard tasks. When this happens it is because the use of the assessment result has been changed from merely being a report on achievement and progress to being a basis for decisions which involve comparison of one pupil with another. It then takes on the character of assessment for selection and certification.

Selection and certification

Assessment for this purpose concerns individuals and is used for providing qualifications, or determining whether progress is allowed to a higher level, or, in some other way, the future opportunities of the pupils. Such assessment has to be seen to be 'fair' to all because either there is some comparison of pupil with pupil or because it is the basis of a qualification which should mean the same for all who hold it. It is important, then, that the assessment is as reliable as possible. Being reliable and being seen to be so are not necessarily the same, however. Teachers' assessments are not necessarily less reliable than formal examinations, but they are often perceived to be so, and some element of formal testing may be included because of this. The emphasis on reliability can be at the expense of validity, however. Pupils may become skilled at taking tests rather than developing the skills and understanding which will really be of use to them.

School evaluation

Use of pupil assessment for this purpose is controversial. It involves summarizing information about pupil assessment to form an average for groups of pupils. The information used is usually that gathered for the summary purpose described above; its use for school evaluation can distort the summary assessment procedure. For example, if comparisons are made between schools on the basis of pupil performance then there will be a demand for 'visible' reliability, resulting in a move towards formal testing rather than the use of teachers' judgements.

A further objection, however, is that average pupil performance is a product not just of the school, but of out-of-school influences, such as the social and educational home background of the pupils. One approach to allowing for this is to take into account pupils' achievement on entering school, but this requires a measure of that achievement and leads to more testing. Although our focus here is on the assessment of pupils, it is important to note the strong plea that other information than about academic performance is taken into account for a balanced view of a school's effectiveness (Riddell and Brown, 1991).

National or regional monitoring

This purpose of assessment is for quality assurance at the level of an educational system as a whole, to review the standards of achievement being attained. Regular monitoring can help to determine whether standards are changing and comparison of sub-groups used to explore the extent to which there may be under-achievement of some pupils. The methods used have to be ones which can be employed reliably in a large number of schools across the country. In many countries (and in projects producing international comparisons of achievement) this has meant multiple-choice tests. However, the Assessment of Performance Unit (APU) used more open-ended items and many practical tasks in their surveys of science performance from 1980 to 1984. Since the results were not used for purposes which affected the individual pupils tested, who were simply representatives of their age group, it was not necessary for them all to take all the tests used. This allowed a much greater number of items to be used than would be possible if every child had to be treated in the same way. The result was to increase the validity of the assessment because a greater sample of questions and tasks could be included.

Principles of assessment

When assessment takes place, some information is gathered about what a pupil has done or produced, a judgement is made about it and it is reported in some way. The various methods of assessment can be described in terms of four parameters:

What the pupils are doing
How the information is gathered
How the judgement is made
How the outcome of the judgement is expressed and reported

Although we shall consider each of these separately, they are not independent of each other. The way in which information is judged is not just a consequence of what is gathered, but a decision which has an impact on what is relevant information to collect. Similarly the mode of reporting has a significant impact on earlier steps in assessment; for example, a descriptive profile of performance requires different procedures for collecting and judging information than a series of test scores.

What the pupils are doing

This can vary from carrying out normal work to sitting a highly formalized examination; between these extremes are several variations. When pupils are put into a situation specially set up and designed to see to what extent they can do something under certain controlled conditions, the process is described as a test or examination. 'Normal work' sometimes includes regular tests; teachers may ensure that particular tasks, designed to reveal children's ideas, are included in the normal work. Many teachers give regular spelling and arithmetic tests and these are recognized by both teachers and pupils as tests, as are more formal and less frequent tests and examinations. In other cases the pupils may be unaware whether or not a particular work card is a test while for the teacher there is a significant difference. Ultimately, as we see in the next chapter, all children's work provides opportunities for assessment; special tasks are used to make this more efficient, being designed to elicit certain ideas or the use of particular skills.

How the information is gathered

The range here extends from observation by the teacher during the usual interactions between teacher and pupils to the reading of written tests or examination papers. Again there are several intermediate positions. Observation, which includes watching and listening, can be structured so that pupils are observed responding to particular tasks or questions. An important variable is whether or not a permanent record of the pupils' ideas or skills is created. Where this is the case, then it can be studied after the event in which it was produced, but if there is no permanent record of actions taken or words spoken, then it is necessary to gather the information by observation at the time. However, even where there are drawings, writing or other products to be assessed, information about when and how these were produced is important in the assessment. This applies particularly to young children, whose products may need to be discussed at the time and annotated by the teacher if they are to convey meaning later.

How the judgement is made

There has to be a basis for making any judgement – a standard or criterion against which an action or product is judged. Three bases for comparison are used in education:

- comparing with the standard of others of the same age and/or experience (norm-referenced)
- comparing with criteria for certain levels of performance (criterion-referenced)
- comparing with the individual's previous performance (pupil-referenced or ipsative).

In the first of these a pupil's assessment will depend on how other pupils perform as well as on his or her own performance. In formal standardized tests the 'norm' is a certain mark derived from testing a representative sample of pupils, but in a less formal way a teacher may apply standards derived from experience of other pupils in deciding what is the expected level of performance.

When criterion-referencing is used, the assessment is in terms of how the pupil's performance matches criteria describing certain kinds of performance. This judgement does not depend on how other pupils perform, although the choice of criteria is likely to be influenced by what it is reasonable to expect of pupils of comparable age and experience.

Ipsative or pupil-referenced assessment judges a pupil's performance against what (s)he has done previously and may result in a teacher appearing to use different standards for different pupils. One pupil who completes a certain piece of work may receive praise because it represents an improved performance while from another pupil this same work would have received a less favourable reaction if it were less than the pupil had already been able to do.

Which of these bases for judgement is appropriate depends on the purpose of the assessment. When the purpose is to encourage individuals and help them see signs of progress in their own work, then pupil-referenced assessment is appropriate. At the same time, however, the teacher needs to be aware of the actual level of skills and abilities a pupil is developing, through criterion-referenced assessment, the same for all pupils. Norm-referencing is used where a limited number or fixed proportion of pupils is allowed to pass or to obtain a particular grade – as used to be the case in the GCE examination and in the 11+. It is also used in arriving at the result of standardized reading and verbal reasoning tests. Here the raw score is converted into a standardized score which indicates how an individual's performance relates to the norm or average for the age group. When assessment is carried out to tell us about the development of various abilities of individual children the most useful judgement is about what the individual child can do. The judgement is therefore best made by comparing what the child does and says against criteria which describe what children do and say at certain points in development of skills, attitudes and ideas.

While compelling in theory the practice of criterion-referenced assessment is not unproblematic. The first problem is arriving at agreed criteria and expressing them at the level of generality that is neither too specific, so that a long list is needed, nor too vague, so that relating particular behaviour to them becomes too slippery. These matters will be taken up again later where some criteria for assessing primary science are offered and discussed.

How the outcome is expressed and reported

There are two aspects to be considered: first, how the assessment is conveyed to the pupils; second, how it is recorded by the teacher. The outcome of assessment may be expressed to the pupils through written or oral comment, by a tick or cross, by a number or letter grade – or indeed by a smile or frown. The cumulative record of assessment for all pupils may take the form of a mark sheet, checklist, comments written to specific headings or a descriptive summary. The appropriate type of expression and record of an assessment is closely related to how it is made and its purpose. We return to this matter in relation to on-going and summary assessment in Chapter 9.

Criteria for assessing science at the primary level

There are certain general points about the selection and use of criteria which must preface the statements proposed below for assessing science. The point of having criteria is so that everyone means much the same when using a particular term. If teachers are asked, for example, to assess their pupils in ability to predict, without defining what is meant by predicting, then inevitably a number of different notions would be used and communication about children's achievement could be hampered not helped. An operational definition, describing what children are doing when they are 'predicting' is the most helpful in this case. But this is not enough if it simply indicates what to look for and not how to judge what is found. The element of progression is missing. We need a description of progression in the skill so that it is possible to judge where children are in developing it, not just whether or not they are using a skill or idea.

There are various issues surrounding the identification of developmental criteria. How is the 'level' of ability in a skill or the grasp of an idea to be determined at different points in development? All those who attempt to define developmental criteria (including the working groups who produced the National Curriculum and the 5–14 Development Programme) face this issue. The answer is that these things are determined, not by theoretical ideas of development but by a pragmatic approach. Those who have helped to produce developmental criteria have drawn on their own and others' observations of children, to judge what kinds of performance would be appropriate for children of certain ages. Furthermore, in development of criteria of any kind there always is some implicit reference to a norm. This conclusion has emerged clearly from research: 'When almost any specific example is looked at in detail, it will be found that information about norms influences the setting of criteria. It is also true, although perhaps less evident, that criteria affect norms.' (Black, Harlen and Orgee, 1984, p. 11). However, in use of the result, in the criterion-referenced assessment discussed here, the behaviour being judged should be assessed against the criteria and not against the norm. In this way we should avoid limiting our goals to the level of development that is the norm for a particular age by allowing 'what is' at present to become 'what ought to be'.

The criteria should define the skill or understanding in operational terms at different points in development as well as directing attention to behaviours that are significant in its development. Thus gathering information for assessment by observation can be made more efficient, by knowing what to look for. This means that a teacher using the criteria must already have them in mind before observations are made. The criteria should affect, and help, the information gathering and not merely be used at the point of making judgements.

There is some danger in focusing too narrowly, of course, and this must be guarded against both in the way the criteria are expressed and in their application. The statements have to be in sufficiently general terms to apply to a particular skill or understanding in a wide range of contexts but sufficiently specific to indicate the characteristic of the behaviour that is significant. When they are used it must be borne in mind that evidence has to be gathered about behaviours in a variety of situations; a snap judgement should not be made on too little evidence.

The criteria for each skill and idea should be applied separately. It is easy to allow knowledge about a child's ability in one skill to influence judgement of another. This can be avoided by using the criteria meticulously and consciously. If a teacher says 'I don't think Joe is very good at hypothesizing' she should ask herself 'What have I see Joe do or heard him say that supports this judgement?' It may be that Joe is not very good at some other process skills and this has influenced the teacher's judgement of his hypothesizing without there really being any evidence for it. Behaviour relevant to each skill should be observed and assessed by using only the appropriate criteria.

A further point relates to the delicate issue of the extent to which norms enter into the use of criteria. The point can be illustrated by the example of the criteria relating to science process skills. These are invariably expressed in general terms and are not specific to any content. But in practice skills and attitudes are always applied in relation to some content which influences their deployment. It is not difficult to show, by considering extreme cases, that the influence could be quite large.

For example, an 11-year-old who is able to find and use patterns in data concerning the girth of trees and their height might not be able to pick out patterns in the chemical properties of elements that explain their arrangement in groups. It would be unreasonable to judge the 11-year-old's pattern-finding ability in the latter context, but quite reasonable to do so for a sixth-former studying chemistry.

Table 3 Criteria for assessing progress in the main areas of understanding in science at the primary level

Area of understanding	Age 7/8 criteria	Age 11/12 criteria
The characteristics of living things	That there are different kinds of living things called plants; that there are different kinds of living things called animals.	That living things can be grouped according to their general characteristics; that different species of plants and animals can be found in different locations; that competition for life-supporting resources determines which survive where; that human activity can interfere in the balance between resources and the plants and animals depending on them.
Processes of life	That plants and animals grow, develop and reproduce themselves and need food, air and water to live; that animals have senses which respond to different signals from the environment, that human beings must have enough of certain kinds of food for healthy growth and activity.	That all living things, including human beings, have ways of carrying out the same life processes; that the organs of the bodies of mammals are arranged in systems which carry out the major life processes; that flowering plants also have organ systems; that the human body needs certain conditions to remain healthy; that animals and plants depend on each other in various ways.
Materials, their properties and interactions	That materials can be divided into groups such as metals, wood, plastic, with certain properties; that materials vary in properties; that they are used for different purposes because of their properties	That materials are classified according to their origins and composition; that the properties of materials (including solid, liquid and gas) can be explained by their composition and structure; that manufactured materials can be designed to have required properties; that materials are changed (sometimes reversibly, sometimes irreversibly) through reaction with each other, erosion and energy.
Energy sources, transmission and transfer	That objects are seen if they give out light or reflect it; that objects that stop light cause shadows; that sounds are caused by objects vibrating; that heating and cooling things can change them.	That light, sound, electricity, mechanical energy, etc. are forms of energy which can be changed from one form to another; that different materials affect the transmission, absorption or reflection of these forms in different ways; that things are made to work by transfer of some forms of energy; that change of energy from one form to another always results in loss of useful energy; that some sources of energy are renewable but fuels are being used up and so need to be used carefully.
Forces and movement	That to make anything move or stop moving, there has to be something pushing, pulling or twisting it; that speed means how far something moves in a certain time.	That forces are needed to change the shape or the motion of objects; that when several forces are acting their effect is combined and if the object is at rest, they cancel each other out; that gravity is the force which pulls objects towards the Earth and this force (the weight) differs in places where gravity is different; that it takes more force to start or stop a heavy object moving than a lighter one.

The Earth and its place in the Universe	That the sun, moon and Earth are three-dimensional bodies which move relative to each other in regular patterns; that there are patterns in the weather; that soil is a mixture of material derived from rocks and living things.	That the Earth is surrounded by a layer of air and water vapour which in various conditions produces different kinds of weather; that the Earth is one of nine known planets orbiting the Sun; that the Earth spins on its axis; that the moon orbits the Earth; that days, months and years are related to these movements; that objects used in everyday life are derived from materials taken from the Earth and their supply is limited.

What we are saying is that we judge the 11-year-old's skill in pattern-finding in contexts where the skill would be reasonably expected to be used. What can be 'reasonably expected' is different for an 11-year-old and a sixth-former. Thus to some extent a consideration of what can be expected, what is the 'norm' for the child, is brought to bear.

In this case the interdependence of processes and content help to make the point but the issue of applying general criteria to specific contexts arises widely in science, as it does also in other subjects, particularly English language.

To sum up, to be useful criteria should provide:

• clear indications of the meaning of the abilities to be assessed so that teachers can have these in mind.
• descriptions of progress in terms of differences in actions and ideas of pupils at different points.
• guidelines brief enough for teachers to keep in mind rather than always having to refer to a document.
• reference points for judging the context in which the criteria are relevant.

These points have guided the selection of the criteria which are given in Tables 3 and 4. They represent a compromise between the sometimes conflicting requirements of desirable features of developmental criteria. They attempt to describe progress and at the same time to link the criteria to the context of work at particular ages. The progression of ideas and skills discussed in Chapters 3 and 4 is indicated by criteria considered appropriate at about the end of the first three years of school (at the age of 7 to 8) and at the end of the primary phase (at the age 11 to 12).

Comparison with the National Curriculum

Comparison of the criteria in Tables 3 and 4 with the National Curriculum statements of attainment shows that there is much in common between the statements here and those at about levels 2/3 and 4/5. So why produce an alternative formulation? There are three main reasons. First, that having only two points does not suggest a linear progression, which is implied in the multiple levels of the National Curriculum and conflicts

Table 4 Criteria for assessing science process skills at the primary level

Process skill	Age 7/8 criteria	Age 11/12 criteria
Observing	Use more than one sense and simple instruments to obtain information in reasonable detail	Make wide-ranging observations and select from them the information relevant to a particular problem or enquiry
Hypothesizing	Make an attempt to explain observations	Use of relevant ideas from previous experience to suggest explanations of new phenomena which are consistent with observations
Predicting	Predict from simple patterns in observations	Use previous knowledge or patterns in observations to make a prediction which can be tested
Investigating	Plan and carry out a simple investigation within everyday experience through actions appropriate to what is to be found out	Plan and carry out an investigation in a familiar context where there is a single independent variable separable from those which have to be controlled, with attention to variables and observation of the appropriate dependent variable
Drawing conclusions	Link together simple observations or pieces of information	Draw conclusion relevant to the enquiry based on observations and/or information gathered
Communicating	Describe work carried out so that the important points can be understood by others, using drawings and models where appropriate	Give orally or in writing a clear account of an investigation using graphs and tables to summarize findings

with the experience of children's learning. Second, we do not really know enough about pupils' learning to describe it in such close detail as the 10 levels, but what we do know is that it varies from pupil to pupil and the achievements of some are in the reverse order to the statements at some of the levels. Third, arising from the previous two points, is that when there is no attempt to force progression into a series of specific targets to be reached, teachers are free to work from children's starting points and help children to develop their ideas, skills and attitudes in the direction of progress in whatever way is most effective for learning with understanding.

9

Techniques for On-going and Summary Assessment

The intention in this chapter is to apply the theoretical concepts about assessment, discussed in Chapter 8, to assessment that is most closely concerned with teaching – on-going (or formative/diagnostic) and summary (summative) assessment. To be of most use in helping teaching decisions, assessment for these purposes needs to be criterion-referenced and curriculum-related. The gathering of information should also be planned at the same time as activities are planned, keeping in mind the type of record to be made. Various approaches to gathering, interpreting and recording are described, including the involvement of pupils in their own assessment.

On-going assessment

Throughout this discussion it is important to keep in mind that the purpose of on-going assessment is to gather information which can be used to help learning *at the time*, and which can contribute to a record of performance which will inform longer-term planning. Perhaps the first of these is the one to emphasize, since if it is carried out thoroughly, the creation of a record is a straightforward matter, while the collection of information for a record does not necessarily mean that it helps teaching and learning.

What information?

To develop a picture of what kinds of information are needed to help teaching, we can think through a typical series of activities. Once it is clear what information is required we can consider the methods which are appropriate for gathering it. The activities in this example took place with a class of 9/10-year-old children within an overall topic about clothing.

The teacher planned that the children should discuss and investigate the selection of different fabrics and materials for different purposes. He had in mind that the children should undertake some investigations of different fabrics, so he provided a collection of suitable pieces of fabric, etc. to which the children contributed. He wanted the investigations to advance the children's ideas and therefore to be based on their ideas and questions. It would have been easy to ask, for instance: Which is the most waterproof material? Which is the most wind-proof?, etc. and to start the children's investigations from these questions. These are perfectly good questions for children to investigate and likely to be among those the children ended up investigating, but he wanted to hold back his questions to find out what the children would ask and what ideas they had.

So the first part of the work was an exploratory phase of looking at the range of materials. In groups, the children were given samples of the materials, some hand-lenses and some very open instructions: to put the pieces of material into groups according to what they would be used for and then to explain what was the same about the items in each group and how the groups differed from each other. This task required children to use the ideas the teacher wanted to develop in making their observations, it encouraged them to look closely at the materials and to think about the differences they found. It was not a long activity but gave the teacher time to visit each group to listen in to what the children were saying about the materials. Many of their statements at this stage contained hypotheses and predictions. There was then a whole-class discussion, pooling ideas from different groups. Two groups were interested in investigating one of the ideas emerging from the initial exploration, that natural materials are harder wearing than manufactured ones. Others followed up ideas about warmth and thickness and others did indeed investigate what makes some materials more waterproof than others. Although having different foci, the investigations of all the groups were relevant to developing the idea that 'the uses of materials are related to their properties' (see p. 40).

In the investigation phase the teacher used information about the children's ideas to set them going on investigations which addressed these ideas. The investigations provided opportunities to help the children develop their process skills, in order to carry out systematic and 'fair' tests through which they would arrive at findings useful in developing their ideas. So during the investigation the teacher needed to gather information about the children's process skills and to use this to give them any help they may have needed in thinking through how to collect evidence and make a record of it. At the stage where results had been obtained, the teacher needed information about how the children were interpreting what they had found out and whether their initial ideas had been changed. More information about this and about the children's communication skills was available at the stage when the children made a report of the work, which they shared with the rest of the class. This also gave the teacher the opportunity to ask questions which challenged children to apply their ideas to closely related phenomena to find out the extent to which the children's ideas were becoming more widely applicable.

In summary, then, the teacher would be collecting information at various phases of the work, roughly as follows:

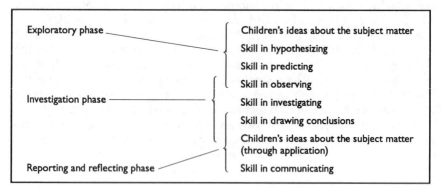

Exploratory phase — Children's ideas about the subject matter / Skill in hypothesizing / Skill in predicting

Investigation phase — Skill in observing / Skill in investigating

Reporting and reflecting phase — Skill in drawing conclusions / Children's ideas about the subject matter (through application) / Skill in communicating

How to gather the information

There are significant differences in methods used for gathering information about children's ideas and about their process skills, so these will be discussed separately. The methods suggested include those referred to in the example just described but go beyond these.

Children's ideas

In the example, the teacher was using two methods: listening and looking at the products of the children's actions. To these we can add others: using children's drawing, writing and concept maps.

Listening, without saying anything, to children while they are working in groups can enable a teacher to pick up the words being used; in this example they might be: 'manufactured', 'natural', 'see-through', 'strong' (or, in other topics, words such as melt, dissolve, disappear and so on). None of these words is unambiguous and some questioning may be helpful to find out what the children mean by them. Open questions are required:

> What is it about these materials that made you decide that they are manufactured?
> What do you think this was before it was made into this piece of cloth?

Using children's products (in the case of the example, the piles of pieces of fabric grouped together) can indicate the way the children are thinking. Do the groups of fabrics indicate that they considered other properties than just the appearance? Were consistent groups produced? Products arising at all parts of an investigation, not just at the exploratory stage, indicate the children's ideas – the way a tower is constructed to support something, the shape used for a boat, how plasticine is moulded to make it float, etc.

Children's drawing, which may not at first seem to give particularly rich information about their ideas, can be made to do so if they are asked to draw not just what they see, but what they think is happening or what makes something work. The drawing in Figure 14 (on p. 52) might well have shown just the container of water with the level going down had the children been asked to 'draw what happened', but instead the request was 'draw what you think made the water go down'. Framing a drawing task so that children have to express their ideas makes a very great difference to the value of the drawing to both pupil and teacher. Figure 20 shows a considerable insight into a child's ideas about the needs of living things through asking for a drawing of 'where you think would be the best place for a snail to live?'

Figure 20   (SPACE research, unpublished)

For young children expressing ideas through drawings, with labels, may not be easy, of course, but it is then useful for the teacher to discuss the drawing with the child and to annotate it as a result of asking questions (as was done in Figure 20).

In the same way, children's writing may be made more productive for revealing children's ideas if the task requires ideas to be expressed. The same request which led to the drawing in Figure 20 led another child to produce the piece of writing in Figure 21.

Accounts of investigations also reveal information about ideas, providing the children are encouraged to reflect upon and not just report their findings. All too often, however, the account describes events somewhat uncritically. The account in Figure 22 by an 11-year-old shows understanding of insulation, but a surprising acceptance of the apparent rise in temperature during cooling of one of the cups.

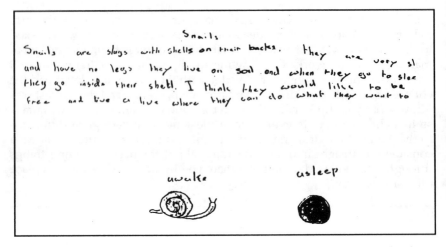

Snails are slugs with shells on their backs. they are very slow and have no legs. they lie on soil and when they go to sleep they go inside their shell. I think they would like to be free and live a live where they can do what they want to.

Figure 21

Concept maps have a wide variety of applications (Novak and Gowan, 1984) and the one suggested here is a limited one. It makes use of the device as a means of showing links between concepts, but does not depend on notions of hierarchies among concepts. The simple approach is to represent relationships between words by means of arrows, thus:

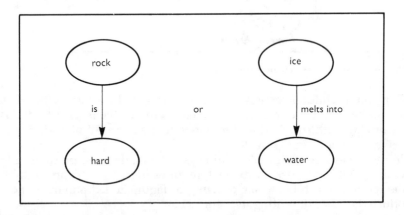

These are propositions of a one-way relationship between the concepts 'rock' and 'hard' and between ice and water. The arrow indicates the relationship. The reverse, 'hard is rock' and 'water melts into ice' do not make sense. When several concepts are linked together, the relationships

Water Experiment

Donald, Sharon and I did an experiment to see which material could keep water hottest.

We had four polystyrene cups and filled them with hot water. We put a different material over each one. We put polystyrene over one, polythene over another, cotton wool on another, and aluminium over the last.

We left it for five minutes and checked the temperature with a thermometer.

The foil was 50°C, so were the polythene and the polystyrene, but the cotton wool was only 40°C.

After another five minutes the cotton wool was the same, but the other three had fallen.

We left them a further five minutes to get a final result.

Aluminium foil came out at 41°C, the cotton wool had risen to 43°C and the polystyrene and the polythene were equal at 45°C.

This shows that the polythene and polystyrene are best.

I think polystyrene was best as it started off at 50°C and fell by only two or three degrees at a time.

I think the polystyrene being best could of had something to do with the cups also being made from polystyrene.

Insulation is good because it saves energy. If something isn't heated, it needs heated more often, but if something is insulated, heat can not escape so easily.

Figure 22

form a web or map. The process is very easy even for the youngest children to grasp and the product gives some insight into the way they associate things together or see cause and effect.

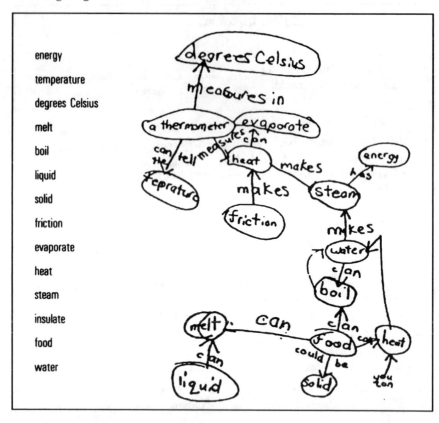

energy

temperature

degrees Celsius

melt

boil

liquid

solid

friction

evaporate

heat

steam

insulate

food

water

Figure 23   (reproduced from Harlen, 1992, p. 179)

The map in Figure 23 was drawn by a 6-year-old. After some activities about heat, the teacher listed words which they had been using and then asked the children to draw arrows to link them together and write 'joining words' on the arrows. From reading Lennie's map it would appear that he has useful ideas about the effects of heat but sees a thermometer as measuring both heat and temperature and has not distinguished between these two. Although this is to be expected from a child of this age, to be sure of the interpretation it would be necessary to talk through his map with him. As with drawings, the value of the product is greater if it is a basis for discussion between teacher and child.

Process skills

Process skills show in what children think and do. In some cases the products of this thought and action are useful indicators that they have taken place. In other cases, particularly for young children, it is necessary to observe the action as it takes place. This can seem a formidable and even impossible task for a whole class unless it is planned and well focused. Planning, as we suggest later, includes not attempting to collect information about the process skills of more than a few children in any one activity. Focusing involves having a mental or physical checklist of what to look for. The criteria proposed in Chapter 8 (p. 147) could be used directly to focus observation, or it may be helpful to create checklists of more specific items related to the same criteria. For example, for children up to 7–8 years old, such a checklist might be:

Did the child
- have a clear idea of what (s)he was trying to find out?
- make at least one relevant observation?
- observe using more than one sense?
- use a simple instrument such as a hand lens to aid observation?
- make relevant changes in something and observe the effect of changing it?
- link together simple observations in describing what happened?
- attempt an explanation consistent with observations?
- produce a report which conveyed what was done and found out?

For older children, the list might be:

Did the child
- make wide-ranging but relevant observations in the initial stages?
- suggest hypotheses for explaining initial observations?
- make predictions based on observed patterns or hypotheses or previous experience?
- set up the investigation so that one variable was changed at a time?
- control at least one variable to give a fair test?
- make observations or measurements of the relevant independent variable?
- make measurements within appropriate limits of accuracy?
- make sufficient observations or measurements?
- use aids to observation to improve precision?
- notice patterns or regularities in the results?
- keep adequate records during the investigation?
- draw justified conclusions?
- try to explain findings?
- reflect on outcomes in relation to initial ideas?
- make a clear report of important aspects of the investigation, using graphs, tables, etc. to show findings?

It may not be possible to observe behaviour in relation to all items in the lists within one activity; not all will be relevant. Thus the observations need to be spread over a period of time and different activities. The task becomes very much simpler when the list is internalized, focusing observation almost unconsciously. The list should be an aid, not become a burden. It only exists to help the application of more general criteria (such as the ones suggested in Chapter 8 or those in the National Curriculum) so as to identify more specifically the help children may need. If it turns out that it is consistently not possible to make observations relating to certain items then action needs to be taken to ensure that children are having opportunity to use process skills (see Chapter 7).

Natural	Rubs	Manmade	Rubs
felt (woo¹)	20	cotton + poly.te.	108
rubber	2 10	Viscose	57
cotton	67	Satin	20
linen	15	nylon	2

rubber was the strongest material it took 210 rubs. Nylon was the weakest material it took two rubs rubber took 208 rubs more than nylon

Figure 24

The records and reports that children write will add to the information obtained by observation. However, rarely do the reports of primary children indicate the detail that is needed to judge the extent to which various skills have been used. For example, in the investigation of materials described earlier, p. 149, one group of girls took eight pieces of different kinds of material and compared them by rubbing them against the ground. The teacher observed that they chose the same piece of ground to test all the materials and they counted the number of rubs it took to make a hole. They kept to the same procedures and the same person rubbing. This method took a considerable time, however, and Michelle suggested it would be quicker if they put a stone inside the material. So they wrapped each sample round a stone and started again. Their results were entered in a table drawn up for them by the teacher. Figure 24 shows the results recorded by Michelle's group.

They used these results, first to conclude that 'natural material is better than man-made' but later, after discussing their results with their teacher, they wrote:

> We don't know what's the best Material because when we done our second test Natural got the most points And man-made got the least points. But man made material got the most point's with our first test so we think Man-made and Natural have strong points.

The written work alone gives no information about the extent to which they attempted to control variables or how they came to their first conclusion. The discussion with the teacher caused them to have second thoughts about this. Through the discussion the teacher was able to judge their use of evidence in arriving at conclusions and, with the data from observation, collected a good deal of information which enabled him to see where these girls needed more experience.

Planning assessment as part of teaching

Gathering information when the appropriate opportunity is there – and thus avoiding having to set up special tasks – means planning the assessment as part of the lesson planning. The plan should take account of the *frequency of opportunities* for assessing different aspects and the potential for using the information.

Opportunities (should) arise frequently for children to use process skills. Most science activities should involve children in thinking and doing and thus provide the teacher with opportunities to assess and children to help to develop process skills. All activities should involve children in thinking and using most of the process skills. If this is not the case then there is need for serious evaluation of the learning opportunities being provided. But assuming that there are *frequent opportunities*, this means that it is not necessary to assess all children at a particular time. It is better to observe a small number of children thoroughly throughout an activity so as to achieve a detailed picture of their skills than to attempt to cover a larger number more superficially.

It may take two or three months to complete the observation of all children in the class, and it will mean that different children are assessed when carrying out different activities. This is not a problem in the present context for two main reasons. First, since no comparison is being made between children then, providing the activities give opportunity for the skills to be used, one activity context is as good as another. If the purpose were to assign a grade or label to the children then the variation in content of the activities would be a source of error in the results, but when observations can be repeated and the purpose is to help the children's learning, it is not a problem. Second, the skills we are concerned with are ones which are assumed to be generally applicable and so, again, it is the case that one context is as valid as another, given that they provide similar opportunity for skills to be used. This is not to deny the context-dependence of the use of skills, however, and with this in mind it should be emphasized that no one activity alone is sufficient to give a reliable assessment. Observations should be made during various activities over a period of time.

Focusing on a small target group at one time does not mean that other pupils are neglected. The pupils will be unaware of when they are targets, for the teacher interacts with all pupils in the normal way. When interacting with the targets, (s)he will observe, question and probe with the criteria in mind and keep a record, or make one as soon as possible after the event.

When it comes to assessing children's ideas, the opportunities are far *less frequent*. Ideas are linked to the subject matter and particular ideas will tend to be expressed in activities relating to the appropriate subject matter. Thus the opportunities to assess ideas have to be taken when they occur. This means assessing as many pupils as are working on that subject matter at any one time. Fortunately it is far more feasible to use the products of children's work for assessing ideas than it is for assessing process skills. Children's reports, other writing and drawing and other products can be collected and studied after the event. This is not to deny the importance of the context, which should be noted, and the added value that comes if the work can be discussed with the pupils.

Groups or individuals?

In referring to a group of pupils here the meaning has been a small number of individual children and the assumption that information is gathered about each individually. Teachers generally have no difficulty in identifying the separate contributions of children even when they are combining their ideas and skills in a group enterprise. However, we might question whether, *for the purpose of informing teaching*, it is necessary always to assess individual pupils. If the information is used to make decisions about the activities and help to be given to children *as a group*, then assessment of the group is all that is needed – for this purpose. As reported on p. 112, there is convincing evidence that in heterogeneous groups all pupils benefit when they are encouraged to share ideas and skills. Thus a group assessment may be considered to be all that is necessary in certain circumstances.

The position is different for summary assessment, where the focus is clearly on the individual child, and this is the subject to which we now turn.

Summary assessment

As indicated briefly in Chapter 8 (p. 139) there are two main ways of arriving at a summary assessment of children's achievement at a particular time. One is by forming a summary of the records of on-going assessment; the other is by 'checking up' through giving some special tasks which are designed to find out the extent to which children have developed certain skills or ideas.

Summarizing can preserve the detail of the on-going assessment and enable summary statements to be made about progress during the period in question over a wide range of ideas, skills and attitudes. At the same time two less favourable aspects need to be considered: first, that some of the information may be out of date if areas of work at the beginning of the year have not been revisited later; second, that it may be difficult to produce a descriptive summary which enables pupils' achievement to be compared, for their opportunities may have varied.

Checking up has the attraction of providing apparently equal opportunities for children to show what they can do at a particular time, although necessarily over a reduced range of experiences. It must be remembered, though, that giving children the same tasks is not the same as giving them the same opportunities since learning opportunity implies a match between the activity and the child's ability to engage with it.

Ways of summarizing are considered later, within the discussion of making and using records (p. 169)

Methods for checking up

While special tasks or tests may seem the obvious approach to providing this information, their use has many disadvantages:

- they lack validity since the tasks are restricted to those which can be done in the test context
- there is a restricted range of skills and ideas that can be included, partly because of the practical limitation on length of a test and partly because some skills are only revealed in extended activities
- they require considerable teacher time for organization and marking
- they take up learning time
- they can induce anxiety in children.

Because of these disadvantages teachers who wish to check up on children's progress through giving special tasks try to present these to children as part of their usual work rather than as formal tests. Examples of such tasks have been provided by the work of the Science Teaching Action Research Project (STAR) and published in Schilling *et al.* (1990). The materials devised and used in the STAR project take the form of a small class project about an imaginary 'walled garden'. The children are introduced to various features of the walled garden – water (in a pond with a fountain), walls, wood, minibeasts, leaves, bark, sun-dial. For each of these seven features a poster was produced which could be displayed in the classroom, giving suggestions for activities and posing some questions. Pupils work on one poster at a time and answer the questions in the answer booklet linked to the activities for that feature. Pupils can carry out the activities in any sequence and so a whole class can be working at the same time without interfering with each other's work. The questions were designed for written answers, but the element of active exploration in arriving at the answers extends the range of skills which can be tested. The questions are process-based and the different content provided by the seven features creates opportunities for the skills to be used in different contexts and so avoid to some extent the problem of validity which arises when skills are used on limited content. Since the activities are well designed, attractively presented and intriguing to children there is no problem in children engaging with the tasks as if they were normal work. Thus in various ways, many of the disadvantages of tests are avoided.

The approach embodied in the 'walled garden' materials can be readily adapted in the classroom perhaps avoiding the expensive individual pupil booklet. Other questions and tasks could be designed using the original material as a pattern. As examples the questions on leaves are reproduced in Figure 25.

For checking on children's developing ideas the important aim is to ensure that children are applying their ideas, working out their answer from their own thinking rather than simply recalling it. The decision as to what children are likely to be able to recall and what they will have to work out depends on the experiences of the children. For some, an answer to the question 'How would you try to stop an ice cube from melting for as long as possible without using a fridge?' may require application of ideas about the need for heat to bring about melting and transfer of heat through different materials. For others, however, who may have undertaken such an activity, it may be a matter of recalling what was done and the reasons put forward for it at that time. However, there are many variations in ways of ensuring that *application* of ideas is required and it should be possible to avoid questions which ask for straight recall of facts or for applications which can be recalled. The examples in Figures 26 and 27 illustrate useful approaches.

Involving pupils in assessment

One of the factors associated with good practice in assessment, reported by HMI in a study of the implementation of the requirements of the Education Reform Act, was 'the involvement of pupils in both setting their learning objectives and assessing their achievements' (DES, 1991b, p. 10). This involvement has been given more attention at the secondary level than at the primary level, probably on the assumption that younger pupils are less able to stand back from and reflect upon their own learning. As this may well be the case, expectations of what can be done at the primary school must be pitched at an appropriate level; nevertheless a useful start can be made.

Communicating learning aims and encouraging self-assessment can be developed together. Indeed this already happens, with unintended outcomes, when children are involved, say, in marking their own tests of arithmetic or spelling. They can gain the impression that all that is important is

Figure 25

Leaves

the Holly
and the Ivy

Sue, Nicky, Vince and Eddie saw a holly tree and some ivy
covering a wall near to it. They carefully picked one
leaf from each and compared them.

Look at a <u>real</u> holly leaf and a <u>real</u> ivy leaf.

1. Look for three ways in which they are the same, and three
    ways in which they are different.

	Same		Different
1.	....	1.	....
	....		....
	....		....
	....		....
	....		....
2.	....		....
	....		....
	....		....
	....		....
	....		....
3.	....		....
	....		....
	....		....
	....		....
	....		....

2. Nicky and Vince noticed that there were lots of different
    sized leaves in the ivy growing up the garden wall. They
    asked everyone in their group to pick a leaf. Back at school
    they drew round their leaves on squared paper to find the area
    of each leaf.

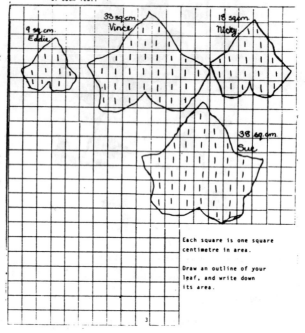

Each square is one square
centimetre in area.

Draw an outline of your
leaf, and write down
its area.

Sue wondered, "Are holly leaves different sizes?"

They asked their teacher to cut a holly twig for them. There
is a picture of it in the project folder.

The holly leaves were too prickly to draw round so the children
decided to measure the length of each leaf instead.

leaf position	leaf length
1	7 cm
2	9 cm
3	10 cm
4	9 cm
5	cm
6	6 cm
7	5 cm

3.   a)   The children had found that the IVY leaves were larger
          the further they were from the tip of the twig.

          Are HOLLY leaves arranged that way? What do you notice
          about the length of the leaves and the distance from the
          tip of the twig?
          ....
          ....
          ....

     b)   What do you <u>think</u> the length of leaf 5 might have been?
          .... cm.   (The picture is NOT the right size.)

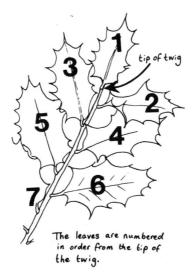

tip of twig

The leaves are numbered
in order from the tip of
the twig.

Sue and Jack were interested in the holly tree. They planned
to find the area of some holly leaves but the leaves were too
prickly.

The prickles were such a nuisance that they decided to count
how many were on each leaf. They made a table of their
results.

leaf length	number of prickles
10 cm	17
9 cm	16
7.5 cm	14
6 cm	12
5 cm	10

Figure 25 contd.

They used the results in the table to draw a line graph.

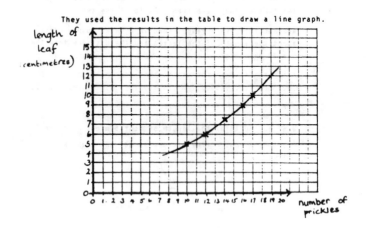

4. How many prickles do you think there would be on a leaf 12 cm long? ....

    How did you decide your answer?

    ....
    ....
    ....
    ....

5. The children made two discoveries. The first was:

    <u>Holly leaves do not all have the same number of prickles</u>.

    See if you can work out the second discovery. It is about leaf lengths and prickle numbers. Write it down.

    ....
    ....
    ....
    ....

```
     John washed four handkerchiefs and hung them up in
     different places to dry.   He wanted to see if the
     places made any difference to how quickly they dried.

  a)  In which of these places do you think the handkerchief
      would dry quickest?   Tick one of these:

         ┌──┐    In the corridor where it was cool and
         └──┘    sheltered
         ┌──┐
         └──┘    In a warm room by a closed window
         ┌──┐
         └──┘    In a warm room by an open window
         ┌──┐
         └──┘    In a cool room by an open window
         ┌──┐
         └──┘    All the same

  b)  What is your reason for ticking this one?

      . . . . . . . . . . . . . . . . . . . . . . . . . . . . .

      . . . . . . . . . . . . . . . . . . . . . . . . . . . . .

      . . . . . . . . . . . . . . . . . . . . . . . . . . . . .

      . . . . . . . . . . . . . . . . . . . . . . . . . . . . .

      . . . . . . . . . . . . . . . . . . . . . . . . . . . . .
```

Figure 26   (DES, 1984, p. 252)

learning by rote and getting the answers right. An approach is required which enables pupils gradually to realize the range of objectives of learning and particularly the value given to their own thinking. These things cannot be communicated directly and an approach through concrete examples has been found effective, described as follows:

> The process can begin usefully if children from about the age of 8 are encouraged to select their 'best' work and to put this in a folder or bag. Part of the time for 'bagging' should be set aside for the teacher to talk to each child about why certain pieces of work were selected. The criteria which the children are using will become clear. These should be accepted and they may have messages for the teacher. For example, if work seems to be selected only on the basis of being 'tidy' and not in terms of content, then perhaps this aspect is being over-emphasized.
>
> At first the discussion should only be to clarify the criteria the children use. 'Tell me what you particularly liked about this piece of work?' Gradually it will be possible to suggest criteria without dictating what the children should be selecting. This can be done through comments on the work. 'That was a very good way of showing your results, I could see at a glance which was best.' 'I'm glad you think that was your best investigation because although you didn't get the result you expected, you did it very carefully and made sure that the result was fair.'

166   *Teaching and Learning Primary Science*

Through such an approach as this children may begin to share the understanding of the objectives of their work and will be able to comment usefully on what they have achieved. It then becomes easier to be explicit about further targets and for the children to recognize when they have achieved them.

(Harlen, 1992, p. 171)

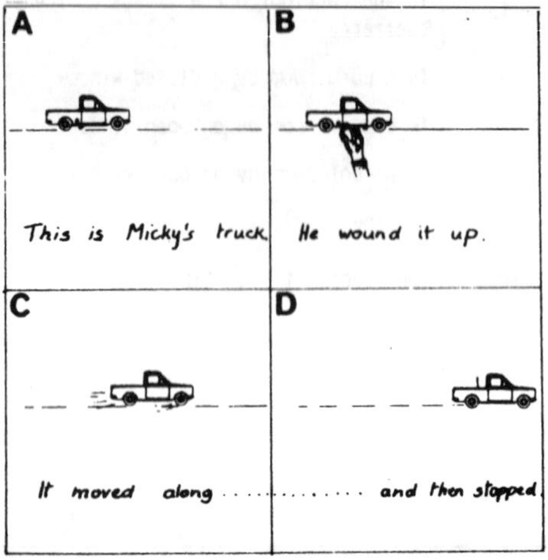

A   This is Micky's truck.

B   He wound it up.

C   It moved along .... and then stopped.

a) When did Micky's truck have the most energy?
   Tick in the box next to the one you choose.

   ☐ A Before it was wound up
   ☐ B After it had been wound up
   ☐ C When it was moving along
   ☐ D When it had stopped
   ☐ Same all the time

b) Give the reason for choosing the one you did.
   Because . . . .
   . . . .
   . . . .
   . . . .
   . . . .

Figure 27   (DES 1983a, p.27)

The participation of children in assessing their work is integral to the use of Records of Achievement as an aid to teaching and learning. By becoming involved in reviewing their work and recognizing progress, children gradually take more responsibility for future learning. The London Record of Achievement team, which has done much to pioneer Records of

Achievement in primary schools, see the review as central to the approach. A review is 'a special time set aside for individual children to talk privately with their teacher about their achievements, hopes and concerns' (Johnson, Hill and Tunstall, 1992, p. 11). According to preference, teachers might arrange reviews with one or two children daily, or set aside a regular time each week or conduct reviews less frequently but for a longer time with each child. During the review the teacher might start by talking about a particular piece of work, or an activity the child has enjoyed. Open and person-centred questions (see p. 84) are used to encourage the child to talk and take a leading role in the discussion, moving from what the child enjoys about the work to what (s)he would like to be able to do and what help (s)he thinks is needed.

> As children begin to reflect on what they would like to be able to do, what they think they are good at and what kinds of help they have needed, this gives you the basis for considering in a practical way how each child's work in class might be improved and the support needed to bring this about. These considerations are formalized in the setting and writing down of agreed targets.
>
> (Johnson, Hill and Tunstall, 1992, p. 16)

The London Record of Achievement team attach particular importance to encouraging children to focus on achievement, which they see as what children are able to do or participate in with varying degrees of help (as opposed to attainment, which is what they can do without help). Achievement in this sense is more child-referenced and related to potential to make progress than is attainment. They also emphasize that self-assessment flourishes within a supportive class ethos which recognizes everyone's need for recognition. The suggestions made in Chapters 4 and 7 for fostering positive attitudes in science are consistent with this approach described in more general terms both by Johnson *et al.* and in the Schools Examinations and Assessment Council's booklet on *Records of Achievement in the Primary School* (SEAC, 1990).

Making and using records

The form of record is an integral part of an assessment. It is in making the record that the actual performance is replaced by some representation of it. The record may attempt to capture the richness and variety of children's performance through description and collection of examples of work, or it may take the form of symbols representing the achievement of certain criteria, or a combination of these. For records of on-going assessment, which are essentially for the teacher to remind him/herself of where children are, the amount of detail and the exact form are individual matters. Circumstances and experience as well as personal preference influence the amount of information teachers can keep in their heads and what it is essential to put down on paper. However, when records are used for communication with others, it is usual for them to have some agreed format and structure. This is where it is important for any symbols or summary phrases that are used to be interpreted in the same way by the teachers and others who will receive and use the record.

In the case of summary records it is common for these to include symbols which represent criteria. For example, the following way of creating a profile of a child's performance originated in the project which produced the Match and Mismatch materials (1977). Criteria were identified for three progressive points in development for each of various skills, concepts and attitudes. For 'observation', for example, these were:

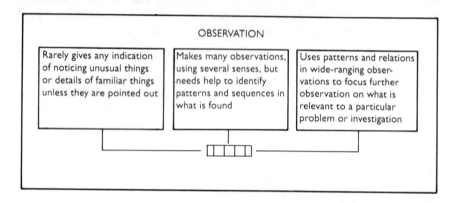

For each skill or concept or attitude, each of the three statements is linked to one of five boxes beneath. These boxes can then be used to record the development along a scale from left to right. The second and fourth boxes allow for some interpolation between the statements. Teachers have devised their own ways of completing the record to incorporate some indication of how sure they feel of it.

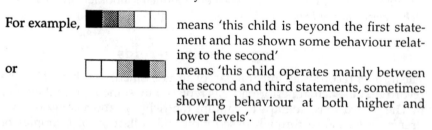

For example, [filled boxes] means 'this child is beyond the first statement and has shown some behaviour relating to the second'

or [filled boxes] means 'this child operates mainly between the second and third statements, sometimes showing behaviour at both higher and lower levels'.

The diagrammatic representation has an advantage as it can be used as a cumulative record. Further information can be added on the same record, simply by increasing the shading when there is some certainty about what a child can do, or making subsequent records in a different colour.

Note that the meaning of the record comes from the criteria used in making it. If a record is made which simply records a rating of a child's ability on a five-point scale, then a rating of 2, say, does not give information about what the child can do. A change from a rating of 2 to 3 would show that a child had made progress but would not describe the quality of the change or suggest what he can now do that he could not do previously. The record therefore has to be read with the same criteria in mind as used in making the observations. For this reason it is important that all those using this record are aware of the criteria which have been employed in creating it. Similar points apply to the use of the criteria in the National Curriculum Statements of Attainment, particularly when the shorthand of 'levels' is used in communication with parents and pupils.

It is not enough to be aware of the criteria, however, but to share the same interpretation. No criteria in a list of manageable length can be so specific that they can be used with total agreement. Useful criteria have to be couched in general terms so that they can apply in the wide variety of contexts in which learning takes place and this means that they are inevitably ambiguous to some extent. For example, it could be said of the third statement concerning observation, above, that it could apply as equally to a research scientist as to an 8-year-old. The same could be said of almost any statement from Attainment Target 1 of the National Curriculum, such as: 'observe closely and quantify by measuring using appropriate instruments'. In using such statements, therefore, there must be some consideration of what it is reasonable to expect of children at certain ages, thus an element of norm-referencing intrudes into a criterion-referenced judgement.

Clearly it is essential for there to be as near uniformity as possible in the interpretation of criteria if they are to be useful in practice. Ideally one teacher's judgement of whether a child has achieved, say, level 2 must be the same as another's. In practice it is very difficult to achieve this and even to find out the extent to which there is agreement. Examples of work, which can be judged against the criteria by several teachers independently, are useful, but such examples rarely evoke the context, background and conditions in which the work was done – all of which influence judgements in real situations. However, the publication of exemplars and discussion of them is valuable as a basis for helping teachers to adjust their judgements to be in line with others'. The example in Figure 28 comes from the SPACE project materials.

Many teachers keep records of their summary judgements by making reference to the Statements of Attainment; for example, by indicating 'approaching', 'attempted', 'achieved', or similar, on a form as in Figure 29. While this may be appropriate for in-school records, where usually teachers have taken steps to make their judgements consistent, it is not a friendly form for a report to parents. A more appropriate form is proposed by the Scottish Office in draft guidelines for reporting performance in the 5–14 Development Programme. An exemplar page of a hypothetical report for parents on environmental studies takes the form indicated in Figure 30. There is official recognition that parents nay need help in interpreting their children's report in the publication *Your Child's Report – What it means and how it can help* (DES, 1991b).

Groups of children had been exploring how sounds could be produced
by flicking a ruler. During the reporting back session, one of the
children explained that a sound was made as the ruler vibrated.

Teacher   *What do you think happens when it vibrates?*

Sue   *It makes a sound, it wobbles the air and the sound waves
            go all over the place.*

Teacher   *Do you always get vibrations when you hear a sound?*

Sue   *Yes.*

Teacher   *Do you ever get a sound and no vibrations?*

Sue   *No, it's the vibrations that make the sound.*

Sue has clearly made the link between the vibrations and sound and
can understand that the sound travels through air as a vibration. She
has therefore achieved level 5.

Joe made an annotated drawing which suggests his work is moving
towards level 5. He mentions that the skin of the drum vibrates as
sounds are produced. The sounds are then explained as turning into
sound waves which travel to an ear. It would be necessary to explore
these ideas with Joe in order to find out whether he regards sound as
vibrations in the air (level 5) or still sees them as different, with sound
turning into vibrations at certain points.

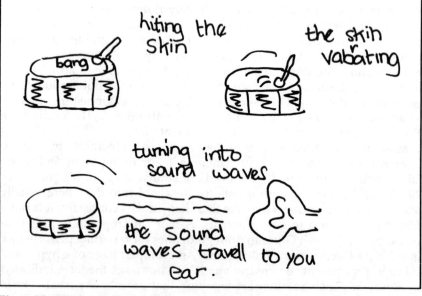

Figure 28   (Nuffield Primary Science Key Stage 2 Teachers' Guide: Sound and Music, p.
66)

Science record				a attempted 🗷 approaching 🗷 achieved	
Name _____					
Attainment target	level 1	level 2	level 3	level 4	level 5
Scientific investigation	a	abc	abcd	abc	abc
Life and living processes	ab	abcd	abc	abcd	abcd
Materials and their properties	a	ab	abc	abcde	abcd
Physical processes	abcd	abcde	abcde	abcde	abcdefg

Figure 29

Environmental Studies is composed of: science in the environment, place, time and society, healthy and safe living, living with technology.

Teacher's Comment:

Jane enjoyed this part of her work especially the visit to the industrial museum. She was particularly successful in interviewing the steel workers and in comparing and commenting on the amount of space given to different topics in various newspapers.
Observation and understanding of the idea of an experiment are developing well. A good step forward would be to note main points in reference material and not copy out of books.
Jane's presentation of information and observations is better here than in mathematics — generally clear and neat.

In Environmental Studies:
Jane is working at level C in scientific investigation, at level D in social studies and some of her reporting is approaching level E.

Figure 30

10

Resources for Learning Science

The kind of learning discussed in this book cannot take place without there being the materials necessary for children to observe, investigate and actively engage with. Both tools to use in inquiry and objects for study or experimentation are essential at some time. These living and non-living resources for children to use in their learning take some effort to obtain, organize and store. There is, however, plenty of help available in the form of lists of equipment, advice about obtaining and maintaining it and useful addresses, to be found in published programmes (for example, Ginn Science Resource File, 1989; Collins Primary Science, 1991; Bath Science 5–16, 1992, Nuffield Primary Science (SPACE) Teachers' Guides, 1993), in HMI documents (DES 1983a, DES 1989) and in publications of the ASE (1991). It is not the intention here to repeat or review this information; rather the concern is with the principles guiding decisions about resources.

Handling and investigating material at first hand are not the only experiences children need to help their learning, however. We have frequently referred to the value of access to ideas of others which can come through various channels. As well as discussion with other children and the teacher, it is valuable for children to have access to suitable books and non-book sources of information such as posters, photographs, slides, films, television, video-disc, radio and microcomputer programs. This may appear a long list but it is not unmanageable. The key factor is setting up a system for organization and control of the resources which is kept up to date and known to all those who use them, children as well as teachers. Indeed, it can be seen as a significant part of the children's experience to help in the care of living material and the organization of other resources. We shall discuss this wide range of resources under three main headings: resources for studying real things, including both living and non-living things, in-school and out-of-school; written (text) materials; non-text materials including radio, television and video-disc and the microcomputer. We shall also consider the role of human resources in the school, specifically that of the co-ordinator for science.

Resources for first-hand study

Safety first

Much of this book has provided a rationale for giving children opportunity to handle, explore and investigate things directly. For this they
themselves need access to the objects of study and sometimes to tools and
equipment to help in their investigation. It also follows from much of the
discussion of the importance of children using and testing their own
ideas, that activities will not be standard ones but ones devised to test
particular ideas or solve problems. Most such activities can be anticipated
from accumulated experience and research; children's ideas and what
follows from them bear a remarkable similarity across the globe.
However, it is the essence of helping children to develop *their* ideas that
activities are open-ended rather than 'following the book'. Unexpected
problems will occur and the overriding consideration at such times
should be safety. Children's natural curiosity may lead them to try certain
things which could be dangerous or to pick up objects out of the classroom which may harm themselves, as well as collecting things which may
harm the environment.

It is essential, therefore, for teachers to be aware of potential dangers,
and, without confining children's activities unnecessarily, to avoid situations which could lead to injury. There is comprehensive advice available
in the excellent booklet *Be Safe* published by the ASE (1991). This covers
use of tools, sources of heat, chemicals, suitable and unsuitable animals
for keeping in the classroom, poisonous plants, and work out of doors. It
suggests that children should be taught to recognize and observe warning
symbols, and be encouraged to consider safety when they plan and carry
out investigations and 'arising from their awareness of safety in their own
environment . . . should develop a concern for global issues which affect
the safety and well-being of all living things' (ASE, 1991). Helping children to act responsibly in matters of safety is part of helping them to take
responsibility for their learning.

Planning and provision of equipment

Rarely does a school have the task of drawing up a shopping list of
requisites for science starting from scratch. Almost always it is a matter of
augmenting an existing collection which has often been assembled in an
unplanned way. But it is important for there to be a regular review of what
exists so that this can be compared with what is required for implemen-
ting the programme for science, resulting from planning at the school
level. Unless the school policy is to follow a particular set of curriculum
materials it will be necessary for the school to draw up its own list of
necessary resources to support its own programme.

A considerable amount of material used in science will be common with other areas of the curriculum and so need not be listed. This includes paper, paint, Plasticine, Sellotape, string, scissors, glue, rulers, etc.

The list of science-specific equipment is not in fact very long, the reason being that many activities can be carried out with materials already in the school. For example, no specialized equipment is required for the wide range of activities young children can engage in that help their awareness that there is air all around (they can 'feel' air moving as they rush through it or fan it onto each other, make paper gliders, parachutes, kites, windmills, make bubbles in water, try blowing a pellet of paper into an 'empty' bottle) all without using any materials other than those which can be collected at school or home. Similarly, there are many activities concerning sound and hearing which make use of everyday objects or containers, rubber bands and any musical instruments already in the school.

There is virtue in keeping the specialized equipment to a minimum and not merely on grounds of economy. Special equipment that is used only in science and not found in other parts of children's school or everyday experience can isolate science from the 'real' world around children. If a special set of instruments has to be used for weather observations, for example, the impression may be given that useful measurements depend on that set. It can come between the things being measured and the child. A better understanding of what is being measured may come from a home-made rain gauge, a windsock made from a stocking and an ane-mometer made with yoghurt containers rather than from more sophistic-ated equipment. These will be designed by the children to do the job that they have defined; they will not be starting with an instrument whose function they have to learn. The more children help in designing the ways they interact with their surroundings the more they will realize that they can investigate and learn about the world around through their own activity.

Storage of equipment

Storing equipment centrally in the school is an obvious way to make best use of items which have to be purchased. Items such as hand lenses, mirrors and magnets need only be obtained in sufficient quantities for one class or for two in a large school. The disadvantages of keeping equipment in a central store can be overcome by systematic labelling and indexing, keeping records and providing easy access and ways of transporting equipment. Before dealing with these points, however, there may be the prior question of how and where to find space. In some cases ingenuity may be required, but there are many examples (some published in the Learning Through Science project's excellent book *Science Resources*, 1982) of under-used store rooms or corners partitioned off which have been most successfully transformed into resource storage areas.

Often parents are only too willing to clean and paint and put up shelves and hooks. Sometimes these activities can be encouraged to extend to constructing multipurpose frames for equipment that needs to be supported and even purpose-built trolleys for particular sets of equipment.

The organization of equipment in the store requires some thought. The notion of 'topic boxes' has been adopted in some schools, particularly where the work is organized round workcards used throughout the school. It seems wasteful, however, for materials to lie in boxes when they could well be of use in topics other than that for which they are ear-marked. Further, this organization would not suit more open-ended activities where equipment demands cannot be anticipated. The opposite extreme is to have all items stored in separate sets and for the collection needed at any time to be gathered by the teacher. This could be wasteful of time, too, since it could be anticipated that bulbs, bulb holders, wires and batteries would probably always be used together.

A compromise is probably possible, in which some equipment is kept in topic collections and other more general equipment kept in separate sets. Careful cataloguing is the key to the success of this, or indeed any, system. A listing of every item should be available to all staff showing where it can be found if stored as general equipment or in which topic box it is stored.

In addition the contents and storage position of each topic box should be listed. This may seem a great deal of cataloguing but almost every school now has a microcomputer which should be used for this purpose. A simple computer database can easily be kept up to date as new equipment is added and can be designed to enable items to be viewed alphabetically, by shelf or whatever variable is appropriate. In large schools the computer may also be used to 'book' equipment at certain times, so that a planned lesson involving the microscope, for instance, is not frustrated by finding it already in use in another classroom. For transporting equipment a trolley, or preferably more than one, is almost a necessity. If several can be obtained, some can be converted as the permanent and mobile store for certain commonly used materials, or for particularly heavy topic equipment. Most often, though, a teacher will load the trolley with the collection needed at a particular time. When a chosen collection is in use in a classroom for a few days or longer, details of what is there should be left in the store.

In setting up a store it is well to remember that collections of material generally grow quite rapidly, they rarely diminish. Items brought to school to add to a display or to the range of materials being investigated are generally donated. In this way useful items such as an old camera, clock, clockwork or battery-driven toys, metal and wood off-cuts are added to the store and room has to be available for them. The store should also house a range of containers and other general equipment that is above that required in each classroom for activities other than science.

This collection can swell quite quickly, too, once parents are aware that squeezy bottles, yoghurt pots, foil pie tins and plastic bottles are all useful for school activities.

Living things

Animals kept in the school for an extended period of time require specialized housing and regular care. It is worthwhile planning the provision of these non-human members of the school so that they make the most contribution to children's experience of the variety of living things. In one school there were salamanders in one classroom, fish in another, gerbils in another and so on. Each year the children changed classroom, so that they lived with each type of animal in turn. In other cases an agreed rota for exchanging classroom animals might be more appropriate, with teachers planning children's activities to suit the animals in residence at different times.

As well as captive animals in the classroom it should be possible to provide access to animals in natural habitats set up in the school grounds. Many schools are now using a small part of the grounds for an outdoor study area, where plants are grown and where birds, insects or other 'minibeasts' can find food and shelter. Few schools are unable to find the few square metres where plants can be grown, even if it is only in a chequerboard garden formed by taking up one or two patio slabs. Generally, much more can be done, so that nesting boxes can be provided, shrubs planted to attract butterflies, a bed for planting seeds with larger areas of garden for planting out seedlings and, quite important, a semi-wild area where wild flowers and grass can grow up round a pile of stones, giving shelter to a range of insects and other invertebrates. A good example of such an area is given in *Science Resources* (Learning Through Science, 1982, p. 30).

An outdoor resource area provides a valuable opportunity for children to study creatures without disturbing them too much. But if brought into the classroom for further study, temporary housing can be improvised from a variety of clear plastic containers.

Display

A great deal of attention has been given to storing equipment and materials tidily away, but not all of it should be always out of sight. As mentioned in Chapter 7, p. 120, displays can provide starting points for activities and give children a useful way to pass odd moments. Displays can feature anything from a collection of tools, measuring instruments, or materials taken from the store, to special items on loan from the museum, local craft centre or industry. There should always be information provided about the exhibits in a suitable form and if possible invitations for children to handle and explore them or to inquire further in other ways.

Using out-of-school resources

Since the overall aim of science activities is to help children understand the world around them, getting out into that world has an important part to play. This is not to deny that the classroom and school and all that is in them are part of the child's environment, but this is a selected and controlled part and to make connections between children's activities in school and the larger environment it is necessary regularly to observe and interact with parts of it at first hand.

There are good practical reasons for taking children out of school. Visits are highly motivating to children, who bring back to school many vivid impressions which sustain follow-up work and often persist over several weeks.

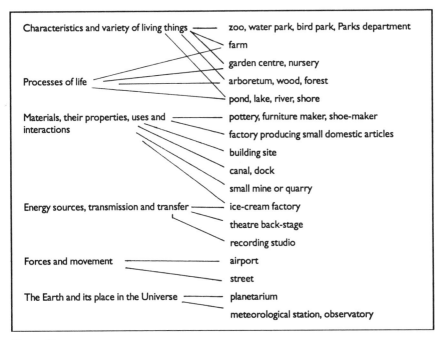

Figure 31

They contribute, of course, to work in other areas of the curriculum and this is not being forgotten in concentrating here on the science work. A most successful teacher of primary science (incidentally not trained in science) always began every topic with a visit; he said it was the equivalent to charging a battery, giving the work for 5 or 6 weeks energy and vitality. Each visit was chosen to suit the programme planned and to provide opportunities for children to develop science concepts during follow-up investigations. It is not difficult to select a site for a visit in this way since most venues provide opportunities for development of any of a whole range of ideas. Figure 31 illustrates this, showing just some of the links between the possibilities for visits and the main areas of basic science concepts. (This does not include museums or special exhibitions which could relate to any or all of the concepts; these have a valuable role in children's learning in addition to and not as a substitute for visiting places which are more a part of everyday life.)

A considerable amount of work for the teacher is involved in planning and organizing a visit but this is rewarded several times over by the quality of the ensuing work of the children. The necessary preparation varies according to whether the visit will be entirely under the control of the teacher (as in field work at a pond or in a wood) or whether people at the site will be involved in giving access and information (as in a visit to a work place).

Where the teacher is the sole person involved in planning (even if helping parents or others accompany the party) the preparation must involve an initial survey of possibilities, having in mind the characteristics of the children who will be visiting. For example, infants will want things to watch, touch, smell, handle and so there should be plenty of opportunity for being able to do these things safely; children need to be shown very clearly any dangerous plants or objects that should not be touched. Lower juniors will not be satisfied with just looking and feeling; they will want to explore how things are related, to make more systematic observations in which patterns can be detected. Upper juniors are capable of concentrating on a particular question and can use the visit to gather evidence systematically, for example, about the different communities of plants and animals to be found in different habitats. Some useful ideas for exploring possibilities in the environment near the school are given by Elstgeest and Harlen (1990):

(1) Which landscape or elements of landscape do you find around your school?
   A landscape is a piece of earth, small or large, that can be recognized as a complex whole. There are many kinds and many sizes. We think of the large rural, agrarian, mountainous, forested or prairie-type landscapes, not forgetting seascapes. Landscapes may be wild like moors, or cultured like a park. But there are small landscapes, too. Think of your own playground and its surrounding shrubbery as a landscape. Or take a footpath and its verge, or a piece of wasteland; the village green, or town square, or a front garden; a hill side, a brook, a bank or a copse, a lawn or a flowerbed. These are all landscapes, each forming a complex entity, each recognizable by its own particular characteristics.
   On a still smaller scale, look for minilandscapes, such as an overgrown wall, a mouldered, mossy stump of treetrunk, a hollow tree such as an ancient pollard willow. Anything might raise questions about what grows and flourishes (or not), about what is happening or what has recently happened, about what has been erected, constructed or put in order. Don't just look for green or bloom; non-living things also speak a language. Notice, for instance, the pattern of the bricks in the buildings or the paving slabs in the streets. Since our focus here *is* the living environment we won't pursue

the avenues opened up by non-living materials in great detail, but they should not be ignored when working with children.

(2) Don't only search at ground level. Look up! A tree, a hedge, a shrub in the shrubbery already takes the eye upward, but let it go further; there is so much to explore above eye level. There are colours and shapes and constructions of many kinds; kites fly, as do birds, aeroplanes, flies and other winged creatures. The sky, with its clouds and rainbows stretches above, and the whole world is filled with sounds and fragrances. Feel changes in temperature as the winds veer in new directions; watch how the sun seems to move, and how the moon changes place and face.

(3) If your school is near the coast, there may be a beach nearby where the high water mark is full of treasure. Or a sandy plain where the wind moulds wave patterns, or where the rains leave little river systems and patterns of erosion.

(4) If your school has a farm nearby, this can be an enormously rich experience and it is very worthwhile to cultivate the friendship and interest of the farmer so that children can visit and investigate. What grows in the fields? Did the farmer intend all of it to grow in the field? Does only grass grow in the meadows? What else grows there? If it is a dairy farm, what animals are kept? How? Where? What animals does the farmer keep? Cattle? Sheep? Goats? Are there more animals belonging to the farm? Pigs? Fowl? Turkeys? Rabbits? Dogs? Cats? Which other animals walk, fly, scurry, and sneak about the farm? Does the farmer want those? And . . .? One can keep asking and looking and finding out on a farm.

(5) If there is an interesting industry, suitably small and safe, it will be valuable for children to visit and to observe how things are manufactured, or investigate the raw materials that are delivered, stored and used. Visits to industry offer many other opportunities for education in other areas of the curriculum . . .

(6) If houses are being built in the neighbourhood, make use of this whenever you can. Not only are there many skilled people working together (which can be observed from a safe distance), but many problems of space and construction are actually being solved right there! It isn't difficult to obtain (by showing interest) samples of the interesting materials to be found there: cement, bricks, wood, metals, plastics and so on, for the children to investigate in the classroom.

(7) Is there a garage, car-works, repairshop, bus station, airport or railway station with a shunting yard?

(8) Are there other interesting structures such as a swing bridge, or a lift bridge, a sluice or a lock, a pier or a ferry-boat installation? Is there a belfry or a carillon?

In the search for potential in the environment, don't ignore tourist guides or local and national societies which exist to study, protect and preserve the environment. These often produce posters, pamphlets and brochures, and sometimes produce other valuable learning materials to buy or borrow, such as books, films and videotapes.

(Elstgeest and Harlen, 1990, p. 24)

Once the site for a visit has been selected the particular aspects to be observed or investigated have to be fully planned, possibly involving another visit. A few selected places for working and talking are better than a tourist guide approach. The teacher needs to think out questions for children to answer actively in relation to what can be found at the selected spots (see Chapter 5).

Where the visit will involve those at the site, then the preparation must involve correspondence and close communication between the school and those who will be involved in the visit. A prior visit by the teacher is essential, not only for the teacher to find out what the children may experience and what safety precautions need to be made beforehand, but to tell those in the place to be visited who may be acting as guide, demonstrator or informer, something about the children. In some cases those involved may have little idea of the level of background knowledge, length of attention span and interests of primary school children. The teacher can help them with their preparation by suggesting some of the questions the children might ask and the sorts of things that will need to be explained in simple terms.

Some useful hints for preparing visits of primary school children to industry have come out of the exploratory study of schools–industry work for the age range 8–13 years carried out by the Schools Council Industry Project (Jamieson, 1984). Primary school teachers may be more familiar with visits to parks, woods and streets than with visits to factories or small industries. However, many of the guidelines have relevance for visits of all kinds. The study identified these points as helping to make a visit successful:

- It should not be an isolated event, but the centrepiece of extended work which begins beforehand and continues afterwards.
- The type of industry visited should preferably be one producing something which children recognize and relate to, for example bicycles, toys or domestic utensils. It was found that complex processes involving huge machinery, often very noisy, did not make for successful visits.
- The best size of group to take round a work place was found to be six to eight children, so to break a class down into groups of this size requires the help of parents or people from the industry being visited.
- When children were issued with worksheets, either by the school or the place being visited, it was found that these:

tended to unduly narrow the observational powers of the children. Many children were observed spending most of their time buried in their notebooks (or even worse, other children's notebooks!) rather than listening to and observing the operation of the factory or workplace.

(Jamieson, 1984, p. 12)

The approach that appeared to be a useful compromise between too much and too little prior instruction was to indicate to children beforehand the main areas of interest and enquiry and to leave the children scope to frame their own questions. The value of this approach for process-skill development is shown clearly in the report that: 'Several schools dealt with this problem by preparation time on the development of questioning and observational skills.' (Jamieson, 1984, p. 12)

- In many cases it was useful follow-up work for the children to create a model of the place visited. As well as the problems of scale and construction to be overcome, the activity helps children to realize the sequence of events. For older children flow diagrams would have similar benefits.
- Inviting someone from the industry back to the school to talk to the children some time after the visit gives them opportunity to pose questions which have occurred later during reflection on the visit. The double benefit here is that the adult from the industry has the chance to learn about the children's work and the school environment, which can improve school–industry communication to the good of later visiting groups.

Written materials

Books for pupils

Most programmes produced since about 1989 include books for pupils, in contrast with the earlier programmes of the 1960s which considered that pupils' books might stifle spontaneity in children's activities. Since that time, however, considerable developments have taken place in presentation and reproduction, releasing ingenuity in using the printed word to engage children's thinking and activity. Many pupils' books combine the purposes of providing information, extending experience (through photographs), showing applications of science in the world around and relating science to other areas of the curriculum, through, for example, stories, drawings and poems. Such books can be least successful when they suggest activities, since these are often a matter of confirming information given rather than testing children's own ideas. It is essential that pupils' books are seen as supplementary to, and not as replacing, pupils' own investigations of events and objects around them.

Children need access to reference books for information beyond that which a teacher can supply to satisfy their curiosity and sometimes their appetite for collecting names and facts. Information books for young children are difficult to write. Finding a way to present information in simple understandable terms requires an expert in the subject matter; the best such books are written by scientists or doctors (for example, the award-winning books by Balkwill and Rolph, 1990). Introducing fantasy as a vehicle for telling 'the story of a meal' or 'the life of a drop of water' does not necessarily aid understanding.

The qualities of good reference books for children are not very different from those of good reference books for adults – large, clear, coloured photographs, with straightforward text and an easily used index or other way of locating information. Reference books can usefully be kept to-gether in a central school library and borrowed by classes, perhaps for an extended time such as half a term, on those occasions when they are likely to be in constant demand for the topic in hand. With this type of use in mind it may be preferable to purchase smallish books restricted to one topic (such as the Observer's Books published by Warne) rather than large encyclopaedic volumes.

Not all reference material is in book form. Wallcharts, although less durable than books, have some advantages over them. Several children can consult them at one time and each can see all the information avail-able: useful either for identifying a specimen by matching or for seeing the parts of a process linked together in a large flow diagram.

Sets of materials to support science activities

Sets of materials which purport to cover the whole of the science curricu-lum for the primary years fall into two kinds: those (such as Ginn Science) which set out activities year by year and those (such as Nuffield Junior Science (SPACE)) which are organized by Key Stages. Despite the appar-ent attractions of having all the planning done by following a programme year by year, many schools are reluctant to adopt a single one, for any of the following reasons. In the first place the programme may not emphas-ize those aspects of learning which the school particularly wishes to em-phasize. Secondly, adopting a set science scheme separates science from other areas of work more than a teacher might wish. If there is integra-tion, it will be the other work which has to fit into the science framework. The notion of topic work spreading across science and several other subjects would be difficult to reconcile with the adoption of the course. Thirdly, there would be some pressure to cover the ground at a pace necessary to finish the prescribed activities within a certain time, for otherwise the continuity in the programme might be in danger. Finally, there is the problem of catering for a range of interests, abilities and rates of working.

Programmes organized by Key Stages only provide greater flexibility for being planned into a school's own programme while providing a suggested structure for those who wish to use it.

The suitability of all materials, whatever their claims, should be evalu-ated within the school. Although it is not always easy to envisage from the written word what the activity is like in practice, an evaluation of proposed activities can reveal their strengths and limitations. A simple grid, such as in Figure 32, can be used to assess the potential for involving pupils in using process skills, developing attitudes and furthering under-standing of basic ideas. Some clear and shared understanding of what the skills and attitudes mean in practice, as discussed in Chapter 4, must lie behind the simple listing of these at the left of the grid. Some measure of the extent of involvement of the skills, attitudes and concepts may be devised so that there is more information than a single tick.

	Activities							
	I	2	3	4	5	6	7	etc.
Observing Hypothesizing - - - - - - - - -								
Curiosity Respect for evidence - - - - - - - - -								
Characteristics and variety of living things Processes of life - - - - - - - - -								

Figure 32

Once the limitations of a certain set of activities are known, it becomes possible to adapt them in the way suitable to the school. Ideas which can be used in
doing this may be found in some of the older but enduring sets of materials,
such as *Science 5/13* and *Learning Through Science*, which need not be discarded
just because they pre-date the introduction of national curricula.

Non-written resources

Computers

When first introduced into primary schools in the early 1980s computers
were seen as a mixed blessing in relation to science. Whereas computer
simulations and models could be useful in science at the secondary and
more advanced levels, it was thought that primary pupils might well
regard them as games, with no more relevance to real life than 'Space
Invaders' and the like. A related concern was that the computer would
take children away from contact with the real world and they would sit at
a screen exploring things which could only represent rather crudely the
things around them.

It was recognized that the potential was there for computers to take a
more useful part in, rather than taking over, pupils' investigations by, for
example, extending the range of data available beyond that which they
had time or opportunity to gather, or by enabling them to display their
findings in different forms at the touch of a key. But few good programs
were written to realize this potential, mainly because of the limitations of
the hardware available in primary schools. So during the 1980s the most
useful role of the computer in science was in data processing and word
processing. Even in this limited capacity it was recognized that the computer can be a stimulus to pupils sharing ideas and working together. A
group of three children working together at the computer have to agree
on their action at each step and usefully argue their point to convince the
others when there is disagreement. There is immediate feedback as to the
effect of their decision which they can use in later interaction with the

program. A gradual increase in the numbers of computers available (an average of four per primary school, meaning one per 40 pupils in 1990, compared with an average of one per 18 pupils in secondary schools (DES, 1991c)) has enabled almost every pupil to have hands-on experience of a computer in the primary school.

Since the beginning of the 1990s, however, there has been the possibility of using computer technology in primary schools to extend the range and sensitivity of information that pupils can use in their science investigations. Sensitive and rapidly responding detectors of temperature, light, sound, rotation, position, humidity and pressure, linked to the computer via a universal interface, can become the means for pupils to investigate phenomena to which the tools previously available to them were quite insensitive (e.g. First Sense, 1991). For example, a probe that can measure temperature precisely can be used to test the idea that dark surfaces heat up more quickly than light ones when exposed to sunshine, or to find out whether the skin on different parts of the body is at the same temperature, or whether metal objects that feel cold really are at a different temperature from their surroundings. Light-sensitive probes can be used to compare intensities associated with changes in the size of the pupil of the eye, to investigate regular and irregular reflection from surfaces, the effect of placing a filter between a light source and the probe, etc. In all cases the measurements can be displayed in numerical, symbolic or graphical form.

These are just some examples of the wealth of possibilities opened up by using the computer to extend the senses, to help in measurement and recording data. Such uses increase dramatically pupils' ability to use evidence in testing ideas, both their own and others'. The speed with which the computer accomplishes the drudgery of measurement, tabulation and display enables pupils' attention to be focused on the interpretation of data, on making sense of what they are finding. This is just the aspect of investigating which is neglected in the absence of this help, when obtaining results seems an end in itself, the climax of the work rather than the beginning of thinking, as should be the case. The construction and testing of ideas by children can become more central to their scientific activity when they control the technology and are not confined by it.

There may well be other roles, as yet unsuspected. It is appropriate for science educators to keep an open mind about the kinds of learning that the new technology may make available. With such a powerful force at hand we should not restrict use of it to replacing aspects of a teacher's role. It may be that children's undoubted ease in communication with computers facilitates modes of learning not tapped and made accessible in any other way.

Slides, films and television

The widespread use of video-recorders has extended the flexibility of use of television programmes in primary schools and many schools make some use of science programmes. The problems of using the whole of a series of broad-cast programmes are similar to those discussed in relation to adopting a written scheme in full. There are some additional points, however. The programmes use only very carefully selected and tried-out activities and audience-reaction evaluation during development of a series has been used to ensure that both the content and its treatment will be interesting to children. (This is not to say that writers of written materials may not go to similar lengths, but it is nonetheless possible – and does happen – that activities are included which do not work in practice, whereas this would not happen on a television programme.) Furthermore, television programmes can, and often do, show children engaged in investigations, so they can indicate methods of working as well as content.

On the negative side, apart from any problems raised by arranging television viewing conveniently, the main additional point is the danger of science becoming a spectator sport. To avoid this the programmes require careful building into the curriculum and there is help in doing this in the written guides for teachers which accompany the programmes, giving detailed suggestions for preparatory and follow-up work.

Greater flexibility in the use of television to extend children's experience to things which it would be too difficult or dangerous for them to experience otherwise, is provided by the use of sequences on video-disc. The MIST (Modular Investigations into Science and Technology) materials provide 40 two-minute modules – short visual sequences each dealing with a scientific idea. The material is culled from the best natural history television material developed commercially and presented with two alternative sound tracks, or none at all, leaving the teacher to provide comment. The video-disc technology enables modules or individual frames to be called up instantly, loops can be set up for groups of pupils to study as required, with easy facility for slow motion or fast-forward running (Mably and Attfield, 1990). The hardware chosen for the MIST development limits its wide application, but video-disc is no doubt a medium that will be developed further in the future as a resource for teachers and pupils.

The role of the science co-ordinator

Resources for teaching include all the materials, objects and aids that can be used in helping children learn. In science the use of resources is essential to help children to explore and to develop ideas about their environment; it is not just a matter of making learning more interesting. There is a variety of resources that are needed; some to be investigated, some to be used as tools in investigations, some to give information, some to give ideas of how to tackle problems, some to pose questions and challenge children to justify and support their own ideas. A well-informed teacher is the best resource of all, but every teacher cannot be an expert in every area of the primary curriculum. Thus the role of the school co-ordinator for science is important to the development and implementation of a school's programme in science.

The co-ordinator will take a leading role in developing the school's policy and reviewing its working, but there are many other ways in which the other staff can be helped by the co-ordinator. The main ones are:

- providing support for teachers who lack confidence to make a start; this may involve giving specific ideas for topics, class organization, displays, etc
- sharing the teaching in a class (when the co-ordinator is able to leave her class in the hands of someone else, perhaps the head) or inviting another teacher into her own class to observe science in action
- acting as a source of information to other teachers, being available to discuss science content as well as teaching approaches
- liaising with receiving secondary schools and neighbourhood primary schools
- collecting and organizing books, materials and information useful to teachers including audio-visual aids, radio and television programmes, microcomputer software and safety regulations
- making proposals for enriching the school environment as a resource for scientific investigation (growing interesting plants, making habitats, places for weather observations, bird watching, etc.)
- being the link between the school and sources of help such as advisory teachers, services provided by museums, zoos and industry
- compiling useful information on places of scientific interest for class visits and a list of interesting people willing to visit
- extending the staff's competence in teaching science by school-based workshops, discussions on specific issues or the study of current reports and relevant research
- generally keeping the school in touch with new thinking and new developments in the field of primary science.

The role of the co-ordinator not only in doing these things but in being able to communicate with and lead other teachers effectively has been somewhat belatedly recognized. It is one thing to know what to do oneself but another to be able to help others to do it for themselves. As ASE document designed to help co-ordinators (ASE, 1981) comes down heavily against the co-ordinator teaching science in other classes than his or her own, describing the role as that of a consultant in the school. It notes that the co-ordinator needs 'qualities of leadership, tact and enthusiasm for science learning' as well as 'a good background of scientific knowledge and understanding of science as a way of working'. The ASE has several publications aimed at helping the work of co-ordinators, in particular its compendium of information, ideas for involving parents and the community in the school's science work and comprehensive list of resources (ASE, 1992).

11

Evaluating Provision for Science

Placing this chapter on evaluation at the end of the book is not to be interpreted as suggesting either that evaluation is an activity that comes after teaching and learning or that it is of lesser importance than the topics of preceding chapters. The concern here is with evaluation that is formative in function in that it helps decisions as to whether, and if so what, changes need to be made. More specifically it is a review of what is being done that enables intentions to be compared with practice and identifies areas where the match is unsatisfactory and requires attention.

We are not concerned with evaluation designed to compare school with school or with measures of school effectiveness. There are important debates about these forms of school evaluation, heightened by the policy decision to publish 'league tables' of schools based on the performance of pupils, but it is not the intention to enter into these here (see, for example, Riddell and Brown, 1991).

However, some of the issues relating to the concept of evaluation are common to all types of evaluation exercises and are discussed in the first part of this chapter. Following this, two further sections deal with evaluation of provision for primary science both at the class level and at the school level.

Concepts and issues of evaluation

Meaning

Evaluation is the process of gathering and using information to help in making decisions or judgements. Schematically:

INFORMATION is judged against CRITERIA → EVALUATION

The distinction between the information and the criteria used to judge it is important, although the two are connected, as discussed later. Making explicit the criteria on which the judgement is based identifies evaluation as quite different from passing an opinion which does not need to be justified.

Nevertheless evaluation is by no means the value-free process that some might have supposed and others would wish it to be. The selection of criteria, the kind of information and the way the two are brought together will all affect the judgement that is made. Indeed it might well be said that understanding the nature and limitations of evaluation is essential to its usefulness. Naive assumptions as to what can be achieved by evaluation, what faith can be placed on its results, must be avoided. If this can be done then it has an important part to play in the many decisions that have to be made in teaching.

Moreover the purpose of the evaluation will also be influential and is one of the general aspects to be considered in a little more detail.

Purposes

As suggested, evaluation involves collection of some information that is relevant to a decision to be made and judging it against appropriate criteria. Just what information is collected and criteria used depend partly on the nature of the problem and partly on the purpose of the evaluation. One can evaluate a new play, for example, by collecting information by going to the theatre to see it, asking opinions of others, reading reviews, etc.; this information could then be judged against different sets of criteria: Would it be suitable for a party of tourists after a hard day's sight-seeing? Would it be understood by/ interest/frighten young children or very old people? Would you feel comfortable seeing it in the company of a sweet but narrow-minded older relative? Knowing the decisions to be taken and the criteria to be used would also influence the information gathered and reported about the play. For instance, one might particularly take note of verbal innuendo and jokes that play on words if suitability for foreign visitors or young children had to be judged.

The range of purposes of evaluation in education is extensive and even if we narrow down concern to evaluation within a school the list is still quite long, including some purposes which have direct effect on the school and some having little direct effect. For instance, the work in a school could be evaluated as part of a wider research into the use of certain curriculum materials or the effects of a certain kind of class organization. The findings would add to the information generally available about the materials or the organization but not necessarily have direct impact on the school. In contrast an evaluation can be carried out in a school solely for the purpose of informing decisions to be taken in that school, when the results would not necessarily have value to others unconnected with it.

Since it is difficult for those outside the schools to have access to the detail that is required to evaluate their performance, reports provided by the schools themselves are an important source of information that parents and the general public use in evaluating them. The requirement for schools in the UK to report annually to their governors or school board and the publication of inspectors' reports has opened up schools to much greater public scrutiny. At the same time, the information thus made available is complex and not easy to interpret. To avoid inappropriate judgements being made it is import-

ant to extend the understanding about the less than precise nature of evaluation to those using information about schools.

Criteria and indicators

Criteria that are usable in making judgements have to make clear for each
aspect evaluated the particular quality or quantity that is to be taken as successful performance. In other words, the indicators – the aspects or type of
performance to be judged – have to be spelled out in detail. For example, for
evaluating the extent to which effective learning experiences are being provided for science in a class, the indicators might include:

- use of a range of equipment and materials
- discussion of key scientific ideas
- use of process skills
- access to information
- etc.

However, to make a judgement about a particular classroom it would be
necessary to decide what should be the criteria for success for that classroom,
that is: How and how often should materials be used? Who should discuss
which ideas? and so on. Success criteria are described by Hargreaves and
Hopkins (1991, p. 50) as 'a form of school-generated performance indicator'
which should spell out more precisely what it is intended to achieve, in what
time-scale, and provide warning of the kind of evidence that will need to be
collected for the judgement of success to be made.

It is likely to be easier to agree the broad aspects or *indicators*, which could
apply to all classrooms and indeed to almost all schools, than the *success
criteria*, that will vary from class to class and are more dependent on value
positions. For instance, in the example above it would be possible to interpret
'use of materials' as demonstrations by the teacher and not use by the children; discussion could be seen as limited to teacher–pupil rather than pupil–
pupil. With only a little exaggeration it would be possible to imagine two
different sets of success criteria for these indicators, such as:

A	B
Teacher gives regular demonstrations using materials and equipment	Pupils use materials and equipment themselves
Pupils comment on ideas presented by the teacher	Pupils discuss their own ideas with each other and the teacher
Pupils observe and keep accurate records	Pupils suggest hypotheses, make predictions, plan and carry out investigations and record their work
Pupils read passages as directed by teachers from class books	Pupils find information from reference books in the classroom or library

It is not difficult to see that the judgement of a particular class would be different according to whether set A or set B criteria were used. The selection of criteria is therefore of considerable import. Not only can criteria based on contrasting values lead to different judgements about the same information, but the choice will influence what information is gathered. Since information cannot be gathered about everything the selection will be made in terms of what is thought or known to be significant and is to be aimed for. This changes as our understanding of schools and teaching grows. For example, various research studies into how schools adapt to change have shown that schools coping most effectively usually have:

- good arrangements for feedback, communication and sharing among all those involved within and outside the school – headteachers, teachers, parents, pupils and the general public;
- teachers working co-operatively;
- pupils involved in assessing their own work;
- a clarity about goals and yet tolerance of different ways of achieving them;
- the practice of checking that each step is in place before the next is taken.

With these findings in mind it would be important to include these aspects as criteria of success and to gather information about them in designing an evaluation to help a school adapt to change.

Types of information

Quantitative information, expressed in terms of figures, describes performance, conditions or situations in terms of how much, how often, how many, etc. It may appear to be more definite, more dependable, more objective, than qualitative information which conveys perceptions, impressions and explanations. On the other hand, quantitative data often oversimplify what are complex matters and may force information into categories which seem arbitrarily chosen.

In evaluation, success criteria are required in order to use either kind of information. To report that x% of time is, for example, spent on science, is only useful in evaluation when judged against a percentage of time that is thought to be appropriate in a particular case. The point at issue is whether quantity of time is a relevant indicator for evaluation or whether it is more important to know how the time is spent. In this case, as in most similar ones, both are desirable. In general a multiplicity of types of information is required, including both quantitative and qualitative.

One of the main areas of contention about information for educational evaluation, bearing on the qualitative-quantitative issue, concerns the relevance of information about pupils' learning. Some of the early evaluations, particularly those carried out in the United States, were based on a view of education where the outcomes of learning, that is, what children do or do not know, what they can or cannot do, are assumed to give the only rational basis for deciding the quality of classroom experiences:

However, since educational objectives are essentially changes in human beings, that is, the objectives aimed at are to produce certain desirable changes in the behavior patterns of the student, then evaluation is the process for determining the degree to which these changes in behavior are actually taking place.

This conception of evaluation has two important aspects. In the first place, it implies that evaluation must appraise the behavior of students since it is change in these behaviors which is sought in education. In the second place, it implies that evaluation must involve more than a single appraisal at any one time since to see whether change has taken place, it is necessary to make an appraisal at an early point and other appraisals at later points to identify changes that may be occurring.

(Tyler, 1949, p. 106)

So Tyler advocated testing ('appraising behaviour of students') before and after children have experienced certain activities to see whether expected changes in their performance are found. Decisions have to be made about what the expected changes are and the level of change that would be considered acceptable. If the changes were found to be below that level then the learning activities would be judged to have been inadequate.

This may sound a reasonable approach to evaluation at first; it is attractively logical (we do wish to change children's skills, ideas and attitudes: all things which influence their behaviour); it is neatly scientific, too, using measurement of a dependent variable (knowledge) to test the effect of an independent variable (children's classroom experience). What it ignores is that education concerns people, not objects that can be treated and tested under controlled conditions in a scientific laboratory. Learning does not depend only on what activities are provided, but on how the individual interacts with them and on what sense they make of them in the light of their previous experience and ideas. Furthermore some of the changes in behaviour that we hope to bring about are long term, difficult to assess and quantify, so the 'instruments' needed for measuring the dependent variable would be hard to find.

There is another serious set of objections to the Tyler approach to evaluation, which concerns the other question which has to be considered at this point in an evaluation: 'How will the information be used?' Even supposing that appropriate and valid tests were available and were used, the results would indicate only that certain outcomes were or were not found; this information would have little value for the purpose of improving the learning activities. Tyler makes the assumption that there is consistency between the 'treatment' and the 'outcomes'. The link is provided by the learning objectives which are stated in terms of changes in children's behaviour and used for devising the activities being evaluated. In the context of curriculum materials development it could be argued, perhaps, that this assumption is justified, though many would disagree. In the context of evaluation of the existing curriculum, however, one of the main purposes is to question whether opportunities for certain kinds of learning are actually being provided, not to assume their existence. Evaluation thus has to be more diagnostic than is possible if it relies on information about outcomes alone.

Arguments such as these (and experience of applying the 'measurement of objectives' approach and finding it wanting, see e.g. Harlen, 1975) have led to a series of alternative approaches to evaluation being proposed. The most useful for the present purpose is an approach depending on information about the classroom processes rather than the outcomes, or products. To put it another way, the evaluation is investigating the extent to which the independent variable (the provision of intended learning experiences) is in operation and is not concerned with the dependent variable (outcomes or changes in children's behaviour). This is not to deny the value of finding out what knowledge and abilities children have, but to acknowledge that there is not really any point in doing this until there is some confidence that related learning opportunities are being provided. It would be as ridiculous as testing pupils to see if they had learned to swim regardless of whether they had ever had a chance to learn. We can still agree with Tyler that the purpose of education is to change children's behaviour but disagree that this means that useful information for evaluation of education has to concern these behavioural changes only.

At the same time it must be acknowledged that there are equally strong arguments against an approach to evaluation which depends wholly on information about classroom processes and ignores the products. For a start the whole notion of 'learning opportunity' implies an identification of the expected learning and it would seem ingenuous to make such judgements without establishing that 'opportunity to learn X' can lead to 'learning X'. Thus at some stage it is necessary to relate process and product. If we ignore one or the other then assumptions are being made that may not be justified.

A second point is that obtaining the information about classroom processes is not easy, either for a teacher or for an outsider. The teacher is a central figure in the very transactions being examined and thus experiences both practical and psychological difficulty in gathering information that is not so biased by subjective judgement as to be useless, or even dangerous. An observer, who must be an 'outsider' to the classroom climate, experiences different but equally serious problems in attempting to gather information that is not distorted by his or her presence and provides an adequate sample of the variety of activities going on.

A third, related, point is the difficulty of deciding exactly what information about classroom processes is required and what would constitute an adequate sample of the events being evaluated. Until the developments in school self-evaluation beginning in the late 1970s (e.g. ILEA, 1982) little had been done to establish methodology for collecting information about school and classroom processes. Since that time, however, a considerable amount of work has been done and published so that guidelines and examples are now readily available (Hopkins, 1987; Hargreaves and

Hopkins, 1991). We shall now look at some of the approaches suggested for use at the class level and at the school level.

Evaluation at the class level

The purpose in mind in this discussion is evaluation to help a teacher answer in relation to science a question such as: How can the pupils' learning opportunities be improved? The intention is for the teacher to judge how well (s)he is doing and what improvements may be made. It is not so that others can judge how well the teacher is doing.

It is useful to start from the criteria relating to the learning opportunities and teaching processes intended. The information that is required has to enable these criteria to be applied. Some criteria concerned with the nature of pupils' science activities have been suggested (p. 101). To these can be added others relating to the way in which pupils engage with their activities and more general criteria which reflect the approach to learning, assessment, recording and planning. The resulting list which follows is intended only as an example, being based on the particular values behind the approach to learning and teaching embraced in this book.

Examples of criteria

- Pupils are involved regularly (every week) in handling materials and investigating at first hand.
- They understand what they are doing, and are not just following instructions or what others do.
- The demands of activities and the support given are matched to individual pupils.
- They are interested and intrigued by their work and feel it is important.
- They spend a high proportion of time on the task.
- Activities over a period of time provide opportunity for developing basic scientific ideas about the world (as listed in Chapter 3).
- Activities relate to pupils' everyday experience and help them understand it.
- Activities give opportunity for using and developing process skills and for fostering scientific attitudes (as listed in Chapter 4).
- Pupils participate in the assessment of their work.
- Records show what children are achieving through their activities as well as what they have completed.
- Information about pupils is used diagnostically in planning further learning experiences.

Examples of methods of gathering information

There has to be a compromise between the desire for as much information as possible about the pupils' experiences and the amount of information that can realistically be dealt with. It is necessary to take a sample; to collect several different kinds of information during a series of short periods is preferable to an extended and perhaps repetitive record of a limited kind. The sampling depends on whether:

- the main interest is in the class as a whole or one group or one child
- various groups or individuals are working on similar or different activities at one time
- science activities are discrete and well defined or are integral parts of topic work.

The circumstances of particular cases will decide the convenient and useful sample of activities to be considered. For this sample of activities we need some record to be kept of what the children did, what they felt about it, what the teacher did, what the teacher felt about it, etc.

The methods that can be used to gather this information are clearly more limited if a teacher is trying to evaluate the events in the classroom single-handed. In such a case the methods that can be used include the following:

Making notes during lessons.

These can only be the briefest jottings made at the time and should be written up more fully immediately after the lesson. They can include factual details, such as what each observed group did, how many children the teacher spoke to, for how long, what difficulties arose, whether they were overcome satisfactorily, to what extent the teacher's intentions for the lesson were realized.

Collecting any worksheet, textbook or other written material used by pupils.

These would be analysed later to determine the kinds of mental and physical activity they encouraged or allowed. It is important to note at the time the extent to which children used them, how they followed or departed from the activities offered, etc.

Collecting any written notes, drawings or other products made by the children.

These provide some record of what the children did and may also indicate whether there has been any productive thinking or, in contrast, show where time has been spent in straight copying from books or cards. Analysing pupils' work in this way is quite different from 'marking' it and might well be supplemented by a discussion with the pupils.

Discussing their work with children.

A quiet moment after a lesson might be used to talk to two or three children about what they had been doing, when the equipment and notes are still at hand. The teacher has to try to turn into an interviewer, to listen and encourage the children to talk about their work, what they understood and did not understand of it, what they found interesting, what was easy, how they arrived at any result or solution. The teacher can either make notes immediately afterwards or tape record the conversation. This discussion could also be part of a review of work of individual children in the context of creating records of achievement (see p. 167).

Tape recording

A tape recorder is a most useful piece of equipment for the teacher attempting any self-evaluation. Its use should be carefully planned, however, for too much recorded tape will be a deterrent to the use of recorded information. It is better to record two or three samples of 5 minutes' conversation with a group than to be faced with 60 minutes of tape and no basis for sampling from it. However, when recording pupils' conversations without the teacher present there is a case for placing the tape recorder near a group and letting it run. The children soon forget its presence if attention is not drawn to it by continued switching on and off. In listening to the tape it is then necessary to listen consciously for 5-minute periods, running on 10 minutes or so between each section.

The methods just discussed are the main ones available to the teacher working single-handed. If help with gathering information can be given by a colleague or a visitor then these same methods can be used with less effort and other methods can be added. Often a pair of teachers in a school can arrange to help each other in this matter. Such a reciprocal situation has many advantages; each then knows from experience the problems of being the observer and the teacher and will interpret the information accordingly. More important, however, is that when the purpose, process and findings of the class observations are shared between observer and teacher the anxiety that usually accompanies being observed while teaching is dispelled.

The main additional methods of gathering information that can be used by an observer but not by the teacher are systematic and detailed observations of pupils and teacher. These can range from a simple record of the movements of the teacher or a few selected children (made on a plan of the classroom) to a structured observation schedule for recording previously defined behaviours or events.

An example of such co-operative evaluation took place in the context of an in-service course in primary science where teachers were organized in groups of four all from different schools. Each week the four met in one school and observed the lesson of the teacher in that school. The next week they visited another member's school, so each was observed in turn. The three observers had well-defined tasks to carry out. One observed one group of children, using the schedule shown in Figure 33. Another made a plan of the classroom and recorded the movements of the teacher and at the same time made regular assessments of the proportion of

Class: .... Topic: ....

No. in group: .... Date: ....

	1-2	3-4	5-6	7-8	9-10	11-12	13-14	15-16	17-18	19-20	21-22	23-24	25-26	27-28	29-30	31-32	33-34	35-36	37-38	39-40	41-42	43-44	45-46
Observation of group (group work)																							
Relating to task																							
Making observations																							
Using measuring instruments																							
Handling other materials/equipment																							
Interpreting observations (pattern finding)																							
Suggesting explanations (hypothesizing)																							
Posing question																							
Proposing investigation																							
Proposing procedure (variable control, measurement)																							
Recording																							
Reading worksheet																							
Relating to teacher																							
Asking about topic																							
Asking for help/about procedure																							
Answering teacher's questions (fact/recall)																							
Answering teacher's questions (ideas)																							
Reporting/explaining actions																							
Listening to teacher																							
Relating to each other																							
Organizing task (co-operatively)																							
Organizing task (argument)																							
Talk about topic/task																							
Talk about record/report																							
Non-topic/task talk																							
Listening/responding to others' ideas																							
Independent working																							
Number actively/purposefully working																							
Other (specify)																							

Figure 33 Schedule for observing a group of children involved in science activities.

children appearing to be working purposefully, noting the possible reasons for non-task activity. The third observed the teacher, recording on a schedule similar in design to the one used for the group of pupils, the verbal and non-verbal behaviour of the teacher.

The observation schedules asked for a record to be made for successive 2-minute intervals throughout the lesson. If any of the listed behaviours was observed during a 2-minute interval it was ticked, whether it occurred once or several times. At the end of the 2 minutes the observer moved to the next column. Observers were instructed constantly to scan the list to remind themselves of the behaviours to look for and to add any of significance which were not included. However, the schedules were not designed to record everything happening, only those behaviours which were of interest for the purpose of the evaluation.

Analysing the information; applying the criteria

The use of several of the methods just discussed can result in a mass of varied and apparently disparate information. Some of it will need further analysis before it can be used in making evaluative judgements. The collection of worksheets and pupils' records provides information in this unanalysed form, as do any tape recordings of conversations. By contrast, the observation schedules contain information that has already been 'filtered' since the criteria were used in deciding what behaviours to record and what to ignore.

To analyse the 'unfiltered' information it has to be reviewed to find out whether children did any of the things that are suggested by the criteria on p. 147. In using some of the items on this list it will be necessary to refer to more detailed descriptions, such as those of process skills and attitudes given in Chapter 4 and the criteria for assessing process skills in Table 4 on p. 147. Using these more detailed criteria the information about the children's activities over the selected period of time (perhaps a term) can be sifted systematically to see to what extent and in what ways the criteria were met. This can be done by taking each subdivision of an activity and all information relating to it, including the teacher's interventions and relevant information about the class organization, and then ticking each criterion which is met. Some measure of the extent of meeting the criteria could then be provided by the number of ticks across all the activities. The disadvantage here is that the interaction of one activity with a subsequent one may be ignored. The alternative procedure, avoiding this disadvantage, is to take the criteria one at a time and to scan across all the activities, noting how often it is met.

These procedures may seem rather rough and subjective, as indeed they are, but in practice greater refinement is not needed for the purpose being considered. It is usually the case that the areas where there is a gap between what we would like to be happening (as represented by the criteria) and what is happening (evident in the information gathered) are large and obvious. Evaluation in this context is not intended to produce fine judgements of the extent of success, but to help those who carry it out to make their work more effective. The process of gathering information and sifting it systematically is likely to be of more value in bringing shortcomings to the attention and in suggesting ways of improvement than the end product. Indeed the end product is only the beginning of the next cycle in what should be an on-going review.

Evaluation is an essential aspect of a scientific approach to teaching science. We would do well to regard all our teaching, all the activities we provide for children as hypothesized solutions to the perpetual problem of how best to develop their process skills, ideas and attitudes. We should constantly be putting these hypotheses to the test, looking for alternatives and then testing them out. Evaluation is the means for testing our ideas about teaching.

Evaluation at the school level

Evaluation of a school for the purposes of improving the quality of teaching and learning is most usefully considered in the context of school development planning. 'Development *planning* is more than a development *plan*, the document: it is the process of creating the plan and then ensuring that it is put into effect. The plan is a statement of intentions which reflect the school's vision for the future. The process involves reaching agreement on a sensible set of priorities for the school and then taking action to realize the plan' (Hargreaves and Hopkins, 1991, p. 3).

An important and often initial process in development planning is evaluating or auditing the existing procedures and performance of the school. In school development planning the audit provides information for the school to use in establishing its priorities for areas needing development, which in turn lead to preparation and implementation of action plans. After a time for implementation, specified in the plan, the success of the action taken is evaluated, but this does not replace the regular audit.

School audit should cover all aspects of the teaching and learning, management, staffing, buildings, resources, relationships with parents and governors, links with the education authority and other institutions. Hargreaves and Hopkins suggest that it is not appropriate to spend the enormous amount of time required to audit all these aspects at once, but rather to focus successively on key areas and carry out specific audits. At the same time, information about pupils' learning opportunities needs regular annual review. Information collated from the class-level evaluation will enable review of such things as the time spent on science in each class and the relationship of each class programme to the overall school plan for science. A specific audit relating to science would supplement this information with the following:

• the nature and use being made of the school's policy for science

- the extent of continuity in pupils' experience from class to class
- the progress being made in learning by pupils from class to class
- the adequacy of resources and equipment
- the support and development of staff
- assessment and record keeping in science.

A school audit or specific audit is usually best custom-designed to suit the context, staff and previous history of the school. However, there are schemes available for schools to take as starting points and to adapt. These include the GRIDS approach (McMahon *et al.*, 1984), the advice offered by the NCC (1990), by SOED (1992) and the guidance provided by Hargreaves and Hopkins (1991). None of these deals specifically with primary science but the principles could be applied.

For a specific audit of science provision, information is required in relation to the indicators suggested above. Performance criteria might be such as:

- Teachers are aware of and use the school policy on science.
- Teaching methods are consistent with those agreed and expressed in the school policy.
- The programmes of individual classes cover the relevant part of the National Curriculum or guidelines without gaps or unnecessary repetition.
- Records of pupils' experiences and learning are kept consistently in every class.
- Teachers are satisfied with the amount, quality and accessibility of equipment.
- Teachers can find the help they need in planning and teaching their science programmes.
- Teachers are satisfied with in-service provision within and outwith the school.
- Pupils' performance shows regular progress at the levels expected.
- Pupils are enthusiastic about science.
- Parents are satisfied with their children's experiences and performance in science.

Sources of information are signalled in these criteria. Teachers are clearly a major source. Their records and opinions need to be collected and reviewed systematically. In addition, their views on the adequacy of support, equipment, in-service, etc. can be sought by questionnaire or interview. Documents provide a second source of information. School programmes and procedures and National Curriculum and assessment requirements or guidelines have to be analysed and compared. Then there are the perceptions of pupils, parents and others, such as governors, local inspectors or advisers, which can be elicited by questionnaire or interview. Where time allows, semi-structured interviews held with a well-selected sample are probably most helpful, since they can probe reasons for satisfaction or dissatisfaction and so suggest action to be considered.

The question as to whether the information is collected and analysed by someone inside the school or by an outsider may be a real one in some cases; in others there may be no alternative to the head or a deputy undertaking this work. If an outsider is involved this is likely to be part of a deliberate strategy for providing an external perspective rather than relying wholly on self-evaluation. Hargreaves and Hopkins provide a useful summary of the strengths and limitations of this strategy, reproduced in Figure 34.

Strengths	Limitations
• provides a dispassionate view, and a chance for staff to talk through problems with outsiders	• timing of visit/inspection may be inappropriate for school needs or planning cycle
• limited time-scale reduces demands on staff	• might not focus on school's concerns and may result in breadth rather than depth
• tells schools what they are doing well besides highlighting weaknesses	• external perspectives on their own do not necessarily lead to development
• provides the possibility of bringing new ideas into the school and encourages staff to question what they take for granted	• may neglect the existing inner strengths of the school

Figure 34 (Reproduced with permission from Hargreaves and Hopkins, 1991, p. 35.)

A further point to be taken into account is that the purpose is not to provide an overall judgement but to identify areas needing improvement. Participation is likely to increase the feeling of ownership over the decisions about action to be taken. An open and shared evaluation, in which everyone is aware of the purpose, the process and the findings, is itself a large step in the direction of school development.

References

Alexander, R., Rose, J. and Woodhead, C. (1992) *Curriculum Organisation and Classroom Practice in Primary Schools*, DES, London.

APU (1988) *Science at Age 11: A Review of Survey Findings 1980–84*, HMSO, London.

ASE (1980) *Language in Science*, Study Series No. 16, Association for Science Education, Hatfield, Herts.

ASE (1981) *A Post of Responsibility in Science*, Science and Primary Education Paper No. 3, Association for Science Education, Hatfield, Herts.

ASE (1991) *Be Safe* (2nd edn), Association for Science Education, Hatfield, Herts.

ASE (1992) *Primary Science: A Shared Experience*, Association for Science Education, Hatfield, Herts.

ASE/NCC (1990) *Opening Doors for Science – some aspects of environmental education and science in the National Curriculum for 5–16*, ASE/NCC, Hatfield, Herts.

Ausubel, D.P. (1968) *Educational Psychology: A Cognitive View*, Holt, Rinehart and Winston, New York.

Balkwill, F. and Rolph, M. (1990) *Cell Wars* and *Cells are Us*, Collins, London.

Barnes, D. (1976) *From Communication to Curriculum*, Penguin, Harmondsworth.

Bath Science 5–16 (1992) *Discovering Science* (Key Stage 1) and (Key Stage 2), Teachers' and Pupils' Materials, Nelson, Walton–on–Thames.

Bell, B. (1981) *Video: Animals*, Working Paper No. 51, Science Education Research Unit, University of Waikato, Hamilton, New Zealand.

Bell, B. and Barker, M. (1982) Towards a scientific concept of 'animal', *Journal of Biological Education*, Vol. 16, no. 3, pp. 197–200.

Bennett, N., Desforges, C., Cockburn, A. and Wilkinson, B. (1984) *The Quality of Pupil Learning Experiences*, Lawrence Erlbaum Associates, London.

Biddulph, F. and Osborne, R. (1984) Pupils' ideas about floating and sinking, *Research in Science Education*, Vol. 14, pp. 114–24.

Black, P.J., Harlen, W. and Orgee, A.G. (1984) *Standards of Performance: Expectations and Reality*, APU Occasional Paper No. 3, DES, London.

Bruner, J.S. (1964a) *On Knowing. Essays for the Left Hand*, Harvard University Press, Cambridge, MA.

Bruner, J.S. (1964b) The course of cognitive growth, *American Psychologist*, Vol. 19, pp. 1–15.

Bruner, J.S., Goodnow, J.J. and Austin, G.A. (1966) *A Study of Thinking*, Wiley, New York.

CACE (1967) *Children and Their Primary Schools* (Plowden Report), HMSO, London.

Clift, P., Weiner, G. and Wilson, E. (1981) *Record Keeping in Primary Schools*, Macmillan, London.

Collins Primary Science (1991) *Teacher's Guide for Key Stage 1* and *Teacher's Guide for Key Stage 2* and Pupils' Books, Collins, London.

Comber, L. C. and Keeves, J. P. (1973) *Science Education in Nineteen Countries: An Empirical Study*, Almqvist and Wiskell, Stockholm.

Davis, B. and Robards, J. (1989) Progress in primary science: the assessment of topic work, *Primary Science Review*, no. 9, pp. 7, 8.

DES (1978) *Primary Education in England*, HMSO, London.

DES (1981) *Science in Schools. Age 11*, APU Report No. 1, HMSO, London.

DES (1983a) *Science in Schools. Age 11*, APU Report No. 2, DES Research Report, DES, London.

DES (1983b) *Science in Primary Schools*, A discussion paper produced by the HMI Science Committee, DES, London.

DES (1984) *Science in Schools. Age 11*, APU Report No. 3, DES Research Report, DES, London.

DES (1989) *Aspects of Primary Education. The Teaching of Science*, HMSO, London.

DES (1991a) *Science in the National Curriculum*, HMSO, London.

DES (1991b) *Your Child's Report – What it means and how it can help*, HMSO, London.

DES (1991c) *Statistical Bulletin 11/91*, DES, London.

Driver, R. (1985) *The Pupil as Scientist?* Open University Press, Milton Keynes.

Duckworth, D. (1972) The choice of science subjects by grammar school pupils. Unpublished Ph.D. thesis, University of Lancaster.

Einstein, A. (1933) preface to M. Plank, *Where is Science Going?* Allen & Unwin, London.

Elstgeest, J. (1985) The right question at the right time, in W. Harlen (ed.) *Primary Science: Taking the Plunge*, Heinemann, London.

Elstgeest, J. (1992) Questions and questioning, *Primary Science Review*, no. 23, pp. 8, 9.

Elstgeest, J. and Harlen, W. (1990) *Environmental Science in the Primary Curriculum*, Paul Chapman, London.

Finlay, F.N. (1983) Science processes, *Journal of Research in Science Teaching*, Vol. 20, no. 1, p. 51.

First Sense (1991) Philip Harris Education, Lichfield.

Galton, M.J., Simon, B. and Croll, P. (1980) *Inside the Primary Classroom*, Routledge & Kegan Paul, London.

Ginn Science (1991) Resources File, Pupils' Books and Assessment Booklets for Years 1–7, Ginn, Aylesbury.

Glover, J. (1985) Case Study 1. Science and project work in the infant school, in Open University, *EP531: Primary Science – Why and How?* Block 1 Study Book, Open University Press, Milton Keynes.

Gunstone, R. and Watts, M. (1985) Force and Motion, in Driver, Guesne and Tiberghien (eds.) *Children's Ideas in Science*, Open University Press, Milton Keynes.

Hargreaves, D.H. and Hopkins, D. (1991) *The Empowered School*, Cassell, London.

Harlen, W. (1975) *Science 5/13: A Formative Evaluation*, Macmillan, London.

Harlen, W. (ed.) (1985) *Primary Science: Taking the Plunge*, Heinemann, London.

Harlen, W. and Symington, D. (1985) Helping children to observe, in W. Harlen (ed.) *Primary Science: Taking the Plunge*, Heinemann, London.

Harlen, W. (1992) *The Teaching of Science*, Fulton, London.

Hawking, S.W. (1988) *A Brief History of Time*, Bantam Press, London.

Hopkins, D. (ed.) (1987) *Improving the Quality of Schooling*, Falmer Press, Lewes.

Howe, C. (1990) Grouping children for effective learning in science, *Primary Science Review*, no. 13, pp. 26–7.

ILEA (Inner London Education Authority) (1982) *Keeping the School Under Review*, Learning Materials Service, ILEA.

International Educational Achievement (1988) *Science Achievement in 17 Countries: A Preliminary Report*, National Science Foundation, Washington.

Jamieson, I. (ed.) (1984) *We Make Kettles: Studying Industry in the Primary School*, Schools Council, London.

Jelly, S.J. (1985) Helping children to raise questions – and answering them, in W. Harlen (ed.) *Primary Science: Taking the Plunge*, Heinemann, London.

Johnson, G., Hill, B. and Tunstall, P. (1992) *Primary Records of Achievement: A Teacher's Guide to Recording and Reviewing*, Hodder & Stoughton, London.

Johnstone, A.H., MacDonald, J.J. and Webb, G. (1977) Misconceptions in school thermodynamics, *Physics Education*, no. 12, pp. 248–51.

Kelly, P.J. (1959) An investigation of the factors which influence grammar school pupils to prefer science subjects. Unpublished MA thesis, University of London.

Lapointe, A., Mead, N. and Askew, J. (1992) *Learning Science, The Second International Assessment of Educational Progress*, Educational Testing Service, Princeton.

Layton, D. (1990) *Inarticulate Science?* Occasional Paper No. 17. University of Liverpool Department of Education.

Learning Through Science (1982) *Science Resources*, Macdonald Educational, London.

Mably, C. and Attfield, J. (1990) Two views of MIST, *Primary Science Review*, no. 12, pp. 22–3.

Match and Mismatch (1977) Materials include three books: *Raising Questions, Teacher's Guide, Finding Answers*, Oliver & Boyd, Edinburgh.

McMahon, A., Bolam, R., Abbot, R. and Holly, P. (1984) *Guidelines for Review and Internal Development in Schools (GRIDS) Primary School Handbook*, Longman, York.

Morris, R. (1990) *Science Education Worldwide*, UNESCO, Paris.

National Curriculum Council (NCC) (1990) *The Whole Curriculum*, NCC, York.

New Zealand Ministry of Education (1992) *Science in the National Curriculum, Draft*, Wellington, New Zealand.

Novak, J.D. and Gowan, D.B. (1984) *Learning How to Learn*, Cambridge University Press.

Nuffield Junior Science Project (1967) *Teachers' Guide I, Apparatus and Animals and Plants*, Collins, London.

Nuffield Primary Science (SPACE) (1993) 11 Teacher's Guides and 22 Pupils' Books for Key Stage 2, Teacher's Guide for Key Stage 1, Teacher's Handbook and INSET Pack, Collins, London.

Ormerod, M.B. and Duckworth, D. (1975) *Pupils' Attitudes to Science*, NFER, Windsor.

Osborne, R.J. (1985) Children's own concepts, in W. Harlen (ed.) *Primary Science: Taking the Plunge*, Heinemann, London.

Osborne, R.J. and Freyberg, P. (1982) *Learning in Science Project (Forms 1–4) Final Report*, Science Education Research Unit, University of Waikato, Hamilton, New Zealand.

Osborne, R.J. and Freyberg, P. (1985) *Learning in Science: The Implications of 'Children's Science'*, Heinemann, New Zealand.

Osborne, R.J., Biddulph, F., Freyberg, P. and Symington, D. (1982) *Confronting the Problems of Primary School Science*, Working Paper No. 110, Science Education Research Unit, University of Waikato, Hamilton, New Zealand.

Piaget, J. (1929) *The Child's Conception of the World*, Harcourt, Brace, New York.
Piaget, J. (1964) Cognitive development in children: Piaget papers, in R.E. Ripple and D.N. Rockcastle (eds.) Piaget Rediscovered: Report on the Conference on Cognitive Studies and Curriculum Development, School of Education, Cornell University, Ithaca, New York.
Riddell, S. and Brown, S. (eds.) (1991) *School Effectiveness Research*, HMSO, Scottish Office Education Department, Edinburgh.
Russell, T. and Harlen, W. (1990) *Assessing Science in the Primary Classroom: Practical Tasks*, Paul Chapman, London.
Schilling, M., Hargreaves, L., Harlen, W. with Russell, T. (1990) *Assessing Science in the Primary Classroom: Written Tasks*, Paul Chapman, London.
Science, a Process Approach (1966–1976) Rank Xerox Services.
Science 5/13 Series (1972–1975) *Teachers' Guides* (26 titles), Macdonald Educational, London.
SEAC (1990) *Records of Achievement in the Primary School*, SEAC, London.
Shamos, M.H. (1988) Science literacy is futile: try science appreciation, *The Scientist*, 3 October, p. 9.
SOED (Scottish Office Education Department) (1991) *Environmental Studies 5–14*, Working Paper 13, SOED, Edinburgh.
SOED (Scottish Office Education Department) (1992) *Using Performance Indicators in Primary School Self-Evaluation*, SOED, Edinburgh.
SPACE (Science Processes and Concepts Exploration) Research Reports, *Evaporation and Condensation* (1990), *Growth* (1990), *Light* (1990), *Sound* (1990), *Electricity* (1991), *Materials* (1991) *Processes of Life* (1992), *Rocks, Soil and Weather* (1992), Liverpool University Press.
Thurber, J. (1945) *The Thurber Carnival*, Harper & Row, New York.
Tyler, R.W. (1949) *Basic Principles of Curriculum and Instruction*, University of Chicago Press.
Vygotsky, L.S. (1962) *Thought and Language*, Massachusetts Institute of Technology.

Index